NONVIOLENT COMMUNICATION

TOOLKIT FOR FACILITATORS

Interactive Activities and Awareness Exercises
Based on 18 Key Concepts for the Development
of NVC Skills and Consciousness

By Raj Gill, Lucy Leu, and Judi Morin

Certified Trainers, Center for Nonviolent Communication

PuddleDancer
PRESS

2240 Encinitas Blvd., Ste. D-911, Encinitas, CA 92024
email@PuddleDancer.com • www.PuddleDancer.com

Nonviolent Communication Toolkit for Facilitators
Interactive Activities and Awareness Exercises Based on 18 Key
Concepts for the Development of NVC Skills and Consciousness

PuddleDancer Press, Permissions Dept.
2240 Encinitas Blvd., Ste. D-911, Encinitas, CA 92024
Tel: 760-557-0326, Email@PuddleDancer.com
www.NonviolentCommunication.com

Ordering Information
Please contact Independent Publishers Group, Tel: 312-337-0747;
Fax: 312-337-5985; Email: frontdesk@ipgbook.com or visit www.IPGbook.com
for other contact information and details about ordering online

Authors: Raj Gill, Lucy Leu, and Judi Morin

Find More Online: To access online materials visit: nvctoolkit.org, and enter the
following (lowercase): Username: nvctoolkit, Password: rglljm

Cover and interior design: Numa Marketing, www.numamarketing.com
Cover source photo: Stock Photo, Magdalena Spurek

Manufactured in the United States of America
1st Printing, December 2022

This Toolkit was previously published by the authors as the
Nonviolent Communication (NVC) Toolkit for Facilitators.

26 25 24 23 22   1 2 3 4 5

ISBNs: 978-1-934336-44-1 (print), 978-1-934336-45-8 (ebook)

Library of Congress Cataloging-in-Publication Data
Names: Gill, Raj (Nonviolent communication facilitator), author. | Leu, Lucy, author. | Morin, Judi, author.
Title: Nonviolent communication toolkit for facilitators : interactive activities and awareness exercises
    based on 18 key concepts for the development of NVC skills and consciousness / by Raj Gill, Lucy
    Leu, and Judi Morin, Certified Trainers, Center for Nonviolent Communication.
Description: Encinitas, CA : PuddleDancer Press, [2022] | Summary: "Internationally respected NVC
    trainers, Judi Morin, Raj Gill, and Lucy Leu have come together to codify more than twenty years of
    training experience in one hands-on Nonviolent Communication (NVC) facilitator guide. Whether
    you're a new facilitator, a seasoned trainer looking to incorporate a more experiential approach, or
    a team of trainers, the Nonviolent Communication Toolkit for Facilitators has a wealth of resources
    for you. By breaking Nonviolent Communication down into 18 key concepts, this toolkit provides
    succinct teaching tools that can be used on their own for shorter sessions, or combined for a long-
    term or multi-session training. Your NVC Toolkit purchase includes: Hard Copy Exercise Manual-
    Includes exercises, activities, and facilitator scripts to guide you in sharing 18 key NVC concepts
    Electronic Downloads-Access to 21 Learning Aids and 33 Handouts to create an interactive, hands-
    on learning environment Instructional Video Clips - Access 20 short clips and one 30-minute video
    to help clarify some of the more complex activities"-- Provided by publisher.
Identifiers: LCCN 2022036138 (print) | LCCN 2022036139 (ebook) | ISBN 9781934336441 (trade paperback)
    | ISBN 9781934336458 (ebook)
Subjects: LCSH: Interpersonal communication. | Interpersonal relations. | Nonviolence.
Classification: LCC BF637.C45 G54 2022 (print) | LCC BF637.C45 (ebook) | DDC 153.6--dc23/eng/20220916
LC record available at https://lccn.loc.gov/2022036138
LC ebook record available at https://lccn.loc.gov/2022036139

What People Are Saying About the
Nonviolent Communication Toolkit

"These dynamic trainers have designed a cornucopia of games and exercises to inspire active learning that is fun, concrete, and imbued with NVC consciousness. If you wish to facilitate and practice NVC, here is a resource I recommend with confidence and enthusiasm!"

> **—MARSHALL B. ROSENBERG, PhD,** was the founder and educational director of the Center for Nonviolent Communication

"I am literally on the edge of my seat, eagerly waiting to dig into this treasure chest of 'hands-on' training activities, which I know will prove enormously useful to me in every workshop, class, or study group I facilitate. These tools guide us in 'getting the consciousness' on more than an intellectual level."

> **—DOW GORDON,** Center for Nonviolent Communication Certified Trainer, Freedom Project Prison Training Coordinator, Seattle, WA, USA

"I have used many of the materials and activities in this kit in a variety of locales— schools, community settings, and jails—and am delighted that they are now more widely available. The *Nonviolent Communication Toolkit for Facilitators* brings together the kinesthetic, visual, verbal, and motoric modalities for understanding NVC concepts."

> **—JANE CONNOR, PhD,** Bartle Professor of Human Development, Binghamton University, New York USA

"I am convinced that the world is a safer and more peaceful place because of the work of these three women. For years I have witnessed and been inspired by their skills in bringing humanity into the world of prison, showing the power of Nonviolent Communication when it comes from the heart. I deeply appreciate their willingness to share what they have learned by making this toolkit available to all of us."

> **—KARI BJERKE,** Nonviolent Communication Prison Project Coordinator, Sonderborg, Denmark

"NVC concepts can be challenging to convey inside prison. However, these exercises pack a powerful punch, transforming vague concepts into animated reality with the prisoners I work with. I believe the *Nonviolent Communication Toolkit* will profoundly impact the educational outcome of any NVC program."

> **—REV. DAVID PRICE,** Chaplain, Mission Institution, Mission, B.C., Canada

We dedicate this work to
OUR PARENTS
for being the first to model the primary NVC belief
in the joy of giving:

Jaswant Kaur Dhaliwal
Chanan Singh Dhaliwal

Linda Shen Leu
F. J. Leu

Nancy Joan Sumner Russill
Louis Morin

Contents

Acknowledgments 1

Introduction 3

Accessing the Online Toolkit Materials 9

Key Concept 1:   Intention 19

Key Concept 2:   Attention 31

Key Concept 3:   Communication That Blocks Connection 45

Key Concept 4:   Four Choices in Receiving a Difficult Message 63

Key Concept 5:   Observation 77

Key Concept 6:   Feeling 91

Key Concept 7:   Need 115

Key Concept 8:   Request 129

Key Concept 9:   Connecting With Self 157

Key Concept 10: Honesty 181

Key Concept 11: Empathy 199

Key Concept 12: The NVC Dance 223

Key Concept 13: Making Life Choiceful 243

Key Concept 14: Expressing and Receiving a No 265

Key Concept 15: Appreciation and Celebration 285

Key Concept 16: Anger 307

Key Concept 17: Mourning and Forgiveness 335

Key Concept 18: Resolving Conflicts 351

Appendixes

Cross-References—Toolkit Exercises and Marshall Rosenberg Book 371

The Four-Part Nonviolent Communication Process 372

Some Basic Feelings and Needs We All Have 373

Nonviolent Communication Research and About Nonviolent Communication 374

About PuddleDancer Press 375

About the Center for Nonviolent Communication 376

Trade Books From PuddleDancer Press 377

Trade Booklets From PuddleDancer Press 380

About the *Nonviolent Communication Toolkit* Creators 382

Find More Online! 383

Acknowledgments

It is with joy that we pause to remember the many individuals and organizations that have made this moment possible.

We eagerly thank the **Sisters of St. Ann** for their generosity in offering us two Esther's Dream grants which supported us in initiating and completing this project.

We are grateful for a grant from **Correctional Service of Canada;** their confidence in the potential of the *Nonviolent Communication Toolkit for Facilitators* to enhance the department's mission gives us ongoing encouragement.

Our families, friends, and colleagues have been patient and understanding during the several years it has taken us to create the *Nonviolent Communication Toolkit.* We appreciate their unfailing support and their receptivity to our efforts. To **Linda Leu,** for her faith in the long-range vision of this work, we extend special gratitude.

Tiffany Meyer (Numa Marketing) has been an invaluable partner from beginning to end, helping us visualize and materialize the final product. We are grateful for Tiffany's extensive expertise as well as for her dedication to NVC. We thank **Sandra McCormack** and **Harpreet Patel** for their generous support with website and design elements. **Ruby Phillips, Monica Wood, Chris Rowe**, and **Carla Munro** offered invaluable service editing and proofing the Manual to render it print-ready. Our gratitude goes to **Cedarwood Video** and **Kellie Whitlock** for offering professional skills and pro bono time and to members of the **Freedom Project** and **Victoria NVC practice-group** for serving as actors in the production of the Toolkit video clips.

The **Sisters of St. Ann's Residence** in Victoria, B.C., Canada, fed us, housed us, cheered us on during many intensive writing retreats. Their random acts of kindness, spontaneous tea and empathy, earnest conversations, and hilarity nourished us more than they will ever know.

Finally we would like to acknowledge two sources without whom this project surely would not have been launched. The *Nonviolent Communication Toolkit* is our response to requests from **workshop participants** eager to share NVC in the form of hands-on activities and a large repertoire of exercises. Although we don't have your names, we thank you earnestly for your commitment to practice, your challenge to us to make these exercises available, and your patience in their delivery.

We close with a great garland of gratitude to **Marshall Rosenberg.** The practice of NVC has infused our lives with deep meaning and freedom, peace, and connection. We are inspired by how tirelessly Marshall dedicated his life to bringing these teachings to the far corners of our planetary community. We express our heartfelt thanks to you with the hope that this resource may support our shared vision of a world of peace and compassionate connection.

Introduction

We are excited that you are reading these words right now. Throughout the three years that the three of us have devoted to conceiving, creating, organizing, and producing this *Nonviolent Communication Toolkit for Facilitators* the vision of your presence in this moment has inspired our focus. We are excited because we trust that you who read these words share our profound yearning for a more compassionate world—a world of connection where everyone has a place at the table and where all our needs matter. We are doubly excited because we suspect that like ourselves, you have experienced the power of Nonviolent Communication (NVC) to create that world, both internally within yourself and externally in your community, whether local or global. We especially rejoice that you intend—or are considering the intention—to share your empowering understanding of NVC with others. It is our earnest hope that your intention is realized with joy, clarity, and confidence. We offer you the *Nonviolent Communication Toolkit* with the wish that it may enhance your efforts to effectively engage your community in the practice of NVC. May it contribute to your happiness and the happiness of those with whom you share your compassion, your understanding, and your delight in NVC.

What Does the *Nonviolent Communication Toolkit* Consist Of?

The *Nonviolent Communication Toolkit* consists of three parts: a hard-copy **Exercise Manual,** a collection of **Online Learning Aids,** and a set of **Online Instructional Videos Clips**.

1. The hard-copy **Exercise Manual** presents 74 exercises arranged under 18 key concepts for the development of NVC skills and consciousness.

    *   **Handouts** are used in many activities. The contents of these *Handouts* are included in the *Exercise Manual* for copying, but templates for copy-ready reproduction may be downloaded from the *Nonviolent Communication Toolkit* website at **nvctoolkit.org**, and clicking on "Electronic Downloads."

2. **Learning Aids** enhance the activities included in the *Exercise Manual* and can be accessed on the *Nonviolent Communication Toolkit* website at **nvctoolkit.org** by clicking on "Electronic Downloads." There are two kinds of *Learning Aids*:

    *   **General Learning Aids** are used in a number of Toolkit activities and support general NVC practice in all situations.

    *   **Specific Learning Aids** are used only for a specific Toolkit activity.

3. **Online Instructional Video Clips** are to be viewed on the *Nonviolent Communication Toolkit* website at **nvctoolkit.org**, by clicking on "Video Clips." The clips include:

- A 30-minute video clip illustrating how a practice session might be facilitated in consonance with NVC principles. This video clip enacts a group inside a men's prison practicing a Toolkit activity.

- Twenty short videos clips each demonstrating an interactive Toolkit activity that may be challenging for the reader to grasp through written description alone.

> For detailed information on the *Nonviolent Communication Toolkit* website and its contents, please refer to the section of this manual entitled, "Accessing the Online Toolkit Materials."

Who Is a Facilitator?

The *Nonviolent Communication Toolkit* is designed for individuals who wish to share NVC in group settings. Because of the authors' longtime commitment to support effective NVC practice in prison, this resource is particularly helpful for facilitators working with prisoners or returnees (people returning from prison to the community). All *Nonviolent Communication Toolkit* exercises, however, have been adapted for use in any environment.

We use the term *facilitator* to refer to someone with at least a basic understanding of NVC concepts and consciousness who is actively engaging others in group practice. Whether you are a prison chaplain, a member of a Parent-Teacher Association, team leader, churchgoer, peace activist, soup kitchen volunteer, or simply one of a group of friends, the *Nonviolent Communication Toolkit* can support you in designing meaningful ways to learn, share, and practice the basic principles of NVC.

The *Nonviolent Communication Toolkit* does not address issues of group dynamics or how to develop and nurture a practice group. We assume that facilitators have an established rapport with the groups in which they are introducing toolkit activities.

How Is the *Nonviolent Communication Toolkit* Structured?

The *Nonviolent Communication Toolkit* is organized into 18 sections, covering each of 18 key NVC concepts. Each section contains:

- A short description of the concept.
- At least one **Awareness Exercise**—Awareness Exercises use guided silence and imagery to open us experientially to the concept being introduced.
- Two or more **Activities**—Activities engage us in practicing and applying the concept. They may call for hands-on, interactive, multi-sensory participation as well as solitary reflection.
- Brief facilitator tips.

How Are the Exercises Presented?

Each activity contains a statement of purpose and a brief description. It specifies materials needed, group size, suggested time, space, and literacy level required for participants to engage in the activity. The procedure for each activity is presented in detail and offers facilitators step-by-step guidance on how to introduce the exercise and give clear instructions. Debrief Questions for the group and Suggestions for Practice in Daily Life are included at the end of many activities.

The instructions for guiding the awareness exercises consist of itemized statements that may be read verbatim.

Toolkit exercises may be introduced in any order, depending on the learning needs of the group and the facilitator's preference. Marshall Rosenberg's *Nonviolent Communication: A Language of Life* (3rd edition) is cited as a resource in the *Nonviolent Communication Toolkit*. At the end of an exercise, reference is made to specific chapters which relate to the particular key concept being addressed. (Cross-references of exercises to chapters in Marshall's book are provided at the back of this *Exercise Manual*.)

- **Numbering of Exercises**

  Each exercise is numbered according to its Key Concept and position in the section. For example, 10.2 refers to the second exercise under Key Concept 10 ("Honesty").

- **Explanation of Icons**

  Icons are used in headings to specify the following:

 = This activity uses Handouts.

There are two kinds of Handouts: Group Handouts and Individual Handouts. When a handout consists of scenario for practice, there will be one version for prison use and another for the general community. The contents of all handouts are included in the *Exercise Manual* as part of the exercise for copying.

However, to make clean copies of any handout, please use the electronic downloads available on the *Nonviolent Communication Toolkit* website.

 = This activity requires Learning Aids.

There are two kinds of Learning Aids: **General Learning Aids,** which are used across many activities, and **Specific Learning Aids**, which pertain only to a specific activity. All templates for additional materials and instructions for their production are available as electronic downloads on the *Nonviolent Communication Toolkit* website.

 = This activity is demonstrated in the *Online Instructional Video Clips* on the *Nonviolent Communication Toolkit* website.

- ## Use of Italicized Text

  Italicized text accompanied by a gray bar in the left margin appears in all the Awareness Exercises and many of the Activities. The italics indicate that these words may be spoken verbatim by facilitators when addressing participants. We included italicized text in response to feedback that it is often helpful to hear exactly how instructions might be worded.

Suggestions for Using the *Nonviolent Communication Toolkit*

1. Before introducing an exercise to a group, review it closely. Visualize the entire procedure and then do each step, following the instructions you will be giving to the group. Check to see if the exercise is included in the Online Instructional Video Clips. Thoroughly familiarize yourself with any Handout or Learning Aid that accompanies the activity.

2. We encourage flexibility and creativity in your use of the *Nonviolent Communication Toolkit*, especially when you have had experience with an exercise. For example, although a general estimate of "time needed" is given for each activity, please use your own discretion by monitoring participation in the room. Do participants appear engaged in learning? How is the energy in the room? Note, however, that we *strongly discourage* using flexibility as an opportunity for a discussion. A core intention of the *Nonviolent Communication Toolkit* is to engage participants in *practicing*, rather than *talking about*, NVC.

3. It is very important to us that the *Nonviolent Communication Toolkit* not be used to develop technical skill and fluency divorced from NVC consciousness. We see the NVC model as training wheels that support our skill in nurturing compassionate relationships. Like any powerful tool, NVC mechanics could be used with the intent to hurt, manipulate, or belittle others. We would be chagrined to see the *Nonviolent Communication Toolkit* used without commitment to compassion—of valuing the needs of another as much as our own. With this in mind, we make the following suggestions to facilitators sharing exercises from the toolkit:

   - **Invite pauses and silence in between activities.** Create space for everyone to reconnect with themselves and their intention for attending the group. Bring in frequent reminders of why you and others are engaging in this practice.

   - **As a facilitator, practice vulnerability.** Acknowledge your feelings and needs, especially when you think your needs for competence, effectiveness, or contribution are not being met in your role as facilitator. Be aware of your own triggers and how they might impact the way you are facilitating the group.

- **Honor the needs of both parties in all interactions.** A symbolic gesture that affirms this intention is to spread your hands, visualizing the needs of each party resting in one palm. Try this whenever you notice that your own needs or those of another have been absent in a dialogue. As you lead the exercises, remember to stay open to hearing the needs of the participants.

- **Cultivate shared experiences of gratitude in the group.** Practice articulating NVC appreciation at each session, recognizing especially the common gifts and resources that support us all.

Request for Feedback

Our intention in creating the *Nonviolent Communication Toolkit* is to support facilitators in sharing NVC with confidence, joy, clarity, and effectiveness. We are eager to receive ongoing feedback to know how your needs have or have not been met through the toolkit.

In reviewing feedback, it helps us to have the following information about you and about how you are using the *Nonviolent Communication Toolkit*:
- Name
- Email address
- NVC experience or background
- Size of group and context in which you are sharing Toolkit exercises (e.g., five-person NVC practice group, sixty-person church gathering)
- Group's geographical location (city, country) and language

We appreciate specific references to an exercise or page as well as general comments that help us understand what worked and didn't work for you. We ask for permission to incorporate your feedback for future editions.

ADDRESS FEEDBACK TO: info@nvctoolkit.org

Please specify if you want a response back from us.

Accessing the Online Toolkit Materials

The following essential pieces of the *Nonviolent Communication Toolkit for Facilitators* need to be accessed online:

- **Learning Aids** (comprising **General Learning Aids** and **Specific Learning Aids**)
- **Instructional Video Clips**
- **Handouts** (for individual exercises)

These items are briefly described in the Introduction under "What does the *Nonviolent Communication Toolkit* consist of?" Detailed information about these items are given below:

I.   Instructions for accessing the **Nonviolent Communication Toolkit** website
II. List of 9 **General Learning Aids**, including a description of each and suggestions for its use
III. List of 12 **Specific Learning Aids**
IV. List of 21 **Online Instructional Video Clips**
V.   List of 33 **Handouts** (for individual exercises)

I. TOOLKIT WEBSITE

The Toolkit website, located online at **nvctoolkit.org**, provides purchasers of the hardcopy *Nonviolent Communication Toolkit for Facilitators* **Exercise Manual** with easy access to electronic downloads of the accompanying **General Learning Aids, Specific Learning Aids, Handouts,** and a library of **Online Instructional Video Clips** designed to aid your use of this Toolkit. When partnered with these web-based resources, the manual becomes a complete toolkit of exercises, learning aids, and step-by-step guidelines to fully enhance your NVC teaching experience.

To begin accessing these materials online, follow these instructions:

1. Log on to **nvctoolkit.org**

2. From the homepage, click on either "Electronic Downloads" or "Video Clips" in the top navigation bar. When prompted, enter in the following, all in lowercase:
   USERNAME: nvctoolkit
   PASSWORD: rglljm

3. You now can access electronic PDF downloads of the **General Learning Aids, Specific Learning Aids, Handouts,** and you can view the **Online Instructional Video Clips.** Should you ever need to come back to this section of the website, simply click on "Electronic Downloads" or "Instructional Video Clips" from the top navigation bar, and re-enter the username and password.

II. GENERAL LEARNING AIDS

We recommend that **General Learning Aids** be made available during all NVC practice sessions and we encourage facilitators to develop creative ways of using them. Downloads for each **General Learning Aid** consist of (a) instructions for producing or assembling the **Learning Aid,** and (b) all necessary templates.

List of 9 General Learning Aids Available Online:

- General Learning Aid G1: Learning Guide
- General Learning Aid G2: Finger Map
- General Learning Aid G3: Floor Map
- General Learning Aid G4: Small Floor Map
- General Learning Aid G5: Wall Signs of Feeling Words
- General Learning Aid G6: Set of Feeling Cards
- General Learning Aid G7: Wall Signs of Need Words
- General Learning Aid G8: Set of Need Cards
- General Learning Aid G9: Guidelines for Assembling a Set of Pictures

Description of General Learning Aids and Suggestions for Use:

NOTE: Visit the *Nonviolent Communication Toolkit* website at **nvctoolkit.org** to view in color the photo illustrations given on the next page.

General Learning Aid G1: Learning Guide
When participants are provided with their own copy of a **Learning Guide** during practice, they have at their fingertips a handy reference showing:

- The four components of the NVC model
- A list of universal needs
- A list of feelings when needs are met
- A list of feelings when needs are unmet

Encourage participants to call upon this guide when naming a feeling or connecting to a need. The **Learning Guide** may be used during practice exercises as well as during informal interactions to support participants in translating judgmental or demanding thoughts into the language of feelings and needs.

General Learning Aid G2: Finger Map
The color-coded Finger Map gives a visual overview of the various steps and directions that may be taken when engaging in NVC dialogue. When following a conversation, it is often helpful for participants to track the conversation by pointing to the pieces on the Finger Map. For instance, if a speaker is evaluating someone's words or action, they would point to the orange block on the Finger Map. Or if a

speaker is expressing their own need, they would point to the blue box labeled "Need" under the section "Expressing Honestly."

The Finger Map may also be used during small group exercises to help the whole group focus on the step that is currently being taken or to consciously choose the next step to take.

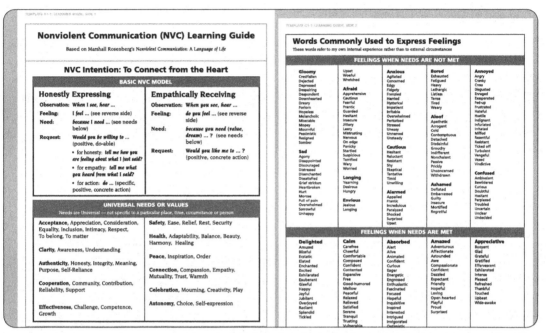

Learning Guide, front and back

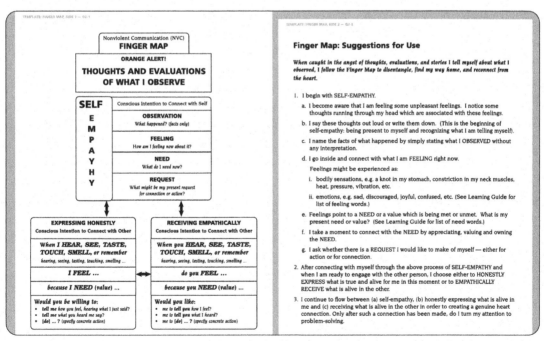

Finger Map

When experimenting on their own to apply NVC to a personal situation, individuals might use a Finger Map to walk themselves through the three steps of self-empathy, honesty, and empathy.

General Learning Aid G3: Floor Map

The contents of the Floor Map are similar to that of the Finger Map, but large enough to be put on the floor or wall for all participants to see. We encourage facilitators to walk along the Floor Map (or point to it on the wall) as they work through scenarios or as they refer to specific aspects of the model. The Floor Map can also be effectively used when two people are demonstrating an interaction for a larger group. The colored Floor Map supports learning by providing a constant visual reference to the NVC model.

The Map includes both orange territory (indicating life-alienating communication) as well as NVC territory, so we can never "fall off the map." It heightens awareness of where we are on the process-level as we engage in contentlively dialogue.

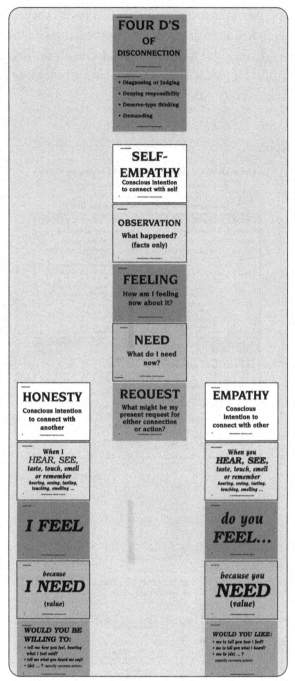

Floor Map

General Learning Aid G4: Small Floor Map

The Small Floor Map is a half-size version of the Floor Map. It is designed to conserve floor space so that small groups may use it to work independently of one another. Consider offering small groups only one or two sections of the Small Floor Map when engaging in exercises focusing on a specific concept that does not require the entire Map.

Small Floor Maps are also preferred by some NVC practitioners who use them at home to navigate through sticky situations or conflicts with family members.

General Learning Aid G5: Wall Signs of Feeling Words
General Learning Aid G7: Wall Signs of Need Words

We have found these bright blue (Needs) and red (Feelings) wall signs to be a wonderful way to decorate and dedicate a space for NVC practice. They provide participants with constant visual access to common feeling and need words. Surrounded by these large colorful word-cards, we are reminded that the purpose of our practice together is to create a world where we think, listen, and express ourselves through the vocabulary of feelings and needs.

Probably the biggest deterrent in using the Wall Signs is the time it takes to attach them to the wall. Consider creating games that incorporate participants taking particular wall signs to post. As people pick, handle, or post a particular Wall Sign, they are further familiarizing themselves with a feeling or need word. We encourage facilitators to experiment with creative ways to use the Walls Signs as well as all other **General Learning Aids** that are provided through the Toolkit. For example, one facilitator spread the Wall Signs on the floor for participants to pick the most prominent feeling or need they were experiencing in that moment.

Wall signs of feeling words

Wall signs of need words

General Learning Aid G6: Set of Feeling Cards
General Learning Aid G8: Set of Need Cards

These color-coded Card Sets are used in several exercises and provide endless variations for practice. They offer participants visual and tactile support when naming and connecting to feelings and needs. The set of Feeling Cards offered through this Toolkit consists of eighty feeling words; the Needs set consists of fifty-four need words (and two wild cards).

There are ready-made sets of Feeling and Need Cards available for sale in the NVC network which offer a diversity of games and activities. For example, "GROK" cards may be obtained though Galloping Giraffe Enterprises at **www.nvcproducts. com**. NOTE: These card sets may not reflect the color-coding used in the Toolkit.

General Learning Aid G9: Guidelines for Assembling a Set of Pictures
Several activities in the *Nonviolent Communication Toolkit* call for a set of images. We find pictures to be very effective learning aids: they provide context and can stimulate a range of feelings and needs. Most participants take pleasure in being offered an opportunity to engage visually as a respite from the spoken words which prevail in most sessions. We hope you will be inspired by the set of pictures you assemble to develop new activities to enhance NVC learning.

Note on colors used for Learning Aids
Although more effort may be required for the production of colored materials, we have found color-coded **Learning Aids** to be more effective for most NVC practitioners. The *Nonviolent Communication Toolkit* uses the following color-coding:

- **ORANGE** for "Orange Alert," alerts us to the kinds of thinking that block connection, e.g., judgment, blame, demand, etc.
- **YELLOW,** the color of the sun, is used for the first component of the NVC model—"observations." It symbolizes light which enables us to see the facts.
- **RED** represents "feelings" which can often be strong and fiery. This is the second component of the NVC model and may refer to either a body sensation or an emotion.
- **BLUE,** the color of the sky, is used to symbolize the universality of "needs," the third component of the NVC model.
- **GREEN,** as in a green traffic light, is used for "requests," the fourth component of the NVC model. NVC requests give clear direction regarding the action we want to take. They indicate "GO" toward the direction of meeting a need.

III. SPECIFIC LEARNING AIDS

Specific Learning Aids are designed to be used with specific *Nonviolent Communication Toolkit* exercises. They are numbered according to the exercises in the *Nonviolent Communication Toolkit* **Exercise Manual**. For example, Specific Learning Aid 2.3 refers to the Learning Aid for Exercise 2.3. Electronic PDF downloads for each **Specific Learning Aid** consist of (a) instructions for producing or assembling the **Learning Aid** and (b) all necessary templates.

List of 12 Specific Learning Aids Available Online

> **2.3 Choosing Where to Place Our Attention**
> Specific Learning Aid 2.3: Accordion-Pleated Handout—Choosing Where I Place My Attention

4.2 Experiencing the Four Choices
Specific Learning Aid 4.2: Set of Four Signs Labeling the Four Choices

5.2 Walking Between Evaluation and Observation
Specific Learning Aid 5.2: Set of Two Signs Labeled *Observation* and *Evaluation*

8.2 Six Stepstones for Making Requests
Specific Learning Aid 8.2: Set of Six Stepstones for Making Requests

8.3 Making Requests in a Group
Specific Learning Aid 8.3: Set of Eight Scenario Cards

10.2 Building Blocks of Honesty
Specific Learning Aid 10.2: Materials for Building Blocks of Honesty

10.4 Components Practice
Specific Learning Aid 10.4: Component Practice Strips

11.5 Empathy Mill
Specific Learning Aid 11.5: Empathy Mill Cards

12.3 Cha-Cha-Cha
Specific Learning Aid 12.3: (A) Tent Cards and (B) Step-Trackers

16.2 Stimulus or Cause?
Specific Learning Aid 16.2: Slap Cards

16.3 SSSTOP
Specific Learning Aid 16.3: SSSTOP Flowchart

16.5 Anger Poker
Specific Learning Aid 16.5: Set of Anger Poker Cue Cards

IV. INSTRUCTIONAL VIDEO CLIPS

A 30-minute video clip "Facilitating an NVC Circle" illustrates how a facilitator might apply NVC principles in leading a practice session. This clip includes a demonstration of Exercise 16.5: Anger Poker. There are also 20 short video clips demonstrating specific activities; these are categorized by key concept in the list below.

List of 21 Online Instructional Video Clips

"Facilitating an NVC Circle" (30-minute clip)

Key Concept 2:   Attention
Video Clip 2.2   Awareness Without Agenda
Video Clip 2.3   Choosing Where to Place Our Attention

Key Concept 3:   **Communication That Blocks Connection**
Video Clip 3.2   Cover-Up

Key Concept 4:   **Four Choices in Receiving a Difficult Message**
Video Clip 4.2   Experiencing the Four Choices
Video Clip 4.3   Choosing How We Hear and Respond

Key Concept 6:   **Feeling**
Video Clip 6.4   Sculpting Feelings

Key Concept 8:   **Request**
Video Clip 8.2   Six Stepstones for Making Requests
Video Clip 8.3   Making Requests in a Group

Key Concept 9:   **Connecting With Self**
Video Clip 9.5   I see, I think, I feel, I sense, I value

Key Concept 10:   **Honesty**
Video Clip 10.2   Building Blocks of Honesty

Key Concept 11:   **Empathy**
Video Clip 11.2   Reflecting Back Empathically
Video Clip 11.3   Practicing Empathy as Connecting Presence
Video Clip 11.4   Empathy Poker
Video Clip 11.5   Empathy Mill

Key Concept 12:   **The NVC Dance**
Video Clip 12.2   Dancing Fingers
Video Clip 12.3   Cha-Cha-Cha

Key Concept 15:   **Appreciation and Celebration**
Video Clip 15.3   Giving Someone an Appreciation

Key Concept 16:   **Anger**
Video Clip 16.4   Powergrounding
Video Clip 16.5   Anger Poker (included in the 30-minute Instructional Video Clip, "Facilitating an NVC Circle")

Key Concept 18:   **Resolving Conflicts**
Video Clip 18.2   Destroying Enemies by Breathing "EH"?
Video Clip 18.3   Conflict Lineup

V. HANDOUTS (FOR INDIVIDUAL EXERCISES)

Please note that **Handout** contents are included with the exercises in the hardcopy **Exercise Manual** itself. For increased convenience, electronic PDF template downloads for copy-ready reproduction of the **Handouts** are available on the Toolkit website by clicking on "Electronic Downloads."

List of 33 Handouts:

Individual Handout 1.3: What's My Intention?

Individual Handout 3.2: Cover-Up

Individual Handout 3.3: Tuning in to the Four Ds

Group Handout 4.2A: Difficult-to-Hear Messages—Prison

Group Handout 4.2B: Difficult-to-Hear Messages—General Community Individual

Handout 6.2: Expensive Emotions Worksheet

Individual Handout 6.5: Words Which Express Thoughts Instead of Feelings

Individual Handout 7.2: Phrases to Express "I Need…"

Individual Handout 8.2A: Six Stepstones for Making Requests

Individual Handout 8.2B: List of Scenarios—Prison

Individual Handout 8.2C: List of Scenarios—General Community

Individual Handout 8.5: What Keeps Me From Making a Request?

Individual Handout 9.1: Self-Empathy Meditation

Individual Handout 9.3: Freeing Myself of Self-Violence

Individual Handout 9.4: Freeing Myself of Self-Demands

Group Handout 9.5: Cue Sheet – I see, I think, …

Group Handout 11.4: Empathy Poker Dealer Instructions

Individual Handout 13.2: Power Against vs. Power With

Individual Handout 13.3A: Cultivating Our Power to Choose

Group Handout 13.3B: Cards Life Has Dealt Us—Prison

Group Handout 13.3C: Cards Life Has Dealt Us—General Community

Group Handout 14.2A: List of "No" Messages—Prison

Group Handout 14.2B: List of "No" Messages—General Community

Group Handout 14.3A: Situations for Expressing No—Prison

Group Handout 14.3B: Situations for Expressing No—General Community Group

Handout 14.3C: Expressing No—Instructions for Pair Practice

Individual Handout 15.4: What Keeps Me From Expressing My Appreciation?

Group Handout 16.2A: Anger: Stimulus or Cause?—Prison

Group Handout 16.2B: Anger: Stimulus or Cause?—General Community Individual

Handout 16.3: SSSTOP

Group Handout 16.5: Anger Poker Dealer Instructions

Group Handout 17.2: Healing the Inner Child—Guidelines for Role-Play

Individual Handout 17.3: Mourning—Healing the Past

INTENTION

1.1 Awareness Exercise:
Cultivating Awareness of
Intention

1.2 Activity: Grounding Our
Intention to Connect

1.3 Activity: What's My Intention?

KEY CONCEPT 1:

Intention

Description: The intention of NVC is to develop a quality of connection that allows us to understand and value one another's needs, and then together explore how to meet both of our needs. We hold this intention to connect heart-to-heart—even when we are angry or "don't feel like connecting"—by remembering that connection is the value we are choosing to live from in this moment. On the other hand, if we are invested only in getting certain results, and have no intention to connect human to human, heart to heart, then no matter how strictly our speech adheres to the NVC model, we are not expressing NVC consciousness.

Toolkit exercises in this section stress how intention is constantly present as we move through daily life. They support us in noticing what our moment-to-moment intention might be, and provide practice in consciously cultivating the intention to connect.

Tips for Facilitators: Without a strong emphasis on intention, NVC practice can become simply a technique. We urge facilitators to introduce reminders at every session to ground practice in NVC consciousness. Facilitators are powerful models. How we lead the practice, relate to participants, connect to our own needs, and handle conflict are all opportunities to demonstrate the NVC intention, which is connection. In any moment we can recommit to this intention by slowing the pace of the group process or by taking a few moments of silence with the group. We recommend doing these, as well as the activities in this section, on a regular basis.

Cultivating Awareness of Intention

AIM OF EXERCISE:

1. To deepen awareness that every word and every action is a choice behind which lies an intention
2. To cultivate awareness of the intention behind my choices

INSTRUCTIONS FOR GUIDING AWARENESS EXERCISE: Read the following slowly, leaving space between each statement for the participant to engage in the guided process:

a. *Sit comfortably. Straighten your spine. Make any necessary adjustments.*

b. *Focus your attention inward by closing your eyes or gently dropping your gaze to the floor in front of you.*

c. *Notice whether you chose to keep your eyes open or closed. Are you aware of the intention behind your choice?*

d. *Where did you sit at dinner? Are you aware of the intention behind that choice?*

e. *Recall something you said or did today. What was your intention?*

f. *Remember your choice to come here today. What was your intention?*

g. *When you are ready, open your eyes and look around the room, aware of each person here being conscious of their intention in coming here today.*

SHARING CIRCLE:

- My name is _____ .

- My intention in coming here today is _____ .

SUGGESTIONS FOR PRACTICE IN DAILY LIFE:

- Before opening your mouth or taking action, ask yourself, "What's my intention here?"

- Every day approach someone with the conscious intention of connecting with them.

REFERENCES: Chapters 1, 13

ACTIVITY 1.2

Grounding Our Intention to Connect

PURPOSE OF ACTIVITY: To practice connecting to others out of a consciousness of our fundamental commonality as fellow human beings

BRIEF DESCRIPTION: Participants sit in a circle and look at one another in silence for 1 to 2 minutes. After a pause for reflection and debrief, they repeat the process, but this time with conscious awareness of their shared humanity.

MATERIALS NEEDED:

❑ A bell and timer would be helpful, but not necessary.

TIME REQUIRED: 30 minutes

GROUP SIZE: Any

SPACE REQUIRED: Adequate for everyone to be seated in circle (either one large circle or several smaller circles)

LITERACY LEVEL REQUIRED: None

PROCEDURE:

1. Invite participants to join this activity saying that the group will have an opportunity to discuss its purpose at the end.

2. Arrange seating in one large circle or several smaller circles so that each person is able to see everyone in the circle.

3. **Part I**—Give the following instructions:

   Please close your eyes and bring your attention inside. In a minute or two you will hear a bell. At that time, open your eyes and look around at the people sitting in your circle. Simply look at each other. Keep looking without speaking, gesturing, smiling, or otherwise communicating with each other. Simply notice what comes up for you. [Use a bell to signal the beginning and end of this 1–2 minute period.]

   Consider giving participants an opportunity to reflect quietly on the following debrief questions before initiating discussion:

   a. *What feelings and needs came up for you?*

   b. *Did anyone notice judgmental thoughts of other people? Of yourself?*

   c. *When you became aware of judging, what feelings and needs came up for you?*

4. **Part II**—Give the following instructions:

a. *We'll take a few moments to work in silence now.*

b. *Ask yourself if any unmet needs got triggered by looking and being looked at in silence.*

c. *Pick the one that is most prominent for you.*

d. *If there were no unmet needs, identify a need that was met either during the silence or is being met in this moment.*

e. *Take whatever need you picked and create a blessing to offer yourself. For example, if the need you chose was "acceptance," a phrase of blessing might be "May I experience full acceptance." If the need was for "belonging," a phrase might be "May I feel completely at home." For "safety," "May I be safe." Create only one phrase.*

Check to see that everyone is clear about the task. After a minute or so, ask participants to go around and say out loud the blessing phrase they created.

5. **Part III**—Give the following instructions:

Once again close your eyes and bring your attention inside. [Pause] *Take a moment to see if you can connect with the innate beauty of who you are, your essence as a living human being in this moment.* [Pause] *Perhaps it's a physical sensation in your body, such as the steady beat of your heart? Perhaps it's a phrase that speaks to you, such as "child of God." Perhaps it's an image—ocean waves, being alone in the forest—that reminds you of your essential nature and your place in the universe. Whatever it is, take a moment to feel connected to your own basic humanity or oneness with life.*

- *Now take the blessing you created and offer it to yourself. For example: "May I be safe." "May I be at ease." "May I know that I am accepted just as I am." Whatever blessing you created, offer the words to yourself with sincerity. Do this for a few moments.* [Pause]

I will soon ring the bell as a signal for you to open your eyes. At that time, once again look around the room at the other people. As you do so, take your blessing and offer it to the individuals seated in the circle. So instead of 'May I be safe,' change the word 'I' to 'you' and silently repeat, 'May you be safe.' Or 'May you know you are accepted just as you are.' Use the same phrase and continue to offer your silent blessing to each person as you look around the circle." [1–2 minutes]

Stop. Close your eyes, come home to yourself. [Pause] *In this last minute of the exercise, take your blessing and change the wording so that it includes both yourself and others. Use the words "we all" instead of*

"I" or "you." For example, "May we all be safe." As you repeat this new phrase silently, imagine it spreading to embrace everyone in the circle.
[30 seconds]

- *As we end this exercise, gently open your eyes and look around the room, being aware that each person here is extending to all of us a blessing based on a need that came alive in this circle.*

DEBRIEF QUESTIONS:

1. Was the second round of silent looking different from the first time? If so, describe the differences and what might have caused them.

2. What do you think was the purpose of this activity?

3. Was it successful for you?

4. What would have made it more effective?

REFERENCES: Chapters 1, 13

ACTIVITY 1.3

What's My Intention?

PURPOSE OF ACTIVITY:

1. To deepen awareness of the intention behind our words or silence, our actions or non-actions

2. To practice choosing our intention

BRIEF DESCRIPTION: Working in small groups, participants reflect on the intention(s) behind something they did or said. They are invited to look at how a deeper awareness of intention might affect the situation.

MATERIALS NEEDED:
 ❑ Individual Handout: What's My Intention?

TIME REQUIRED: 30 minutes

GROUP SIZE: Any size

SPACE REQUIRED: Enough for small groups to work without mutual interference

LITERACY LEVEL REQUIRED: One person in each group needs to be able to read if facilitator chooses to use the handout with guiding statements

PROCEDURE:

Part I—Demonstration

1. Introduce the concept of intention:

    There is an intention behind everything we choose to do or not do, say or not say. This activity is designed to develop our awareness of intention. When we are aware of our intention, we then have the freedom to stay with our intention or change our intention.

2. Give an example of how we are sometimes unaware of our intention, and how awareness of intention gives us more choices.

    For example: I decide to wash the dishes that someone has left in the sink. My intention might be to make that person feel guilty and teach them a lesson on how things "should" be done. If I become aware of my intention, I can choose to follow through on it or choose not to. And, if I do decide to wash the dishes, I might then do so because I want to contribute to a cleaner and more pleasant living space.

3. Give a second example.

Another example: I decide to go up to someone whose radio is blaring. An unconscious intention behind my action might be to let that person know who is boss on the range. With awareness, I might choose to change my intention, approaching them with the intention to support them in finding a safer way to live in prison.

4. Give an example of the use of force, distinguishing the intention behind the protective use of force from the intention behind the punitive use of force. NOTE: in the example below, the narrator discovers the subtle intention to punish in an act that was taken with the apparent intention to protect.

When we use force, sometimes our intention is to inflict harm or pain on another person. At other times our intention may be to protect the person. For example, I am grabbing a child who has run out on the road. Annoyed, I squeeze his arm hard while dragging him roughly back to the sidewalk. I am thinking that if it hurts enough, maybe he won't run out again. If asked to state the intention behind my action, I might say it is to protect the child from traffic harm. If asked to reflect further, I might add that my intention was also to impress upon him that running into the street brings unpleasant consequences. Only by looking even more deeply might I see that, in my annoyance, I also intended for him to feel some pain as a form of punishment for what he did.

Part II—Instructions

1. Ask participants to work in groups of three or four.

2. Ask participants to recall something they did or said. Distribute handout if desired.

Bring to mind something you did or did not do, something you said or did not say. If you have difficulty doing this, try recalling something specific you did that involves:

- *The use of force*

- *Offering someone "negative feedback" or "constructive criticism"*

- *Agreeing to do something someone asks of you*

- *Saying no to someone*

- *"Being good," "being nice"*

- *Telling a joke, "being funny," saying something humorous*

- *Attending this and other trainings ("programming")*

3. Ask participants to take turns sharing what they did or said and to state the intention behind it.

4. Ask participants to reflect on whether there were deeper layers of intention beneath the one just named and to take turns sharing whatever they discover.

5. Ask participants,

   When you became aware of an intention, did you want to change your intention? Did you want to change your action? Share with the group any changes you wanted to make in either intention or action.

DEBRIEF QUESTIONS:

1. What did you discover about the power of intention?

2. How might you apply this learning in your life?

SUGGESTIONS FOR PRACTICE IN DAILY LIFE: Several times each day, stop and ask yourself:

1. "What was my intention in what I did or said?"

2. "What is my intention in what I am doing or saying right now?"

3. "What is my intention in what I am planning to do or say?"

REFERENCES: Chapters 1, 13

What's My Intention?

BRING TO MIND one of the following, and share it with the group:

Something you chose **to do** or **not do** and what your intention was
Something you chose **to say** or **not say** and what your intention was

Something you are choosing **to do** or **not do** now and what your intention is
Something you are choosing **to say** or **not say** now and what your intention is

Something you are planning **to do** or **not do** and what your intention is Something you are planning **to say** or **not say** and what your intention is

ASK YOURSELF:

1. Are there other intentions besides the one I gave? (If so, share them with your group.)

2. Given my awareness of the intention behind my words or action, would I want to change the intention? Would I want to change my words or action? (Share with the group any changes in intention, words, or action you would want to make.)

IF YOU HAVE DIFFICULTY RECALLING A SITUATION TO WORK WITH:
Reflect on something you did or said, are doing or saying, plan to do or say, that involves:

- The use of force

- Offering someone "negative feedback," "constructive criticism"

- Agreeing to do something someone asks of you

- Saying no to someone

- "Being good," "being nice"

- Telling a joke, "being funny," saying something humorous

- Attending this and other trainings ("programming")

ATTENTION

**2.1 Awareness Exercise:
Directing Our Attention**

**2.2 Awareness Exercise:
Awareness Without Agenda**

**2.3 Activity: Choosing Where
to Place Our Attention**

KEY CONCEPT 2:

Attention

Description: NVC challenges us to live in the present—to focus on our own or the other person's feelings and needs from moment to moment. Whether we are observing, thinking, evaluating, or judging, our practice is to be aware that this is what we are doing right now. Even when we are thinking about a past or future event, we recognize that we are engaging in the present-moment mental activity of "recalling" or "planning." We recognize that thinking about the past or imagining the future generates present-moment feelings and needs.

Toolkit exercises in this section support us in cultivating mindfulness so we can choose where to focus our attention and to be fully present to ourselves and others.

Tips for Facilitators: Our ability to apply NVC consciousness in daily life is enhanced by practices that help us slow down, stay present, and be self-aware. We urge facilitators to experiment with ways to realize an atmosphere in the group that encourages connection and awareness and serves as a reminder to return over and over again to the present moment. Awareness Exercises included in this Toolkit, as well as brief meditations, activities that ground us in our bodies, poetry, music, and various mindfulness practices, may all be helpful in cultivating this quality of experiencing ourselves in the present moment.

Directing Our Attention

AIM OF EXERCISE:

1. To practice awareness of where we place our attention

2. To practice choosing where we place our attention

INSTRUCTIONS FOR GUIDING AWARENESS EXERCISE: Read the following slowly, leaving space between each statement for the participant to engage in the guided process:

1. *Straighten your spine. Make any necessary adjustments.*

2. *Focus your attention inward by closing your eyes or gently dropping your gaze to the floor in front of you.*

3. *Sit comfortably. Focus your attention on your breathing.*

4. *Notice your breath coming in and going out.*

5. *Now focus on your ribs and notice the movement of your ribs.*

6. *Notice your body sensations as your lungs expand and release.*

7. *Now move your focus to your nostrils. Feel the air coming in and going out. Notice any difference in the quality of the air.*

8. *Now I invite you to focus on imagining being with someone you really enjoy.*

   - *Begin by focusing on your thoughts about that person. Just notice your thinking as you imagine being present to that person.*

   - *Now attend to what you are seeing in your imagination as you look at them. What are they wearing? What expression do you notice on their face?*

   - *Next, change your focus and guess what they might be observing in this situation.*

   - *Now put your attention on your feeling as you are present to them.*

   - *This time focus on what you think they might be feeling in this situation.*

   - *Now come back to your own heart. Be aware of what you are needing or what need is being met as you are present with this person.*

   - *Next turn your attention to what you guess they might be needing. Or what need of theirs is being met in this situation?*

- *In this moment, if you had one request of them, what would it be? Imagine yourself making that request to them.*

- *Now guess what request they might have of you.*

- *As we bring this visualization to a close, take a moment to say goodbye to this person.*

9. *The purpose of this awareness exercise is to practice noticing and choosing where we place our attention. Recall the various times in this exercise when you chose where you placed your attention.*

10. *When you are ready, open your eyes and look around the room at other people with a sense of curiosity as to what each one might have just experienced.*

11. *Take a moment and be conscious of what you learned about yourself and what you chose—or chose not—to be aware of.*

SHARING CIRCLE:

- My name is ⎯⎯⎯⎯⎯⎯⎯⎯⎯ .

- One thing I became aware of during this exercise was ⎯⎯⎯⎯⎯⎯⎯ .

REFERENCE: Chapter 1

Awareness Without Agenda

AIM OF EXERCISE: To open our attention to being simply present to whatever comes up—whether a sight, smell, sound, taste, sensation, or thought. NVC asks us to cultivate the capacity to be aware of what is alive in us. We train our attention so that it is available in the only place where life occurs: in the now.

TIME REQUIRED: For beginners, start with 5 minutes plus a 5-minute debrief. (Consider slowly increasing to 20 minutes as group gains more experience over time.)

INSTRUCTIONS FOR GUIDING AWARENESS EXERCISE: Be aware of your own state of mind and notice (without judging) if your attention wanders as you offer the following instructions. Read slowly, pausing between statements:

1. *Take a moment to adjust your body so that you are sitting comfortably with your back straight.*

2. *If you feel safe doing so, close your eyes. Otherwise, allow your gaze to settle softly on the ground in front of your feet.*

3. *Now bring attention to your breath as it enters and leaves the body . . . Notice what it feels like, either at the nostrils or in your chest or belly.*

4. *We'll take some conscious breaths here . . . Aware of breathing in . . . aware of breathing out. Without forcing the breath or changing it, . . . without judging the way we are breathing or thinking about it, we simply notice what it feels like to be breathing. In and out . . . Belly rising, belly falling . . . Be in this experience . . . The very experience of this breath . . . And this one. . . . And this one? . . .*

5. *Now we'll practice opening our attention to whatever comes up in each moment . . . welcoming each new moment with no agenda . . . As you continue breathing, just notice what comes up for you.*

6. *Are there thoughts coming up? Maybe some thought like, "I am bored stiff," "This is super peaceful," "I don't know what the hell I am doing!" Just notice that you are thinking . . . without reacting to the thought, without judging it, without analyzing it, without believing it or not believing it, without getting lost in it . . . Simply notice that thinking is happening.*

7. *When thoughts subside, go back to the sensation of breathing.*

8. *When sounds come up, simply notice hearing . . . without getting caught up in them . . . The sound of my voice . . . sounds inside the room . . . sounds outside . . . Notice hearing without trying to figure out what the sound is.*

9. When sound subsides, once again return to the sensation of the breath. Just stay with the feeling that comes from breathing in and out until something else appears on the horizon. Perhaps a sensation in your body—an ache, a tingling, warmth, pressure . . .

10. Perhaps a feeling comes up in the form of heaviness . . . sadness . . . tension . . . calm . . . sleepiness . . . Perhaps a smell, a taste in the mouth . . . whatever it is, can we notice what this moment brings without either pushing it away or chasing after it?

11. Let's experiment. Let's welcome these next [30 seconds, or however long] with awareness and curiosity. Whatever it brings. [Allow at least 30 seconds of silence.]

12. This is my life: what is happening right now . . . I am training my attention to be aware of whatever arises and to be able to hold all experiences that arise within this body and mind.

    a. An emotion? . . . Hmm, what does that emotion feel like? . . .

    b. A thought? I'm aware there's thinking going on without getting sucked up in the thoughts.

    c. A sound? I notice hearing happening.

    d. A sensation in the body? Where is it? Let me get close and really feel that feeling in this moment . . . And this moment? And this? [Long pause]

13. The purpose of this awareness exercise is to open our attention to being simply present to whatever comes up—whether a sight, smell, sound, taste, sensation, or thought. NVC calls us to cultivate the capacity to be aware of what is alive in us. We train our attention so that it is available in the only place where life occurs: in the now.

14. For those of you whose eyes are closed, notice the unique experience of this moment as I ask you to slowly open your eyes and become aware of sight . . . of seeing . . . Now everyone, bring your awareness gently back to the room and to the group.

SHARING CIRCLE:

- My name is _____ .

- Something I am aware of, after having done this exercise, is _____ .

SUGGESTIONS FOR PRACTICE IN EVERYDAY LIFE:

- When waiting—in line, in traffic, or for the bell to ring—start by focusing on your breath and then become aware of seeing, hearing, or smelling.

- Take a walk outside. Allow your senses to come alive as you rotate your attention:

— from seeing

— to hearing

— to smelling

— to feeling (either the sensation of the body moving or the feel of the feet pressing into the ground)

— and back to seeing, etc.

Give each of the senses a few seconds to register awareness before moving on to the next.

REFERENCE: Chapter 1

ACTIVITY 2.3

Choosing Where to Place Our Attention

PURPOSE OF ACTIVITY:

1. To practice consciously choosing where to place our attention

2. To practice tracking our attention

BRIEF DESCRIPTION: Participants focus their attention on a sequence of different objects for 6 minutes. There are two parts to this activity; they can be done independently of each other.

Part I—"Inside With People"

Two people carry on a conversation while two others are directed to place their full attention on an object specified in a handout. For example, they are first directed to focus their attention by "looking at the person who is talking." After 20 seconds, the focus may switch to "feeling the feelings in my body," or to "hearing the sounds in the room," or to "intuiting the speaker's needs," etc.

Part II—"Outside Alone"

Participants go outside and take a walk by themselves while rotating attention every 20 seconds from seeing to hearing to smelling to feeling the sensations of the body.

MATERIALS NEEDED:

❑ Specific Learning Aid 2.3: Accordion-Pleated Handout—Choosing Where I Place My Attention; one copy for every two participants in the room.

NOTE: This handout needs to be folded accordion-fashion before use. This process takes approximately 2–3 minutes. Facilitator may provide pre-pleated handouts or give participants an extra few

Accordion-Pleated Handout (finished product)

minutes for each to fold their own. Folding instructions are provided on the reverse side of the handout. See Specific Learning Aid 2.3.

TIME REQUIRED: Part I: 30 minutes (may be conducted independently of Part II) **Part II:** 25 minutes (may be conducted independently of Part I) **Debrief:** 15 minutes

GROUP SIZE: Part I: Four or more, **Part II:** Any size

SPACE REQUIRED: Part I: Enough for groups of four to work without mutual interference. **Part II:** Enough outdoor space for everyone to be able to take a 10-minute walk.

LITERACY LEVEL REQUIRED: Part I requires ability to read short sentences

PROCEDURE:

Part I—Inside With People

1. Explain purpose of activity.

   NVC invites us to be aware moment to moment as to where we place our life energy. We train our minds so that we may consciously choose where to focus our energy rather than be led by our habits of mind and unconscious patterns of behavior. In this activity, we experiment with our power to consciously choose where we place our attention as well as with our mind's tendency to wander.

2. Form groups of four (if there are extra participants, form groups of five).

3. Offer the following instructions to the groups:

   a. *Decide which two persons in your group will be Talkers. Talkers get 6 minutes to talk to each other about something personally meaningful.*

   b. *The others in the group will be Trainers. You will be training your attention on a series of different objects, one after another, over the course of the 6 minutes that the Talkers will be in conversation.*

   c. *Trainers will receive a Handout specifying how and where to focus your attention. The Handout is pleated, accordion-style, so as to reveal only one item at a time.*

   Show participants a pleated handout. Give a pre-folded handout to each Trainer or show them how to fold their own copy.

   d. *There is one item on each fold. Read that item and direct your attention to what it indicates. For example, an item may read: "LOOK at your left hand." Place your full attention on simply looking at the hand. Stay focused on LOOKING for about 20 seconds or until you have difficulty maintaining your attention. Be aware of your mind wandering off or when, instead of LOOKING AT the hand, you start to THINK ABOUT what you are seeing. If this happens, just gently invite your attention back to your intended focus without judging yourself.*

e. *When you are ready to switch focus, use your thumb and flip the pleated Handout upwards to expose the next item. The items are numbered from 1 to 13. When you have completed all thirteen items, you may start from the beginning or flip to any item at random.*

f. *Once again, the purpose of this activity is to train ourselves to consciously choose an object upon which to place our attention. It is likely that Trainers will find their attention drawn to the Talkers' conversation, especially if the dialogue is heartfelt. However, I encourage you, Trainers, to challenge yourselves in focusing your full attention without being distracted by the Talkers' conversation.*

4. Make sure that everyone understands the procedures. Inform groups that you will give a signal in 5 minutes. Talkers may take the last minute to wind down and bring their conversation to a close, after which Talkers and Trainers in each group will switch roles.

5. Upon completion of the first 6-minute round, ask participants if there are questions regarding procedures before launching the second round. Request that Talkers and Trainers switch roles, passing the pleated Handouts to the new pair of Trainers in each group. (If a group has five members, one person will not have a chance to be a Talker.)

Part II—Outside Alone

1. Explain purpose of activity (See Part I, Item #1).

2. Offer the following instructions:

a. *Let's take a 10-minute walk outside. During the walk, I'd like you to rotate your attention:*

- *from SEEING* [Place your hands on your eyes.]

- *to HEARING* [Place your hands on your ears.]

- *to SMELLING* [Place a hand on your nose.]

- *to FEELING THE SENSATIONS IN YOUR BODY* [Sweep your hands from your feet up through your ankles, legs, and hips.]

b. *I'll illustrate.*

- *As I walk, I place my full attention on SEEING. I can move my eyes and let my attention fall on different objects while I walk. But I keep my consciousness focused on what my eyes are seeing. If I find myself naming and identifying objects, guessing and wondering what the object is, I gently remind myself to bring my attention back to just seeing.* [Place your hands around eyes.]

- *After about 20 seconds, I switch to HEARING.* [Place hands around ears.]

  Now I put my full attention on the experience of hearing itself. If I find myself thinking about the sounds, or trying to figure out what they are, I gently re-focus my attention to simply hearing.

- *After another interval of 20 seconds or so, I switch my attention to SMELLING.* [Place a hand on your nose.] *Even if I don't smell anything, I can still focus my attention on smelling at each inhalation.*

- *Now I switch my attention to the PHYSICAL SENSATIONS, especially those in my lower body as I walk . . . the pressure against the ball of my foot as it lifts off the ground, the heaviness in the leg, the constriction in the front of the thigh, the feel of the heel as it makes contact with the earth, the various sensations in the ankles, hips, buttocks, etc. as my legs carry me through space . . .*

- *You may also notice PHYSICAL SENSATIONS such as coolness on your cheeks from a breeze or warmth on top of your head from the sun. However, focus primarily on the sensations you experience as you lift, move, and place your legs and feet when taking your steps.*

c. *After focusing your attention on these physical sensations for about 20 seconds, switch back to seeing, followed by hearing, smelling, and so forth.*

d. *Feel free to walk at a natural pace or experiment with going slowly if it supports your concentration. Please do not communicate with one another while you walk.*

3. Encourage questions to make sure that everyone understands the instructions. Before the group disperses, ask everyone to stand up and review the four areas where they will be placing their attention during the walk. Name each area of focus and invite participants to use the hand gestures you introduced under 2a, above.

   NOTE: Make a clear agreement as to how and when participants will reconvene.

REFERENCE: Chapter 1

Accordion-Pleated Handout (Sample)

(1) LOOK
at whoever is talking

(13) INTUIT
what the speaker is feeling

(2) FEEL
your own feelings: either emotions or physical sensations

(12) FEEL
your body breathing

(3) INTUIT
the emotions of the person who is speaking

(11) INTUIT
the listener's emotions
(Listener may switch from person to person.)

(4) LISTEN
to the sounds in the room

(10) SEND SILENT BLESSING
to someone in your group, e.g. "May you be happy."

(5) LOOK
at your left hand

(6) CONNECT WITH YOUR NEED
whether met or unmet, from moment to moment

(6) LISTEN
to what the speaker is saying

(8) FEEL
what your left hand feels like
(Try closing your eyes.)

(7) INTUIT
the speaker's needs

COMMUNICATION THAT BLOCKS CONNECTION

3.1 Awareness Exercise:
The Impact of Judgmental
Thinking

3.2 Activity: Cover-Up

3.3 Activity: Tuning in to the
Four Ds

KEY CONCEPT 3:

Communication That Blocks Connection

Description: NVC highlights ways in which we think and speak that prevent heart connection. These include:

1. Diagnoses, judgments, labels, criticism, blame

2. Denial of responsibility for our own feelings and behaviors (or depriving another person of their responsibility for their own feelings and behaviors)

3. Demands or demand-energy—asking for compliance without willingness to consider the needs of the party being addressed

4. "Deserve"-oriented thinking—thinking that certain behaviors or individuals deserve certain consequences in the form of reward or punishment

Toolkit exercises in this section cultivate awareness of ways in which we fall into the "Four Ds of Disconnection." These activities provide participants an opportunity to experience how these forms of thinking block compassionate connection.

Tips for Facilitators: Spend time with participants so they see the value of becoming familiar with the four Ds of Disconnection. As we become increasingly aware of how we disconnect ourselves from others by judging, denying responsibility, demanding, and the use of deserve-language, we might begin to criticize ourselves for such behaviors. This generates a "double-disconnect"—we are not only disconnected from the other party, we are also disconnected within ourselves. An image that might be helpful when approaching our own judgmental behaviors is gold-panning. When we pan for gold we focus on the gold in the midst of the refuse and carefully save the precious nuggets of ore so that we can extract what is beautiful and of great worth. In the same way, within a piece of communication that blocks connection we can find valuable clues revealing what our heart needs and how to re-establish connection.

The Impact of Judgmental Thinking

AIM OF EXERCISE: To practice becoming aware of judgmental thoughts and how they affect us

INSTRUCTIONS FOR GUIDING AWARENESS EXERCISE: Read the following slowly, leaving space between each statement for the participant to engage in the guided process.

1. *Sit comfortably. Straighten your spine. Make any necessary adjustments.*

2. *Focus your attention inward by closing your eyes or gazing softly on the floor in front of you.*

3. *Place your attention on your breathing.*

4. *Bring to mind a person who stimulates unpleasant feelings for you.*

5. *Notice the thoughts that come up as you think of this person. Repeat these thoughts to yourself silently by saying the words in your head.*

6. *Return to the memory of the person and let more thoughts arise. With each thought, repeat the words in your head.*

7. *Now focus your attention on sensations in your body. What physical sensations are you aware of? Become aware of your energy while thinking about the person.*

8. *If you notice any judgments, listen to each judgment and repeat it to yourself.*

9. *If you notice blaming thoughts, listen and repeat them to yourself in your head.*

10. *Again, take a moment to notice your energy and body sensations.*

11. *If you notice any demands you want to make of the person, silently state these demands in your head.*

12. *Likewise, if you have thoughts about what they should or should not be doing or saying, repeat these statements in your head.*

13. *If you think they deserve anything, let that come to you and repeat it silently.*

14. *Once more be aware of the physical sensations in your body and muscles, your energy level, and the type of energy available to you as you run through these thoughts.*

15. *Now take a moment and connect with the need or needs that are not being met for you when this person comes to mind. Are you able to identify the universal needs that you would like met in this situation?*
[Pause]

16. *Go back to your body and be aware of physical sensations and the quality of your energy. As you switch your focus from judgmental thoughts to the universal needs underneath those thoughts, do you notice any changes in your body or energy?*

17. *Spend a few moments recognizing the preciousness of the need or needs you have named. Experience how much you treasure the need(s).*

18. *Once more, check in with your body: notice how your muscles and energy feel in this moment.*

SHARING CIRCLE:

- My name is _____ .

- From the exercise, I learned or realized _____ .

SUGGESTION FOR PRACTICE IN DAILY LIFE: When you find your thoughts turning to judgment, blame, demand or "deserve-type thinking," try deliberately repeating the thought to yourself as a way to become fully conscious of it. Then you can give yourself the choice to either continue in judgment-mode or to change your focus.

REFERENCE: Chapter 2

ACTIVITY 3.2
Cover-Up

PURPOSE OF ACTIVITY:

1. To realize how we hide our hearts under stories we make up about ourselves

2. To realize how we prevent ourselves from seeing and hearing another person by hiding them under the stories we make up about them

3. To recognize that we have choice to:
   • continue feeding our stories, or
   • find strategies to meet the needs behind the stories

BRIEF DESCRIPTION: Participants identify thoughts they have about themselves and others. Using a simple visual metaphor, participants are led through a four-part series to recognize how such thoughts cover up what is real and present in a human being—whether it be ourselves or another person. This activity includes a large group demonstration, individual work, reflection, group debriefing, and a short guided meditation.

MATERIALS NEEDED:
   ❑ One large mirror or window
   ❑ One large sheet of newsprint
   ❑ Individual Handout: Cover-Up (two copies for each participant)
   ❑ Fifteen sheets of paper cut in half lengthwise (to produce thirty pieces, about 11" x 4")

TIME REQUIRED: 1 hour

GROUP SIZE: Any

SPACE REQUIRED: Enough to seat all participants

LITERACY LEVEL REQUIRED: Able to read and write words

PROCEDURE:

Part 1

1. Give this information:

   George has been in and out of prison for twelve years. George asks, "Why does my parole officer look at the piece of paper where lots of people have written thoughts about me instead of looking at me and listening to me?"

2. Stand in front of a mirror or window and have on hand a stack of paper (about 11" x 4").

3. Ask participants:

   - *If you were George, what labels might you be putting on yourself?*

   - *When George judges himself, sees himself as undeserving, or blames himself for what he should or shouldn't do, what kinds of things might he be saying about himself in his head?*

4. Encourage participants to respond and have a volunteer record their answers—one thought (label or judgment) per sheet. Stick the sheets on the mirror or window.

5. When the group has finished responding, ask them:

   Can you imagine George trying to see himself—his real self—in this mirror? What does he see? [If you are using a window, ask participants to imagine that it is a large mirror.]

6. Tack a large piece of newsprint on the wall or board. Ask a volunteer to use the newsprint to write down the group's responses to the next question:

   What might be other people's thoughts about George? What words would they use to label, judge, criticize, or blame him? What thoughts might they have about what George deserves and what's wrong with him?

7. When the group has finished responding, ask a volunteer to represent

   George. Have this volunteer hold the newsprint (covered with people's thoughts about George) in front of himself so that nobody can see him.

8. Debrief question:

   Does anyone wish to share what they have learned from this part of the exercise?

Part 2

1. Introduce the next part:

   Now we'll look at how stories we make up about ourselves prevent us from seeing and hearing what is alive in our hearts and similarly, how stories we make up about other people prevent us from seeing them.

2. Guide participants through the following meditation:

- *Close your eyes, take a couple of breaths, and relax your body.*

- *Imagine yourself standing in front of a full-length mirror.*

- *Take all the labels that you give yourself (for example: "stupid," "smart," "compassionate," "mean," "loser," "winner," "drug addict," "facilitator") and paste them on the mirror.*

- *Now add on to that mirror all the self-blaming statements you say to yourself.*

- *Now add all the "should" and "should nots" you give yourself.*

- *Add all the things you think you deserve—both positive and negative.*

- *Now look at the mirror. Can you see yourself? Or do you just see a pile of thoughts about yourself?*

- *Now visualize taking all the thought statements off the mirror. See your own reflection in the mirror clearly and take a moment to be fully present to yourself. [Pause]*

Part 3

1. Give each participant two copies of the handout with the following instructions:

Take one of these handouts and write down thoughts that you have about yourself—all the labels and judgments you believe about yourself—whether positive or negative, all the thoughts about what you deserve or don't deserve, about what you should or should not be thinking, saying, or doing [Give participants time to write.]

2. After the group has completed the handout, ask them:

Do these thoughts about yourself cover up your real self? Is it possible that they are only a story about you—just like the paper that George's parole officer looked at instead of looking at George?

3. Suggest to the participants:

When you think one of these thoughts, you can remind yourself, "This is only a story I make up about me. I can leave the story and return to who I am in this moment and connect with what is alive in me now."

4. Use the following question for participants to debrief:

What is one thought about yourself that most keeps you from seeing and hearing the real you?

Part 4

Offer the following instructions and questions:

1. *Bring to mind someone about whom you entertain a lot of thoughts.*

2. *Write those thoughts on the second handout such that you no longer can see the figure behind the writing.*

3. *Now ask yourself, "Is there any thought I am willing to let go of?" If so, cross it off the paper.*

4. *Circle the thoughts that are most in the way of your seeing and hearing the other person in the present moment.*

5. *Ask yourself, "What need am I trying to meet by holding on to that thought?"*

6. *Now ask yourself, "What is one other strategy that I could use to meet that need?"*

After participants have completed this part of the exercise, debrief by asking them to share what they have learned that might help them see and hear people in the here and now.

DEBRIEF QUESTION: Is there anything you would like to celebrate—either mourn or appreciate—from having completed the four parts of this activity?

REFERENCE: Chapter 2

Cover-Up

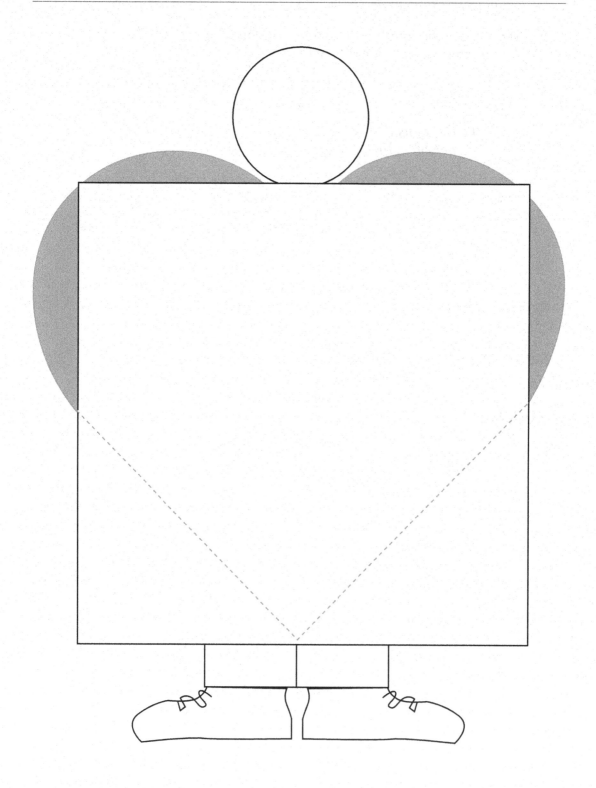

ACTIVITY 3.3

Tuning In to the Four Ds

PURPOSE OF ACTIVITY:

1. To identify four patterns of communication that diminish heart connection

2. To practice recognizing specific instances in everyday speech which fall into these patterns

3. To practice hearing the universal need that may underlie a statement expressing these patterns

4. To experiment with translating statements communicated through these patterns into NVC expression

BRIEF DESCRIPTION: Small teams of participants each create a 3-minute skit containing several statements illustrating the "Four Ds of Disconnection" (see definition of the Four Ds under Procedure Part I, Item #1, below). Teams take turns performing their skit. Audience-teams vie among themselves to identify a "D" as quickly as possible. Any audience member who recognizes a "D" statement in the skit announces it by jubilantly intoning "D-D-D-D" (to the opening notes of Beethoven's Fifth Symphony).

The teams progressively challenge each other to:
    (a) recite the D-statement that generated the chanting of "D-D-D-D,"

    (b) identify which of the four Ds the statement represents,

    (c) guess the need behind the statement, and

    (d) (for groups familiar with the NVC model) translate the D-statement into an NVC expression

MATERIALS NEEDED:
    ❑ Paper and writing instruments; white board or flipchart
    ❑ Individual Handout: Tuning in to the Four Ds

TIME REQUIRED: 2 hours for three groups of four to five participants. Add 20 minutes for each additional group.

GROUP SIZE: Minimum: Nine (three teams with at least three members each). **Maximum** number depends on availability of time and space: allow 2 hours for three teams. Add another 20 minutes for each additional team. If additional rooms are available so that two or more skits may be performed simultaneously, this activity can accommodate any number of participants.

SPACE REQUIRED: Adequate for teams to plan their skits without mutual interference

LITERACY LEVEL REQUIRED: Not required, but ability to write down one's lines may be helpful when performing the skit

PROCEDURE:

Part I—Introduction and Creation of Skits

1. List the "Four Ds of Disconnection" on the board. Review and give an example of each "D." (For additional information on the Four Ds, see Description of Concept #3 at the beginning of this section, p. 47.)

   a. **DIAGNOSE,** judge, label, criticize
      e.g., "The problem with you is that . . ."

   b. **DENY** responsibility for one's actions and feelings
      e.g., "I have to pay taxes." "He made me feel bad."

   c. **DEMAND**
      e.g., "You have to (must, should, got to, ought to, are supposed to) take out the garbage." "You can't wear that."

   d. **DESERVE** as in "You deserve (don't deserve) . . ."

   NOTE: Explain that these four patterns of communication can occur in dialogues we have with others as well as with ourselves. There may be some overlap between (b) and (c). For example, if I say, "I have to pay taxes" to a friend, this would be an example of (b) denial of responsibility. If I say "I have to pay taxes" to myself, this could be either (b) or (c), the common denominator being the absence of choice.

2. Give participants an overview of the activity as offered in the first paragraph of the "Brief Description," above. (Save the details in the second paragraph to present later.)

3. Divide participants into groups of four to five and inform them that they have 30 minutes to create a 3-minute skit, which will be performed twice to an audience. The skit is to contain lines which illustrate the four Ds. However, ask groups to aim for dialogues that sound real or natural rather than exaggerated, and to make their skit challenging for their audience by including both lines which have Ds and those which have no Ds.

4. Distribute and go over the handout "Tuning in to the Four Ds," offer paper and pen, and give participants 30 minutes to create their skits. Double-check that all groups are clear about the task at hand.

Part II—Performance and Challenge

1. Arrange a stage in front of the room where the skits are to be performed.

2. Invite one team to step up to the stage to perform their skit.

3. Ask the referee on the team to stand to one side of the stage. (See #8 below for referee responsibilities)

4. Have the audience face the stage, but clustered in their own teams.

5. Give the following instructions to the audience-teams:

   a. *Audience, you will see the skit performed twice. During the first time, simply listen for "D" statements, but do not interrupt the performance.*

   b. *During the second performance your teams will be challenging each other. Just as soon as any of you hear a "D" statement, stand up, throw both hands over your head, and loudly intone "D-D-D-D" as quickly as possible. [Demonstrate the movements and chant D-D-D-D to the tune and rhythm of the first four notes of Beethoven's Fifth Symphony.]*

   c. *This person will then recite the "D" statement they claim to have identified.*

      • *If they are unable to recite the "D" statement, they forfeit their right to challenge the other team and the skit continues.*

      • *If they are successful in identifying and reciting the "D" statement, they may challenge a specific person from another team to state which of the four Ds the statement represents.*

   d. *The person who is challenged may consult with their teammates before deciding which of the four Ds the statement represents. Please be aware that some "D" statements may qualify under more than one "D" category. What we'll be looking for during the challenge is a clear explanation of why a statement falls into the category that was identified.*

      • *If they are unable to identify the category, their team loses the challenge and the skit continues.*

      • *If they are able to identify the type of D, the challenge continues and moves back to the other team.*

   e. *The original challenger then guesses the need behind the "D" statement. (What universal need might the speaker have had?) The player is allowed to consult with teammates to come up with two guesses.*

      • *If they are unable to make two guesses, the challenge ends and the skit continues.*

      • *If they are able to guess two possible needs, the challenge continues.*

f. The person on the other team is now called to translate the "D" statement into an NVC expression of either honesty or empathy.

- *If they are able to do this, they will have fully succeeded in meeting the challenge from the other team. The skit continues.*

- *If they are not able to do this, the original challenger has an opportunity to give it a try. If the original challenger succeeds in translating the statement into an NVC expression of honesty or empathy, they will have completed their challenge of the other team. The skit continues.*

6. Clarify the following points:

a. *Remember that you may always request assistance from team-mates.*

b. *During the skit, I will take the role of arbiter as to whether a team has satisfactorily responded to a challenge. However, please take notes if you disagree or have a question. We will have a debrief period after each skit to address these concerns.*

7. Ask the audience if they are clear on how they will be challenging one another.

8. Address the following instructions to the team that is performing the skit:

a. *Referee, If more than one person stands up to chant D-D-D-D, please point to the person you believe first completed all three actions: (1) stand up, (2) stretch hands overhead, and (3) chant D-D-D-D.*

b. *Referee, you will also determine how many seconds a team may take to come up with an answer. Use your judgment to give a warning or to "call time."*

c. *Actors, before beginning your performance, please tell us:*

- *The title of your skit*

- *The parties involved, their relationship to each other, and the role each of you are playing*

- *Where (and when) this scenario takes place*

9. Following the performance of each skit, allow time for participants to raise questions or disagreements regarding the challenges that were made.

DEBRIEF QUESTIONS: After all the skits have been completed, ask participants to share what they most enjoyed about the activity, what they learned from either performing or listening to the skits, and how the exercise might be improved.

SUGGESTIONS FOR PRACTICE IN DAILY LIFE:

Listen for Ds

- in the media, when reading signs or hearing public announcements,

- in how you talk to yourself.

Rather than judging the way a message is being expressed, train yourself to guess the need behind the statement.

REFERENCE: Chapter 2

Tuning In to the Four Ds

Your group has 30 minutes to create a scenario which contains a number of "D" statements—statements which *diagnose*, *deny* responsibility, *demand*, or imply that someone *deserves* a particular situation.

Here is a list of the "Four Ds of Disconnection."

1. **DIAGNOSE**, judge, label, criticize
    e.g. "The problem with you is that . . ."

2. **DENY** responsibility for one's actions and feelings
    e.g. "I have to pay taxes." "He made me feel bad."

3. **DEMAND**
    e.g. "You have to (must, should, got to, ought to, are supposed to) take out the garbage." "You can't wear that."

4. **DESERVE** as in "They deserve (don't deserve) . . ."

GUIDELINES FOR CREATING SKIT: In creating the skit, work together in whatever way is most effective for your particular group. Use the following steps as a reference. Time in parentheses are suggestions only.

1. **(2 minutes)** Brainstorm and then pick a scenario involving two or more parties who are not in full harmony with each other. Examples: a parent-child scene over homework, a disagreement between cellmates (neighbors or coworkers), a disciplinary action at school (prison or workplace), a dispute between citizens and government officials, etc.

2. **(5 minutes)** Begin by "playing out" the scenario you picked. Have everyone chime in spontaneously to create the draft of a script-dialogue. At this stage, any person can speak out in any role. Include statements demonstrating the four Ds as well as statements that do not. (Take notes so you can later recall the lines that had been spontaneously generated.)

3. **(3 minutes)** Decide on the outline of your 3-minute skit. Define and write down the following:

    a. Who are the parties involved? How many roles will there be in the skit? Make up a name for each character in the skit. What is their relationship to each other?

    b. Where (and when) does this scenario take place?

c. What appears to be the main issue in the dialogue? Give the skit a title.

d. In what direction do you intend the dialogue to go?

4. **(2 minutes)** Decide who will play which role. Reserve one member of your group to serve as a "referee" during the performance when the audience teams will be challenging each other.

5. **(5–10 minutes)** Create the dialogue. Either:

    a. work together as a team to generate a script; or

    b. have the actors improvise their own lines

6. **(5 minutes)** Have each actor write down the lines they will be delivering which contain a "D." Explore the need(s) that the speaker may be trying to meet by saying that line.

7. **(5 minutes)** Rehearse the skit. You will be performing it twice—once straight through, and the second time with interruptions from the audience.

FOUR CHOICES IN RECEIVING A DIFFICULT MESSAGE

4.1 Awareness Exercise: Awareness of Our Choices

4.2 Activity: Experiencing the Four Choices

4.3 Activity: Choosing How We Hear and Respond

KEY CONCEPT 4:

Four Choices in Receiving a Difficult Message

Description: NVC points to the availability of four choices regarding where we put our attention when we have difficulty enjoying what someone is saying to us.

1. I can hear blame and think what's wrong with them.

2. I can hear blame and think what's wrong with me.

3. I can hear my own feelings and needs as I listen to their words.

4. I can hear their feelings and needs beneath their words.

Toolkit exercises in this section support awareness in recognizing choice, and provide practice in hearing feelings and needs when receiving a difficult message.

Tips for Facilitators:

1. Engage participants by offering "difficult-to-hear" messages that are relevant to their lives.

2. When working with this concept, participants may notice critical thoughts such as, "I shouldn't judge people," or "They shouldn't demand." As mentioned earlier (under Concept 3, Tips for Facilitators), we can "look for the gold" in judgments, demands, and other forms of language that block connection. When a thought about wrongness comes out of someone's mouth (or out of our own), facilitators have an opportunity to model the NVC process if they: (a) stop, (b) name the thought, and (c) check for the feeling and need under that thought.

AWARENESS EXERCISE 4.1

Awareness of Our Choices

AIM OF EXERCISE:

1. To develop awareness of the four ways of hearing a "difficult-to-hear" message

2. To develop the ability to choose how we respond to a message we do not enjoy

INSTRUCTIONS FOR GUIDING THIS EXERCISE: Read the following slowly, leaving space between each statement for the participant to engage in the guided process.

1. *Sit comfortably. Straighten your spine. Make any necessary adjustments.*

2. *Focus your attention inward by closing your eyes or gently dropping your gaze to the floor in front of you.*

3. *Focus your attention on your breathing.*

   - *Simply be aware of how you are breathing.*

   - *Notice breathing in and breathing out. Focus at the nostrils or chest or diaphragm or belly.*

   - *Now, instead of simply being aware of your breathing, think about your breathing. (Judge it, evaluate it, make demands; for example, "I should be breathing more deeply," or "I'm making too much noise with my breath.") Take some time to notice how you may be trying to control your breath now.* [Pause]

   - *Return now to simply being aware of your breathing.*

   - *Alternate between awareness of breathing and thinking about it.*

   - *Notice your body sensations when you're aware of breathing as opposed to when you are thinking about your breath.*

   - *Now focus your attention on what need of yours is being met or not met by the way you are breathing.*

   - *Now go back to your breath and breathe in a way that meets this need.*

4. *At this point recall a "difficult-to-hear" message you have received or are afraid of receiving from another person.*

   - *Say this message silently to yourself or imagine someone else saying it to you.*

   - *Now imagine criticizing or making demands of yourself. Imply that you deserve this message and blame yourself.*

- *Notice any changes in your body: your muscles, your energy.*

- *Hear the message again. This time focus on the one who is giving you the message. Blame or judge them. Make a demand or imply they deserve the negative consequences of their behavior.*

- *Notice any change in your muscles and energy.*

- *Say the message to yourself again for the third time. This time when you hear the message, ask yourself, "What am I feeling and needing?"*

- *Notice any shift in your energy or muscles.*

- *Repeat the message a fourth time, this time imagining the other person saying it to you. What do you guess the speaker is feeling and needing?*

- *Notice if you experience any muscular or energetic changes.*

- *You have just experienced four ways of hearing a "difficult-to-hear" message: blaming yourself, blaming the other, connecting with your own feelings and needs, connecting with the feelings and needs of the other.*

5. *Take a few moments to reflect back on this time and highlight anything you would want to remember.*

6. *When you are ready, return your attention to this room.*

SHARING CIRCLE:

- My name is _____ .

- One thing I'd like to remember from this exercise is _____ .

REFERENCES: Chapters 5, 13

Experiencing the Four Choices

PURPOSE OF ACTIVITY:

1. To practice recognizing and distinguishing four choices in how we hear a difficult message

2. To practice hearing ourselves and others with empathy

BRIEF DESCRIPTION: Working in groups of five, members listen to a "difficult-to-hear" message and practice each of the four options.

MATERIALS NEEDED:

❑ Feeling and need words posted on walls. Use General Learning Aids G5 and G7: Wall Signs

Make copies for each group of the following materials:

❑ Group Handout: Difficult-to-Hear Messages. Choose one of the two handouts: 4.2A is for prison use and 4.2B is for the general community.

❑ Specific Learning Aid 4.2: Set of Four Signs Labeling the Four Choices

---

Choice #1

HEAR BLAME BLAME BACK

Choice #2

HEAR BLAME BLAME SELF

Choice #3

HEAR MY OWN FEELINGS & NEEDS

Choice #4

HEAR SPEAKER'S FEELINGS & NEEDS

Set of Four Signs Labeling the Four Choices

TIME REQUIRED: 30–40 minutes

GROUP SIZE: Ideally five (or a minimum of four) to a group

SPACE REQUIRED: Space for members of each group to hear each other clearly while standing or sitting in a circle

LITERACY LEVEL REQUIRED: Ability to read simple sentences

PROCEDURE:

1. Name the exercise and explain its purpose (see above).

2. Demonstrate the activity using four volunteers:

   - *We'll form groups of five. Members face each other in a circle either standing or sitting. Each group will receive a sheet of "difficult-to-hear" messages and a set of four signs.*

   - *I will hold the "difficult-to-hear" message sheet.*

   - *The person to my left takes the sign "Choice #1: Hear blame and blame back" and places it on the floor, the table or their lap in a way that is visible to other members of the group.*

   - *Continuing clockwise, the next person does the same with the sign "Choice #2: Hear blame and blame self."*

   - *The fourth person does the same with "Choice #3: Hear my own feelings and needs."*

   - *The last person takes "Choice #4: Hear the speaker's feelings and needs."*

   - *We'll start with whoever is holding the sheet of "difficult-to-hear" messages. I am holding it right now so I will read the first message on this sheet to the person on my left. For example, "You're late again!"*
     [Use gestures and tone of voice to accompany the delivery of the message.]

   - *The person on my left practicing Choice #1 will listen to the message, hear blame, and blame back. Please demonstrate by saying a blaming thought about me out loud while shaking a finger or fist at me.*
     [Ask the volunteer on your left to demonstrate this. Do not look at that person. The purpose of this activity is to practice recognizing the kind of thinking that is going on in our minds as listeners, not to practice expressing ourselves to the speaker. Thus encourage the listeners to refer to the speaker in the third person (i.e., to use the words "him/her," "he/she" rather than "you." For example, "Who's she to talk about other people being late!" rather than, "Who are you to talk about other people being late!"].

   - *Now the next volunteer will demonstrate Choice #2 by hearing blame and blaming herself. Please criticize yourself out loud while pointing a finger or shaking a fist at yourself. For example, "I should get my act together."*

- *The next person demonstrates Choice #3 by hearing their own feelings and needs. Please express your feelings and needs while placing your palms on your heart. For example, "I feel discouraged because I need understanding."*

- *The final person demonstrates Choice #4 by hearing the speaker's feelings and needs. For example, "I wonder if they are feeling irritated because they need consideration." Open your palms toward the speaker in a receiving gesture as you focus your attention on what they might be feeling and needing.*

- *After completing a round, everyone will take a step to the left and assume a different role. In five rounds, each person will have had an opportunity to practice all the roles.*

3. Tell participants that if there is a question in their group about anyone's response, they can feel free to interrupt and get clarity before continuing the round.

4. Point participants to feeling and need words posted on walls or available on their Learning Guides.

5. Remind participants to speak softly so groups don't distract one another.

6. Indicate amount of time available for this activity, and ask if there are questions before beginning.

DEBRIEF QUESTIONS:

1. Which of the four choices was easiest for you? The most difficult?

2. Imagine a situation in your life where you see yourself facing these four choices.

   - *What choice would you like to be making in that situation?*

   - *What would support you in doing so effectively?*

REFERENCES: Chapters 5, 13

Difficult-to-Hear Messages: PRISON

1. If you think I'm going to be dumb enough to leave you the keys to my house, you're even stupider than I thought.

2. What good is all this programming doing you? You still can't get along with anyone.

3. Just because you're locked up doesn't mean you have to waste your life rotting in front of the tube, you know.

4. If you don't like the chow, you don't have to eat it.

5. Did it ever occur to you that you blame everything on someone or something else?

6. It's in the books and we've told you clearly: volunteers and inmates are to have no contact whatsoever outside this workshop.

7. When will you ever learn to be considerate of other people? There are fifteen other people on this range, you know.

8. You don't read the chapter and then you expect to understand what's going on in the group. What's wrong with this picture?

9. This group is too intense. I expected to have time to hang out with volunteers here.

10. Why don't you clean up after yourself instead of leaving a mess for others?

11. _____

_____

Difficult-to-Hear Messages: GENERAL COMMUNITY

1. What good is all your NVC practice when you can't even handle a minor crisis like this?

2. Don't let the boys hang around the kitchen. It's time they learned to become men.

3. You really shouldn't waste so much money on workshops. I mean, how much do you have saved up anyway?

4. You want to know what I am feeling and needing? I feel like throwing up and I need to be left alone!

5. I think the government is trying to handle a difficult situation, and it's a shame to have people demonstrating and criticizing our leaders' every move.

6. This is not a playground or a zoo. If you cannot control your children's behavior, we must ask you to leave the premises.

7. Why is it that every time I come home from a trip, the house looks as if a cyclone has hit it?

8. You have no business leading a practice group if you are not qualified and haven't done your personal work.

9. I realize it's the end of the shift and I can't pay you overtime, but I have to have this done for that meeting first thing tomorrow morning.

10. You talk like a robot with all this feelings and needs stuff. Why don't you get real?

11. _____

_____

ACTIVITY 4.3

Choosing How We Hear and Respond

PURPOSE OF ACTIVITY:

1. To recognize the four choices we have in how we hear and respond to a difficult message

2. To practice hearing feelings and needs when receiving a difficult message

BRIEF DESCRIPTION: Participants work in groups of three: the first person makes a difficult-to-hear statement. The second person responds with whatever spontaneously comes up for them. The third person listens to the latter's response and identifies it with one of the four choices listed on the board. If the choice entailed hearing blame, the second person has an opportunity to listen to the message again and to respond differently.

MATERIALS NEEDED:
☐ Board or flipchart

TIME REQUIRED: 30–40 minutes

GROUP SIZE: Three or more

SPACE REQUIRED: Enough for small groups of three to work without mutual interference

LITERACY LEVEL REQUIRED: Ability to read and write sentences desirable, but not necessary

PROCEDURE:

1. Introduce or review the four choices we have in hearing and responding to a difficult message:

    a. Hear blame (judgment, criticism) and blame the speaker

    b. Hear blame (judgment, criticism) and blame myself

    c. Hear my own feelings and needs and (if I so desire) express them honestly

    d. Hear the feelings and needs beneath the other person's words and (if I so desire) reflect back empathically

2. Inform participants that we will work in groups of three to practice identifying the four different responses. Write them in large letters on the board so that they are visible to all:

   a. Hear blame, blame back

   b. Hear blame, blame self

   c. Hear own feelings and needs; express honestly

   d. Hear other's feelings and needs; reflect empathically

3. Give the following instructions:

   a. Person A makes up a difficult-to-hear statement and says it to Person B .

   b. Person B responds to A in whatever manner they wish.

   c. Person C identifies B's response, using the following format: "When A said, "_____," B responded by _____ ." [Point to the board to remind participants to refer to the four choices listed.]

   Example:
   - A to B: "Why are you late?"

   - B to A: "I'm really sorry I screwed up; something's the matter with me that I'm always late."

   - C: "When A said, 'Why are you late?', B heard blame and blamed herself."

4. If B's response was to hear blame, B may ask A to repeat the message. This time B has the opportunity to listen for feelings and needs—either A's feelings and needs or their own.

   Example:
   - A to B: "Why are you late?"

   - B to A: "Are you irritated because you value reliability?"

   - C: "When A said, 'Why are you late?', B listened for A's feeling and need and reflected back empathically."

5. Give another example, if necessary.

   First round:
   - A to B: "You are always picking on your brother."

   - B to A: "You should talk. I have seen you with your sister. She's terrified of you."

- C: "When A said, 'You are always picking on your brother,' B heard blame and blamed back."

Second round:
- A to B: "You are always picking on your brother."

- B to A: "I feel sad hearing you say that because I would like to be better understood for my intentions."

- C: "When A said, 'You are always picking on your brother,' B focused on his own feelings and need, and expressed them honestly."

6. Ask the participants to think of statements that would be difficult to hear and to jot them down.

7. Invite three volunteers to demonstrate the activity by playing the roles of A, B, and C. Person A will begin by addressing B with a difficult-to-hear message.

8. When everyone is clear on the procedures, invite participants to split into groups of three. Ask them to rotate roles so that each person in the group has at least one opportunity to practice each of the three roles. Inform groups that they have 20 minutes.

DEBRIEF QUESTIONS:

1. Which of the four choices did you discover to be most habitual for you?

2. Which of the four choices required the greatest effort for you? What would make it easier for you to respond with that choice?

SUGGESTION FOR PRACTICE IN DAILY LIFE: Review your day, looking for a response you made to a difficult-to-hear message that you are not satisfied with. Notice what you heard in the message and what choice you made in responding. Then write down the way you would prefer to have responded. Reflect on what would support you in making such a response in a similar future situation.

REFERENCE: Chapter 5

OBSERVATION

5.1 Awareness Exercise: Simply
     Observing

5.2 Activity: Walking Between
     Observation and Evaluation

5.3 Activity: Pop-Up—
     Distinguishing Observation
     From Evaluation

5.4 Activity: Using Images to State
     Observations

KEY CONCEPT 5:

Observation

Description: NVC emphasizes the distinction between observation and evaluation. *Observation* refers to what we directly see, hear, smell, taste, and feel through touch. *Evaluation* consists of the thoughts and interpretations in our minds that get triggered by an observation. Observation is the first of the four components of the NVC model. By stating observations, we are defining the stimuli that lead us into a dialogue or action.

Our habit of mixing observation and evaluation contributes to confusion and disconnection. Consider the following ways in which a parent approaches (either in thought or speech) a child regarding a math grade received at school:

a. "You lied to me about your grade."

b. "What you told me about your grade isn't true."

c. "You said you got a B in math, but this report card says it's a D."

d. "I heard you say that you got a B in math, but I am seeing a D on this report card."

The parent makes an evaluation in (a) that the child purposefully gave false information. The parent makes an evaluation in (b) that the report card, rather than the child, gives correct information. The parent makes an observation in (c) based on what was directly heard (from the child) and seen (on the report card.) In (d), the parent states the same observations while also claiming ownership for them. The parent's evaluations in (a) and (b) may or may not turn out to be accurate; what is important, however, is the clarity on both sides as to the observation that is leading the parent to initiate a dialogue with the child.

Toolkit exercises in this section support awareness of the distinction between observation and evaluation and provide practice in making clear NVC observations.

Tips for Facilitators: When you hear a participant stating an evaluation, avoid the temptation to point out, "That's not an observation." Instead, invite them to reflect further by asking, for example, "What did your eyes actually see (or what did your ears actually hear) to lead you to think that?" Ultimately we recognize that our eyes—just like those of newborn babies—can directly see only shapes and colors, and our ears can hear only sounds. "Child," "report card," and "grade" are in fact all mental interpretations of what we observe through our senses. If we keep in mind the purpose of the NVC practice of distinguishing observation from evaluation, we can avoid right/wrong thinking, while developing deeper sensitivity to differences in conventional (cultural, institutional, family, etc.) realities. For example, the word *fail* usually reflects an evaluation, but when applied within a school where there are agreed-on definitions as to what constitutes "fail" and "pass," it could be expressing an observation.

AWARENESS EXERCISE 5.1
Simply Observing

AIM OF EXERCISE: To practice "simply observing" what we see, hear, smell, and feel through touch

INSTRUCTIONS FOR GUIDING AWARENESS EXERCISE: Read the following slowly, leaving space between each statement for the participant to engage in the guided process.

1. *Sit comfortably. Straighten your spine. Make any necessary adjustments.*

2. *Focus your attention inward by closing your eyes or gazing softly on the floor in front of you.*

3. *Place your attention on your breathing.*

   - *Feel the breath at your nostrils.*

   - *Observe any changes in sensation.*

   - *Observe any changes in sound as you breathe in and out.*

4. *Now focus your attention on your lungs. Feel the sensation of your chest expanding and contracting. See how many sensations you can observe.*

5. *Take a moment to open your eyes and look at your hands. What do you observe through your eyes?*

6. *Close your eyes, but continue to focus your attention on your hands. What do you observe through physical sensation and touch?*

7. *Now bring to mind a moment from your childhood.*

   - *In your memory, what do you see? What do you actually see in your mind's eye?*

   - *Notice if you are switching from simply seeing to **thinking** about what you are seeing. When you are aware that you are evaluating and thinking about the situation, simply return to just observing what you see in the scene you are recalling.*

   - *In this memory, are there sounds or voices? What do you hear?*

   - *Are there any smells, body sensations, or tastes that you can remember?*

8. *Now take leave of that childhood memory. Bring your attention back to your breath in the here and now. Take three conscious breaths.*

9. *When you are ready, open your eyes.*

- *Look around the room and notice what you see.*

- *What do you hear?*

- *What do you experience through your sense of touch?*

- *What do you smell?*

- *What do you taste?*

SHARING CIRCLE:

1. My name is _____ .

2. What I learned from practicing "simply observing" in the here-and-now and in my mind's eye is _____ .

REFERENCE: Chapter 3

ACTIVITY 5.2

Walking Between Observation and Evaluation

PURPOSE OF ACTIVITY:

1. To deepen awareness of the difference between observation and evaluation

2. To practice articulating observation that is free from evaluation and moralistic judgment

BRIEF DESCRIPTION: Participants work in pairs standing at one end of the room. One person in the pair makes a statement containing an evaluation and together they walk to the other end of the room. Here, the same participant focuses on the facts behind the previous statement and articulates an observation free of evaluation. The partner provides support or coaching where needed. They take turns doing this for approximately 10 minutes.

MATERIALS NEEDED:

☐ Specific Learning Aid 5.2: Set of Two Signs Labeled *Observation* and *Evaluation*

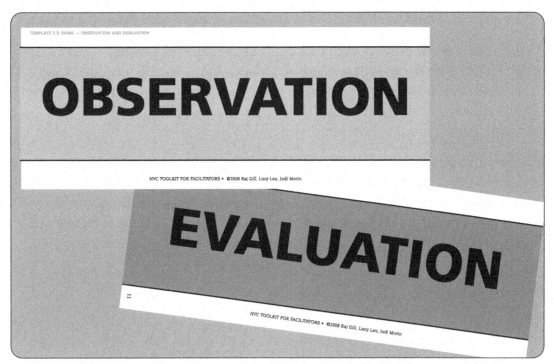

Set of Two Signs Labeled *Observation* and *Evaluation*

TIME REQUIRED: 20 minutes

GROUP SIZE: Two to fifty

SPACE REQUIRED: Enough for participants to comfortably move from one end of the room to the other

LITERACY LEVEL REQUIRED: None

PROCEDURE:

1. Clarify the difference between "observation" and "evaluation."

    NOTE: In this and other exercises where we practice making observations free of evaluation, it may be helpful to acknowledge the concept of "consensual" or "conventional reality." We assume that everyone in the room, for example, shares a common cultural understanding as to the meaning of "green," "room," "wavy," "workshop," etc. Thus, a statement such as, "There are two rooms in the green house where the workshop is being held." would qualify as an "observation" if we are dialoguing in mainstream culture. Theoretically, however, it is possible that people from a remote culture may not share the same meaning that we assign to words such as "room," "green," or "workshop." [For further elaboration on this point, see Exercise 9.5, Procedure #3.]

2. Attach the sign with the word "EVALUATION" on the wall at one end (or one side) of the room. Stand here and state an evaluation, e.g., "This is a cheerful room."

3. Take the "OBSERVATION" sign, walk over to the other end (or side) of the room, and attach it to the wall. Stand here and make an observation related to your previous evaluation, e.g., "There are colored photos of natural scenery and flowers on two sides of this room."

4. Invite a volunteer to step up to the "EVALUATION" sign and state an evaluation. Then walk with them to the other end of the room and ask them to make an observation related to their previous statement. If you perceive evaluation in the volunteer's statement, ask, "What might you be observing—what do your eyes or ears see or hear—that leads you to think that way?" Coach the volunteer until you are both satisfied that their statement consists of an observation free of evaluation.

5. Ask participants to choose a partner and take turns

    *   making an evaluation at one end of the room,

    *   walking together to the other end, and

    *   generating an observation free of evaluation.

6. Inform participants that they have about 10 minutes for this activity.

SUGGESTION FOR PRACTICE IN DAILY LIFE: When you or someone else makes an evaluation or judgment, practice guessing what is being observed behind the thought. In other words, guess what is being seen, heard, smelled, tasted, or felt (through touch or physical sensation). Remember to simply notice the judgment or evaluation without making any judgments about it!

REFERENCE: Chapter 3

ACTIVITY 5.3
Pop-Up—Distinguishing Observation From Evaluation

PURPOSE OF ACTIVITY:

1. To learn the difference between observation and evaluation

2. To practice making observations free of evaluations

BRIEF DESCRIPTION: A participant volunteers to make a statement. Those who consider the statement to be an observation free of evaluation will stay seated. Those who hear evaluation in the statement will stand. Anyone standing can then volunteer a related statement that they consider to be free of evaluation. Those who hear only observation will sit; those who continue to hear evaluation remain standing. Continue until everyone is seated.

MATERIALS NEEDED: None

TIME REQUIRED: 15 minutes

GROUP SIZE: Three to thirty

SPACE REQUIRED: Large enough to seat participants in a circle

LITERACY LEVEL REQUIRED: None

PROCEDURE:

1. Define "observation" and "evaluation."

    NOTE: For this and other exercises where we practice making observations free of evaluation, it may be helpful to acknowledge the concept of "consensual" or "conventional reality." We assume that everyone in the room, for example, shares a common cultural understanding as to the meaning of "green," "room," "wavy," "workshop," etc. Thus, a statement such as, "There are two rooms in the green house where the workshop is being held." would qualify as an "observation" if we are dialoguing in mainstream culture. Theoretically, however, it is possible that people from a remote culture may not share the same meaning that we assign to words such as "room," "green," or "workshop." [For further elaboration on this point, see Exercise 9.5, Procedure #3.]

2. Invite a volunteer to make a statement, either an observation or an evaluation, about someone or something outside of themselves. Examples: "He would make a poor treasurer." "The tree in front of the church is older than the building itself."

3. Ask participants to stand if they hear any evaluation in the statement.

4. Ask those who are standing, "Would someone state an observation that might have led to the evaluation you heard?"

   Example: If the original statement was, "He would make a poor treasurer," someone who heard evaluation and decided to stand up might offer the following statement: "His wife said he bounced three checks last month."

5. Ask participants to sit down if they hear only observation in the new statement and to remain standing if they still hear evaluation.

6. Continue until everyone is seated. Then ask someone to volunteer another statement to start a new round.

7. Take about 10 minutes or until the group seems confident in distinguishing observation from evaluation.

DEBRIEF QUESTIONS:

1. How would you define observation?

2. How would you define evaluation?

3. What did you discover?

SUGGESTIONS FOR PRACTICE IN DAILY LIFE: Practice noticing:

- when you are observing (i.e., seeing, hearing, smelling, tasting, feeling through touch) and

- when you are evaluating (e.g., thinking, judging, interpreting, comparing, etc.).

Remember that our practice is to distinguish observation from evaluation, not to replace one with the other or to judge observation as "correct" and evaluation as "incorrect."

REFERENCE: Chapter 3

ACTIVITY 5.4

Using Images to State Observations

PURPOSE OF ACTIVITY:

1. To gain clarity in distinguishing between observation and evaluation

2. To practice making observations free of evaluation

BRIEF DESCRIPTION: Participants each receive a picture. Working in pairs, they look at each other's picture and make observations. Upon completion, they exchange pictures and seek another partner.

MATERIALS NEEDED:

☐ A stack of pictures, at least one for each participant (more if the group is small). (See General Learning Aid G9: Guidelines for Assembling a Set of Pictures)

☐ Two pictures large enough to be visible to the whole group for use in the initial demonstration of the exercise.

TIME REQUIRED: 20–30 minutes

GROUP SIZE: Any

SPACE REQUIRED: Adequate for participants to move around when seeking partners and for dyads to work without mutual interference

LITERACY REQUIRED: None

PROCEDURE:

1. Show a large picture and invite participants to make observations.

   If you hear evaluation in someone's statement, ask them, "What might you be observing that leads you to think that?"

2. Invite two volunteers (A and B) to demonstrate the procedure.

   • Give a picture to volunteer B.

   • Say to Volunteer A, "Please tell B what you observe in her picture."

   • Say to Volunteer B, "If you hear any evaluation, ask A to tell you what he is observing—what his eyes are seeing in the picture—that leads him to think in that way."

- Request A and B to reverse the process so that B makes an observation of A's picture.

- Ask them to exchange pictures and raise their hands to indicate they are now ready to seek new partners.

- Ask the group if there are any questions regarding the procedure.

3. When you sense that participants have understood the distinction and are ready to make observations free of evaluation, give one picture to each participant.

- Begin the exercise by inviting everyone to find a partner.

- Circulate among the pairs, allowing about 10 minutes for this activity.

SUGGESTION FOR PRACTICE IN DAILY LIFE: As you go about your daily activities, notice what you are receiving of the world through your sense organs— what you actually see, hear, taste, smell, or can feel through touch.

REFERENCE: Chapter 3

FEELING

6.1 Awareness Exercise: Feeling Our Feelings

6.2 Activity: Expensive Emotions

6.3 Activity: Naming Similar Feelings

6.4 Activity: Sculpting Feelings

6.5 Activity: Honing Our Vocabulary of Feeling Words

6.6 Activity: Connecting Feelings With Events

6.7 Activity: Using Images to Connect With Feelings

KEY CONCEPT 6:

Feeling

Description: The second component of the NVC model is "feeling." In NVC, a feeling can be an emotion, body sensation, mood, or state of mind. NVC urges us to "connect with our feelings." We do this by actually feeling our feelings and being aware of what we are feeling, while recognizing the distinction between feelings and thoughts. To verbally express what we are feeling, NVC suggests words that most effectively describe our internal experience without making reference to other people or outer circumstances. For example, saying "I feel scared and lonely" helps us connect more easily with the actual feeling experience than "I feel abandoned" which is primarily a thought about something being done to me. We are also reminded that, in the English language, phrases beginning with "I feel that . . .," "I feel as if . . .," "I feel he/she/it/you," etc., are likely to express thoughts rather than feelings.

Toolkit exercises in this section offer practice in:

- Connecting with feelings

- Noticing and naming feelings

- Increasing vocabulary of words that convey feelings

- Distinguishing feelings from thoughts and expressing feelings effectively

- Recognizing and working with emotions that expend a lot of energy

Tips for Facilitators: When facilitating practice in this section, keep in mind that "sad," "excited," "discouraged," etc., are not feelings in themselves, but simply words we use to convey a particular internal experience. The words are not the experience, and different people may use different words. Thus, if we hear a participant say, "I feel betrayed," instead of telling them, "Betrayed is not a feeling," we can support them in coming closer to the actual experience. For example, we can ask, "If you think that you have been betrayed, what feelings might be stirred up inside of you? . . . Where in the body would you feel it? . . . Are you willing to focus inward, check in with yourself, and get in touch with whatever emotion or physical sensation you discover?"

In the course of practicing NVC, you may hear words such as "abandoned," "betrayed," "violated," "manipulated," etc., referred to as "non-feelings" or "faux-feelings." It is helpful to be aware of the many words in our language that sound like feelings but tend to convey thoughts. However, our purpose is not correctness in using feeling words and shunning "non-feeling" words, but connecting with our own inner feelings and finding words that most effectively convey that experience.

Feeling Our Feelings

AIM OF EXERCISE:

1. To practice noticing and naming feelings

2. To increase our ability to be comfortable with our feelings

INSTRUCTIONS FOR GUIDING THIS EXERCISE: Read the following slowly, leaving space between each statement for the participant to engage in the guided process:

1. *Sit comfortably. Straighten your spine. Make any necessary adjustments.*

2. *Focus your attention inward by closing your eyes or gently dropping your gaze to the floor in front of you.*

3. *Focus your attention on your breathing.*

4. *As you focus on your breathing, notice how you are feeling.*

5. *How does this feeling manifest itself in your body (muscles, energy, pulse)?*

6. *Return to focusing on your breath.*

7. *When you notice a thought arise,*

   - *Say the thought to yourself,*

   - *And notice what you are feeling.*

   - *If you have no word to name the feeling, simply notice the body sensations you are experiencing.*

8. *When complete with that thought, go back to watching your breath and wait for the next thought to arise.*

9. *Repeat by:*

   - *Saying the thought to yourself,*

   - *Noticing your emotion, and*

   - *Any accompanying body sensations*

10. *Continue this process for a few minutes.*

11. *When you hear the bell, take a few moments to remember the feelings you experienced.*

12. Now bring your awareness back to the room.

13. When you are ready, open your eyes and look around the room at other people with a sense of curiosity as to what each one might have just experienced.

SHARING CIRCLE:

- My name is _____ .

- One emotion or body sensation I was aware of during this exercise was _____ .

REFERENCE: Chapter 4

ACTIVITY 6.2

Expensive Emotions

PURPOSE OF ACTIVITY:

1. To recognize how certain emotions can drain our energy without contributing to meeting our needs

2. To practice working with an "expensive emotion" to get in touch with the underlying need

BRIEF DESCRIPTION: Participants are invited to reflect upon emotions (such as anger, shame, and guilt) which exact a heavy toll without contributing to our needs being met. With the guidance of a worksheet, individuals focus on a personal situation, moving beyond "expensive emotions" to underlying needs. They then either (a) explore strategies for meeting a need they have named or (b) practice being compassionately present to their need and whatever feeling it might have generated.

MATERIALS NEEDED:
- ❏ Individual Handout: Expensive Emotions Worksheet
- ❏ Pen or pencil for each participant

TIME REQUIRED: 30 minutes

GROUP SIZE: Any size

SPACE REQUIRED: Enough for participants to be seated

LITERACY LEVEL REQUIRED: Able to read and write

PROCEDURE: Introduce "expensive emotions" as emotions which take a lot of energy from us without offering much in return. Anger, hatred, vengefulness, guilt, shame, and depression are examples of "expensive emotions."

1. Brainstorm with participants:

    Which emotions do you experience as "costly" or "expensive"? Costly emotions drain our energy without contributing to our needs being met.

2. Hand out the worksheet and use an example from your own life to illustrate the instructions you give to the group:

    a. *Think of a time you experienced an expensive emotion.*

    b. *Write down the feeling word(s) by which you identify the emotion.*

c.   Using the pie chart, shade in the portion of your total energy which you spent on that emotion in the situation you are recalling.

d.   In the first column, under "FACTS," write down what actually happened: what you observed (saw with your eyes, heard with your ears, etc.).

e.   In the next column, write down your thoughts and interpretations about what happened. What do (or did) you say or tell yourself about the situation?

f.   In the third column write down the need that was not being met behind each thought or statement. (Write the need next to the statement to which it corresponds.)

g.   Hold each unmet need in your heart for a few moments. Focus only on what you need or value in this situation.

h.   As you do so, are you aware of any feelings being stirred? If so, write them down in the last column (next to the need which stirred that feeling).

i.   Choose one need that is most strong or poignant for you in this moment.

j.   Place your full attention on this need. Hold it and notice how much you value and cherish it—how important this quality is for you.

k.   Brainstorm strategies that would address this need.

l.   Choose one of those strategies and decide how you will carry it through or:

m.   Instead of strategizing, simply hold the need with compassion, being fully present to what you are feeling and acknowledge how deeply you value this need.

SUGGESTION FOR PRACTICE IN DAILY LIFE: When you find yourself experiencing an expensive emotion,

- Stop and take a few deep breaths,

- Check in with yourself by asking, "What am I telling myself?"

- Then sit with the question, "What am I really needing here?"

- Notice any shift in body sensations or emotions.

REFERENCE: Chapter 4

Expensive Emotions Worksheet

Expensive emotion: _____

Fill in the pie chart to indicate how much of your energy was being used on this emotion in the situation you identified.

FACTS—What actually happened that I can observe	WHAT I SAY TO MYSELF about what happened	NEED OR VALUE behind what I tell myself	FEELING GENERATED when I become aware of the need

POSSIBLE STRATEGIES I can choose to address what I need or value:

_____

_____

The ONE STRATEGY I am choosing to try out: what I am going to do, when I will do it, and the concrete steps I will take: _____

_____

_____

ACTIVITY 6.3

Naming Similar Feelings

PURPOSE OF ACTIVITY:

1. To increase our capacity to express feelings

2. To increase our vocabulary of feeling words

BRIEF DESCRIPTION: In groups of three or four, one participant names a feeling and others take turns using another word to express the same or a similar feeling.

MATERIALS NEEDED:
- ❑ General Learning Aid G1: Learning Guide or any list of feeling words, one copy per person

TIME REQUIRED: 25–35 minutes

GROUP SIZE: Any size

SPACE REQUIRED: Enough space for participants to sit in groups of three or four

LITERACY LEVEL REQUIRED: Able to read words on Learning Guide
(If necessary, this activity can be done without the Learning Guide.)

PROCEDURE:

1. Make sure participants understand the difference between (a) feelings and (b) thoughts that might be confused with feelings.

2. Name a feeling and ask participants to give another word to describe the same (or a very similar) feeling. Example: If you say, "I feel delighted," participants might respond with, "I feel pleased," "I'm joyful," or "I am filled with happiness."

3. Demonstrate the activity.
   a. Invite three volunteers to the front and sit in a circle with them.
   b. Express a feeling, e.g., "I feel grumpy."
   c. Ask the next person to name a similar feeling, e.g., "I feel irritable."
   d. The next person continues by using another word to express the same or a very similar feeling, e.g., "I feel cranky."
   e. The fourth person completes the round by saying, e.g., "I feel out of sorts."
   f. If someone has difficulty coming up with a feeling word similar to the original, refer them to the Learning Guide or list of feelings.

4. Verify that everyone is clear about the procedure before inviting them to form groups of three or four. Give the following instructions:

- *After the first person expresses a feeling, go clockwise giving each person a turn to use a different word to express the same or a similar feeling. Begin your sentence with, "I . . ." or "I feel . . ." Remember that we can express a feeling without using the word "feel," and that we sometimes say "I feel . . ." when we are actually expressing a thought.*

- *You may choose either to do one round or to continue with further rounds until all possibilities for synonyms have been exhausted in your group.*

- *When your group is ready, have another participant express a different feeling to begin a new round.*

- *You have 10 minutes for this activity.*

NOTE: After a debrief, you may like to form new groups of three to four and continue the activity for another 10 minutes.

DEBRIEF QUESTION: During this activity, did you come across any feeling words that you had never—or only rarely—used before? Please say those words out loud in any order you wish.

SUGGESTION FOR PRACTICE IN DAILY LIFE: Consider playing this game with family or friends, either individually or in a small group.

REFERENCE: Chapter 4

ACTIVITY 6.4
Sculpting Feelings

PURPOSE OF ACTIVITY:

1. To increase our active vocabulary of feeling words

2. To practice relating body sensations with emotions

3. To connect bodily sensations with vocabulary that expresses feelings

4. To enhance our capacity to connect with another person's feelings from observing their body language and posture

BRIEF DESCRIPTION: Participants take turns picking a feeling and using their bodies to express or "sculpt" it. Others in the group guess the feeling being expressed through the "sculptor's" body stance.

NOTE: Instructions for this activity are given for small group practice but are easily adapted for working with a large group.

MATERIALS NEEDED:

☐ List of feeling words or General Learning Aid G1: Learning Guide, one per person

NOTE: Variation I of this exercise requires cards (or small pieces of paper) with a feeling word written on each. See General Learning Aid G3: Set of Feeling Cards. If participants are practicing in small groups of three to four, provide at least twenty cards for each group. If practicing in one large group, provide at least forty cards.

TIME REQUIRED: 20–30 minutes

GROUP SIZE: Any size

SPACE REQUIRED:
- Large enough for everyone to be able stand and spread their arms
- If working with small groups: additional space so that groups of three to five may work without mutual interference

LITERACY LEVEL REQUIRED: Able to read words on Learning Guide or feeling-cards (However, it is possible to do the primary activity and Variation II without relying on written words.)

PROCEDURE: Introduce this activity by discussing how we experience emotions through physical sensations in the body.

1. Give the following instructions:

   Working in groups of three or four, one of you will choose a feeling word and sculpt it in your body. As the "sculptor," please think of a feeling first, then imagine experiencing it in this moment while using a body stance or a movement to express the feeling. The rest of you in the group are to silently "read" the body language to guess what feeling is being sculpted. You will then check out your guesses by saying the feeling-words out loud. The first person who guesses the feeling the sculptor had in mind becomes the next sculptor and will start a new round.

2. Demonstrate the activity.
   a. Use your body to sculpt a feeling, e.g., "amazement."
   b. Invite the participants to guess what feeling you are sculpting.
   c. Ask the person who guesses the feeling to choose a different feeling, to sculpt it, and then have others guess what that feeling might be.

3. Form groups of three or four to practice this activity for approximately 10 minutes.

4. Invite participants to return to the large group for questions and sharing.

   NOTE: Below are two variations of the above activity with instructions for small group practice. However both variations may be conducted with a large group. If you choose to work in small groups, be sure to demonstrate the activity to the whole group before dividing up the participants.

Variation I

1. Give every group a stack of cards (or small pieces of paper) with a feeling word written on each piece.

2. Ask someone to close their eyes, pick a card, and then sculpt that feeling in their body.

3. Invite others to observe the sculptor's body and to guess the feeling word written on the card.

4. Have participants take turns being the sculptor.

Variation II

1. Ask a participant to say a feeling word out loud.

2. Invite others to use their bodies to "sculpt" that feeling and, while acting out the sculpted stance or movement, to say "I feel" followed by the word that was chosen.

DEBRIEF QUESTION: What did you learn about emotions and body sensations?

SUGGESTIONS FOR PRACTICE IN DAILY LIFE:

1. When you see someone, notice their body language and posture. Guess what they might be feeling in that moment.

2. When you notice your own muscles tense up or relax, name a feeling word that describes what is being expressed through your body.

REFERENCE: Chapter 4

Honing Our Vocabulary of Feeling Words

PURPOSE OF ACTIVITY:

1. To distinguish between words which express feelings and words which express thoughts

2. To differentiate feeling from the experience or event which triggered the feeling

3. To recognize whether we are using the phrase "I am feeling . . ." to express blame and judgment toward myself or others

4. To recognize thoughts as thoughts, to recognize feelings as feelings, and to express them independently from thoughts

BRIEF DESCRIPTION: The facilitator uses a list of words and phrases expressive of thoughts which are often confused as expressions of feelings, and calls them out—one at a time—to pairs of participants who are facing each other in two concentric circles. After each partner has had an opportunity to practice translating the thought into feeling words, those in the outer circle take a step clockwise such that new pairs are formed before the facilitator calls out the next word. At the end of this part of the activity, participants receive a handout: "Words Which Express Thoughts Instead of Feelings." Working in pairs, they generate a list of feeling words that correspond to the thought words given on the page, creating for themselves a resource for future reference.

MATERIALS NEEDED:

- ❑ Individual Handout: Words Which Express Thoughts Instead of Feelings
- ❑ Recommended: General Learning Aid G1: Learning Guide, one per person

TIME REQUIRED: 30–40 minutes

GROUP SIZE: Any size

SPACE REQUIRED: Enough for the group to form two concentric circles, either sitting or standing

LITERACY LEVEL REQUIRED: None

PROCEDURE:

1. Write the following on the board before the session begins:

a. When I experience being _____ , I might be feeling _____ .

b. When I think I am _____ , I might be feeling _____ .

c. When I think _____ , I might be feeling _____ .

2. Discuss the difference between feelings and thoughts.

3. Demonstrate the activity:

    a. Invite two volunteers to the front of the room.

    b. Use the word *betrayed* as an example of a word that expresses a thought rather than a feeling.

    c. Ask a volunteer to read the first statement on the board out loud while filling in the blanks: "When I experience being betrayed, I might be feeling _____ (e.g., angry)."

    d. Ask a second volunteer to do the same. Example: "When I experience being betrayed, I might be feeling _____ (e.g., scared)."

4. Arrange for participants to sit (or stand) in two concentric circles facing one another. Tell the group that those in the inner circle will respond first, followed by a second response from those in the outer circle. Remind them of how the two volunteers had demonstrated the activity earlier.

    NOTE: Encourage participants in this activity to refer to the Learning Guide for a list of feeling words.

5. **Part I**—Use the following list of words for this part of the activity. Say the word *abused* to begin the first round.

    a. abused

        Translate to: "When I experience being abused, I might be feeling _____ (e.g., terrified)."

    b. dismissed

    c. challenged

    d. validated

    e. unseen

    f. bullied

    g. hassled

    h. interrupted

6. Verify that those in the inner circle respond with the statement, "When I experience being abused, I might be feeling _____."

7. After the inner circle has completed the statement, say the word *abused* once again for those in the outer circle to take their turn.

8. When the people in the outer circle have completed their statement, ask them to move a step or a seat to the left (clockwise) so that participants are continually paired up with new partners.

9. When you have completed the eight words, ask if participants have any questions or reflections they wish to share with others.

10. **Part II**—Introduce the next part of the activity which focuses on words we use to judge ourselves. Refer the group to the second statement on the board: "When I think I am _____ , I might be feeling _____."

11. Using the same procedure as before, invite the concentric circles to practice with the words given below. (If desired, those in the outer circle may exchange seats with those inside.)
    a. Clever
       Translate to: "When I think I am clever, I might be feeling _____ (e.g., pleased)."
    b. Uneducated
    c. Dishonest
    d. Useless
    e. Triumphant
    f. Talented
    g. Incapable
    h. Stupid

12. **Part III**—Check for questions and reflections after you have completed the rounds using the eight words above. Then introduce the next part by referring to the third statement on the board: "When I think _____ I might be feeling _____."

13. Using the same procedure as before, invite the concentric circles to practice with the phrases given below. [Notice that participants will drop the words "I feel" from each of the phrases you read out loud; see example below:]
    a. I feel that I am a loser.
       Translate to: "When I think that I am a loser, I might be feeling _____ (e.g., discouraged)."
    b. I feel that you should know better.
    c. I feel it's not worth doing.
    d. I feel that Jose is very responsible.
    e. I feel I am a good player.

f. I feel it's unfair.

g. I feel I am expected to do everything.

h. I feel that most people in the world are trustworthy.

14. Ask participants to reconvene in the large group, and invite any questions or learnings generated.

15. Give each participant a copy of the handout "Words Which Express Thoughts Instead of Feelings."

16. **Part IV**—Ask participants to work in pairs, writing in "possible feelings" next to each experience or evaluation word on the Handout.

17. **Part V**—Invite each pair to generate a list of "Positive Experience or Positive Evaluative Words." Give examples of such words: "loved," "valued," "accepted," "respected," etc.

18. Ask what might be possible feelings associated with the thought "I feel loved," "I feel respected," etc. (Possible responses: "joyful," "safe" "tender," "warm.") Instruct the pairs to write down possible feelings next to the list of "Positive Evaluative Words" they generate on the Handout.

DEBRIEF QUESTION: What are your thoughts and what are your feelings about this exercise?

SUGGESTIONS FOR PRACTICE IN DAILY LIFE:

1. Notice when you use the word *feel*. Ask yourself, "Is this a feeling or a thought?" If it is a thought, say out loud or just to yourself, "When I think _____ , I am actually feeling _____ ."

2. Notice when others use the word *feel*. Again ask yourself, "Is this a feeling or a thought?" Without judging how they talk, simply try and guess their feeling. You can do this without saying a word.

REFERENCE: Chapter 4

Words Which Express Thoughts
Instead of Feelings

THOUGHTS: Experience or Evaluative Words	POSSIBLE FEELINGS:	THOUGHTS: Experience or Evaluative Words	POSSIBLE FEELINGS:
abandoned		manipulated	
abused		mistrusted	
attacked		misunderstood	
belittled		neglected	
betrayed		overpowered	
blamed		overworked	
bullied		patronized	
caged/boxed in		pressured	
cheated		provoked	
coerced		put down	
cornered		rejected	
criticized		ripped off/screwed	
disliked		taken for granted	
disrespected		threatened	
distrusted		thwarted	
dumped on		trampled	
harassed		tricked	
hassled		unappreciated	
ignored		unheard	
insulted		unloved	
interrupted		unseen	
intimidated		unsupported	
invalidated		unwanted	
invisible		used	
isolated		victimized	
judged		violated	
left out		wronged	
let down			

THOUGHTS: Positive Experience or Positive Evaluative Word	POSSIBLE FEELINGS:

ACTIVITY 6.6

Connecting Feelings With Events

PURPOSE OF ACTIVITY:

1. To practice connecting with our feelings

2. To practice expressing what we are feeling

BRIEF DESCRIPTION: In groups of three or four, members choose a feeling card and share a situation in which they experience this feeling.

MATERIALS NEEDED:
   ❏ General Learning Aid G6: Set of Feeling Cards

TIME REQUIRED: 30 minutes

GROUP SIZE: Three or more

SPACE REQUIRED: Space for members of each group to sit and hear one another

LITERACY LEVEL REQUIRED: One person in the group able to read feeling words

PROCEDURE:

1. Offer the following instructions:

    *   *I would like to introduce a game that will help us get in touch with, name, and share our feelings.*

    *   *Form groups of three or four.*

    *   *I will now give each group five or six cards with a feeling word written on the underside of each card.*

    *   *You will take turns: select a card, turn it over, read the feeling word given, and share a situation in which you experience that feeling.*

2. Demonstrate this by choosing a card and saying:

    *   *"I feel [the feeling word on the card] when I remember or think of [name an experience].*

    *   *When I am finished, I pass the card to the person on my right and this person will then say "I feel [same feeling word] when I remember or think of* _____ *."*

3. When this card has gone around the circle once, the group may choose another card. Or they may continue using the same card for additional rounds, recalling yet other situations where they experience this feeling. Continuing with the same card often allows the group to develop a sense of safety and to share more deeply.

4. Take 20 minutes for this activity.

5. Ask if there are any questions before the groups begin.

DEBRIEF QUESTIONS:

1. What are you feeling, having done this exercise?

2. Describe how (or whether) this activity supported you in being more aware of feelings.

SUGGESTION FOR PRACTICE IN DAILY LIFE: You may want to try this activity with your family or friends. Make some cards with feeling words on them. (Some people start with the four basic feelings: sad, mad, glad, scared.) Choose one card at a time to pass around and have each person say, "I feel _____ (for example, sad) when I remember or think of _____ ."

REFERENCE: Chapter 4

ACTIVITY 6.7

Using Images to Connect With Feelings

PURPOSE OF ACTIVITY:

1. To help us connect with our feelings and to name them

2. To remind us that our feelings come from our thoughts and are not caused by the outside situation itself

3. To increase our vocabulary for expressing feelings

BRIEF DESCRIPTION: Working in groups of three, participants look at a picture and name the feelings that come up for them.

MATERIALS NEEDED:

❑   A stack of pictures, at least one for each participant, as well as two large pictures visible to the whole group for use in the initial demonstration of the exercise (see General Learning Aid G9: Guidelines for Assembling a Set of Pictures)

❑   A list of NVC feelings words or General Learning Aid G1: Learning Guide, one per person

TIME REQUIRED: 30 minutes

GROUP SIZE: Any size

SPACE REQUIRED: Enough for the whole group to sit in groups of three without being distracted by each other

LITERACY LEVEL REQUIRED: None required although it would be helpful if participants were able to refer to the list of feeling words on the Learning Guide

PROCEDURE:

1. Review "feelings" as the third component of the NVC model.
    *   Explain that the word *feeling* in NVC refers to an emotion or body sensation.
    *   Give examples of words used in NVC to express feelings.
    *   Illustrate how NVC language distinguishes feelings from thoughts.
    *   Confirm that participants understand that feelings arise from the thoughts we have about a situation and not from the situation itself.

2. Hand each participant a Learning Guide (or any list of NVC feeling words). Ask them to take a few minutes to read each feeling word and imagine feeling that feeling.

3. Show the group a large image. Invite participants to notice what comes up for them as they look at the image.

   a. *Are you aware of any emotions stirring in you?*

   b. *Are you aware of any physical sensations in the body?*

   c. *What words would you use to express these feelings?*

Encourage them to refer to the list of feeling words to increase their comfort level with words they may not frequently use.

4. Now ask several volunteers to say out loud the feelings that come up for them when looking at the picture. If they name different feelings, use this opportunity to remind the group that it is not the picture that generates these feelings, but our individual thoughts and how we interpret what our eyes see.

5. If you wish, repeat Steps 3–4 (above) using a second large picture.

6. Pass out a picture to each participant and ask them to work in groups of three. Give the following instructions:

   a. *Choose one picture at a time to work with. Give everyone a chance to look at the picture closely.*

   b. *Take turns expressing what you feel as you look at the image.*

   c. *When you have worked through all three pictures, share what you have learned and whether there was anything that surprised or challenged you during this activity.*

   d. *You have 15 minutes.*

DEBRIEF QUESTIONS:

1. Did you notice whether the same image stimulated different feelings for different people? If so, how did you experience this difference?

2. What have you noticed about the cause of your feelings? Are they due more to what your mind thinks or what your eyes see?

SUGGESTION FOR PRACTICE IN DAILY LIFE: When you encounter an incident, go inside and notice what you are feeling. Own that feeling as one you generated yourself.

REFERENCE: Chapter 4

NEED

7.1 Awareness Exercise: Appreciating Needs

7.2 Activity: Needs Game

7.3 Activity: What's My Need Here?

7.4 Activity: Using Images to Identify Needs

KEY CONCEPT 7:

Need

Description: "Need" is the third component of the NVC model and the core of NVC consciousness. Besides essential requirements for physical survival, such as water, sleep, food, etc., all human beings across all cultures share the same basic needs in order to thrive and realize themselves. Safety, connection, meaning, respect, caring, etc., are qualities which are universally cherished even though the words for their expression and the means for their fulfillment vary drastically in different cultures and for different individuals. While needs may be expressed as a dream, value, want, or desire, NVC clearly distinguishes universal needs from desires which are tied to a specific person, place, action, or time. The latter comprise strategies and solutions to fulfill needs and are expressed in NVC through the fourth component of the model: request. In NVC, we attribute our feelings to the needs that are stirring in us rather than to external circumstances or to other people.

Toolkit exercises in this section provide practice identifying and connecting with needs—both our own and those of others—as well as practice expressing universal needs in ways that are natural for the speaker.

Tips for Facilitators:

1. In this section, we first support one another in developing fluency in the vocabulary of universal needs. More importantly, however, we aim to develop the capacity to be aware of present-moment needs that are stirring in us or in others, and to fully connect with those energies. While words are necessary to convey needs, we can bear in mind that there may be many different ways of expressing the same universal need. Encourage participants to connect with the energy behind whatever word is chosen to identify a need that is alive in the moment. Even where there is a painful feeling arising from a need not being fulfilled, we can still take time to experience how we cherish and value the particular need we have identified. It is easy for many of us to barely touch the energy of the need as we rush to strategize for solutions. Instead, once we discover the unmet need that a painful feeling is pointing to, we can choose to spend time focusing on the need, sitting with it, acknowledging and experiencing how much we care about it. We might even notice that we are uncomfortable owning this need. (In which case no wonder we haven't put energy into fulfilling it!) Before we head into strategies to meet this need, we might want to ask ourselves what is preventing us from valuing this need. Only when we value a need are we ready to engage strategies for its fulfillment.

2. Experiment with replacing the word *need* with "value." This may be especially helpful when the need extends to other people. For example, if I see someone hurting another person I may feel distressed and express my need by saying, "I value caring" rather than "I need caring."

Appreciating Needs

AIM OF EXERCISE:

1. To be aware of needs

2. To value the universal needs of all human beings

INSTRUCTIONS FOR GUIDING AWARENESS EXERCISE: Read the following slowly, allowing time between each statement for the participant to engage in the guided process:

1. *Sit comfortably. Straighten your spine. Make any necessary adjustments.*

2. *Bring your attention inward by closing your eyes or lowering your gaze.*

3. *Focus your attention on your breathing.*

   - *What are you feeling right now as you focus on your breathing?*

   - *As you breathe, are you aware of any need that is either being met or not being met?*

   - *Hold that need or value—a universal need that is precious to all human beings. Hold it gently in your hands. Take some time to simply honor it.*

4. *Now shift your focus: recall something that happened recently over which you still experience some unresolved feelings.*

   - *What happened? Simply state the observable facts.*

   - *How do you feel about it now?*

   - *What need or value of yours—met or unmet—is this feeling pointing to?*

   - *Hold that need or value. Hold it as if you were holding something precious that you treasure. Take some time to simply appreciate it.*

5. *Go back to focusing on your breathing.*

   - *What are you feeling right now?*

   - *What need is being met or unmet?*

- *Hold this need in your hands with the kind of care and full presence you would hold a special treasure.*

6. *Now bring to mind a need or value that is prominent in your life right now and upon which you spend a lot of energy. Simply hold this need and recognize how much you value it, how important it is in your life.*

7. *In the course of this exercise, you have connected with several needs. Now hold all of them together and take a moment to appreciate how you value these qualities.*

8. *When you are ready, carefully take these needs and place them in your heart. Open your eyes and look around the room, being aware that each person you see here has been holding some precious needs in their hands and heart.*

SHARING CIRCLE:

- My name is _____ .

- In this moment I am appreciating the need for _____ .

REFERENCE: Chapter 5

ACTIVITY 7.2
Needs Game

PURPOSE OF ACTIVITY:

1. To increase facility in expressing needs in ways that seem natural to us

2. To increase our vocabulary of words and phrases for expressing needs

BRIEF DESCRIPTION: Participants brainstorm phrases to replace the words "I need. . . ." Then, in groups of three or four, one person says a need word; others express that need in natural or colloquial speech.

MATERIALS NEEDED:
For each participant:
- ❑ General Learning Aid G1: Learning Guide or list of need words, one per person
- ❑ Individual Handout: Phrases to express "I need . . ."
- ❑ Large black or white poster board

TIME REQUIRED: 20 minutes

GROUP SIZE: Any size

SPACE REQUIRED: Enough space for the people to sit in circles of three or four

LITERACY LEVEL REQUIRED: Ability to read words (If this is a challenge, the activity can be done without the Learning Guide or list of needs.)

PROCEDURE:

1. Review the definition of an NVC "need."

> *Needs are universal. They make no reference to any particular action, time, place, or person. In NVC we distinguish "needs" from "requests"— strategies that indicate specific action, time, place, or person. To make sure I am identifying a universal need, I might ask myself whether it is something that everyone values. For example, nearly everyone would acknowledge that they need light, understanding, peace, and celebration. In contrast, requests consist of specific strategies to meet needs. For example: "Would you please turn the lights on?" "Are you willing to tell me what you heard me say so I know I am communicating effectively?" "Would you be willing to design a ritual with me to celebrate our mother's birthday?" In this exercise we will be working with needs, not requests.*

2. Give examples of how a need may be expressed in different ways.

> • *Sometimes we express a need by simply saying "I need . . ." followed by a single word. There are many examples of such need words on the Learning Guide.*

> • *At other times we may find it more natural to express our needs through phrases and multiple words. For example, instead of "I need respect," we might say, "I want to know that I matter, that I count." "I value acceptance even when people have different points of view." "Taking others people's needs into consideration is so important to me."*

Part I—Various ways to express the words "I need. . . ."

1. Ask participants to brainstorm for phrases to replace "I need . . ." in the context of expressing a universal human need in NVC.

2. Write the phrases on the board.

3. Give each participant a copy of the handout, Phrases to Express "I need . . ."

4. Ask participants to add items from the board that they want included in their repertoire of phrases to express "I need . . ." and to delete those phrases from the handout that they are unlikely to use.

Part II—Various ways to express the need itself

1. Demonstrate the exercise by naming a need from the list on the Learning Guide. Ask participants to express the same need in a colloquial way—in a way that is natural for them.
   • For example: "I need HARMONY. How would you say this in your own way?"
   • Participants might respond with: "I like it when people cooperate with one another;" or "I enjoy it when we can work together toward our goal;" or "I love to experience ease when working with others."

2. After a couple of examples, invite participants to form groups of three or four.

> • *Have one person in your group pick a need word on the Learning Guide,*

> • *The rest of you, take turns expressing that need in a way that is comfortable and natural for you.*

> • *Start a second round with another person picking a different need word from the Learning Guide. Keep going for about 10 minutes.*

DEBRIEF QUESTION: Have you discovered anything from this activity that would make it more comfortable for you to express universal needs?

SUGGESTION FOR PRACTICE IN DAILY LIFE: Play this game with your family or with a small group of friends.

REFERENCE: Chapter 5

Phrases to Express *"I Need . . . "*

NOTE: In choosing a need to go with your phrase, be sure it is universal and not specific to you and the person(s) you are interacting with.

DELETE PHRASES BELOW YOU WOULD NOT USE:

- I value _____
- I hope for _____
- I desire _____
- I long for _____
- I treasure _____
- I relish _____
- I dream of _____
- I am nourished by _____

- I cherish _____
- I wish for _____
- I really enjoy _____
- I dig _____
- I groove on _____
- I yearn for _____
- I care about _____
- I am happy if I _____

- _____ would enhance my life
- _____ makes my life worthwhile
- _____ means a lot to me

- _____ gives me joy
- _____ is important to me
- _____ enriches my life

ADD YOUR OWN PHRASES BELOW:

ACTIVITY 7.3

What's My Need Here?

PURPOSE OF ACTIVITY:

1. To explore the statement that "All judgments are tragic expressions of unmet needs." (Marshall Rosenberg)

2. To practice connecting with the speaker's needs behind the words they are using

BRIEF DESCRIPTION: Facilitator addresses participants with a series of statements. Participants guess possible needs that motivated each.

MATERIALS NEEDED:
- ❑ "List of Statements" (see below) or a similar list

TIME REQUIRED: 20 minutes

GROUP SIZE: Any

SPACE REQUIRED: Minimal

LITERACY LEVEL REQUIRED: None

PROCEDURE:

1. Use this activity to introduce "needs" to a group that is new to NVC or as a review practice for experienced learners.

2. Before leading this activity, review the list of statements given below or make up your own statements.

3. Take one of the statements and say it directly to the group as if it were a real live situation. Use eye contact, expressive body language, gestures, and emotion in the voice rather than just read the words off the paper.

4. After delivering the statement, ask the group, "What's my need here?" and allow different guesses to surface.

5. If this is a group new to NVC, write each need on a large board so that the group will have generated their own "needs inventory" by the end of the activity.

6. This activity works best at a clipped pace. While you may wish to rephrase some of the volunteered responses, try to keep discussion at a minimum as you collect need words being offered. Try to create an inventory of need words which includes everyone's contribution.

LIST OF STATEMENTS: Use the following statements for this activity, or create your own:

1. *You are always judging other people.*

2. *You broke your promise!*

3. *How can you watch those idiotic talk shows?*

4. *Sometimes I am so selfish.*

5. *There's no responsible leadership in sight in this country.*

6. *Why don't you ever remember to turn off the lights?*

7. *Lock 'em up and throw away the keys.*

8. *Save your breath because I'm doing what I damn well please!*

9. *He never likes anything I cook.*

10. *Doesn't it bother you that we haven't spoken to each other for more than three months?*

11. *Mom, do you know how stupid you sound when you talk NVC?*

12. *People here are very cliquish.*

DEBRIEF QUESTIONS:

1. What did you do in order to hear the needs behind the statements?

2. What helps or hinders you from hearing needs?

3. What did you learn from this exercise?

SUGGESTION FOR PRACTICE IN DAILY LIFE: Listen for judgments in the world around and within you. Test and see for yourself whether "All judgments are tragic expressions of unmet needs."

REFERENCE: Chapter 5

ACTIVITY 7.4

Using Images to Identify Needs

PURPOSE OF ACTIVITY:

1. To practice connecting with the needs which our feelings are pointing to

2. To provide opportunity to recognize, own, and value our needs as legitimate and even precious

3. To develop confidence in expressing needs

BRIEF DESCRIPTION: Working in groups of three, participants look at pictures and name the needs that come up for them. The group takes time to consciously acknowledge and appreciate each need that is named.

MATERIALS NEEDED:

- ❑ A stack of pictures, at least one for each participant (more if the group is small). (See General Learning Aid G9: Guidelines for Assembling a Set of Pictures)
- ❑ One or two pictures large enough to be visible to the whole group for use in the initial demonstration of the exercise
- ❑ List of NVC need words or General Learning Aid G1: Learning Guide, one per person

TIME REQUIRED: 30 minutes

GROUP SIZE: Any size

SPACE REQUIRED: Enough for participants to sit in groups of three without mutual distraction

LITERACY LEVEL REQUIRED: None, although ability to read individual need words would be helpful

PROCEDURE:

1. Review the concept of NVC needs or values
    a. Needs are universal.
    b. We are all responsible for meeting our own needs. Emphasize the difficulty of meeting our needs if we don't own them or appreciate their importance.

2. Hand out a list of need words. Give the following instructions:

Read the need words on this list slowly to yourself. Pause at each word and see if you can connect with the preciousness of what it symbolizes. Take a moment to appreciate the universal need or value. Perhaps you can hold it in your heart for a moment and notice how much you treasure it.

3. Show the group a large picture. Ask them to reflect on the following questions:

   a. *What needs or values are you aware of as you look at this picture?*

   b. *Are you able to own and value the needs that come up for you?*

   c. *Are these needs met or unmet for you?*

   d. *Do you find any words on the list of needs that might help you identify the needs that this picture stirs up in you?*

4. Ask volunteers to name their needs out loud. If different needs are expressed for the same image, remind participants that feelings and needs come from within and are related to our thoughts about the image.

5. Repeat Steps 3–4 using a second picture if you sense that participants need more practice before working independently in small groups.

6. Pass out a picture to each participant. (In small groups, participants may enjoy picking out their own picture.)

7. Ask participants to form groups of three and give the following instructions:

   a. *Pass a picture around your group. Take some time to notice what needs come up for you.*

   b. *Begin the first round by having one person express the needs that the picture stirs up in them.*

   c. *Then take a few moments for everyone to silently connect with the need that the person just named. See if you can appreciate the precious nature of this need.*

   d. *Give each person an opportunity to express their need, after which the group holds that particular need in silent appreciation.*

   e. *After the first round, continue with the second and then the third picture.*

   f. *When you have completed all three rounds, share anything that surprised or challenged you. Also share whatever supported your understanding and learning.*

   g. *Take about 15 minutes for this activity.*

DEBRIEF QUESTIONS:

1. Were you able to hold and truly cherish the need you named? How did you feel when you were able to do this?

2. How did you experience the silent moments when your group held and appreciated the need you had named? Were you comfortable or uncomfortable?

SUGGESTION FOR PRACTICE IN DAILY LIFE: When you encounter an incident and notice an emotional reaction, go inside and touch the need that has been stirred. Take a moment to value that need.

REFERENCE: Chapter 5

REQUEST

8.1 Awareness Exercise: Making Requests Grounded in Needs

8.2 Activity: Six Stepstones for Making Requests

8.3 Activity: Making Requests in a Group

8.4 Activity: The Request Behind a Statement

8.5 Activity: What Keeps Us From Making a Request?

KEY CONCEPT 8:

Request

Description: The fourth component of the NVC model is "request." We articulate a request as a concrete means to fulfill a need we have identified. We offer our request in the spirit of a gift—as an opportunity for the other person to use their power to contribute to our well-being. NVC suggests that requests be presented in positive and concrete action language which invites the listener to make an immediate response. As a component of the NVC process, request is a strategy to meet needs in a relationship where the needs of both parties are valued. It is clearly distinguished from "demand" where compliance is expected without consideration of the other party's needs.

NVC reminds us that in addition to requesting that someone take a particular action, we can make "connecting requests" that enhance heart connection—and thus increase the likelihood of meeting both parties' needs.

- Connecting request for empathy: "Would you be willing to tell me what you are hearing me say?"

- Connecting request for honesty: "Would you be willing to tell me what you are feeling and needing when you hear me say this?"

Toolkit exercises in this section offer practice in making requests in NVC, distinguishing action requests and connecting requests, exploring the requests hidden in our conversations, articulating requests to a group, and identifying what keeps us from making requests.

Tips for Facilitators:

1. During role-plays and live situations, encourage participants to check for demand-energy when presenting requests.

2. When a dialogue seems "stuck," consider making connecting requests to move it forward. Many of us are not accustomed to making requests for connection. To increase our comfort level in making connecting requests, practice repeating them over and over—just to hear ourselves articulate our intention for connection. Or create role-plays as opportunities for making connecting requests. Further examples of connecting requests:

   - "Would you mind telling me what you hear me say so I know I've expressed myself accurately?" (request for empathy)

   - "Would you be willing to tell me what you understand me to be feeling and needing right now?" (request for empathy)

- "Would you be willing to tell me what comes up for you when you hear me say this?" (request for honesty)

- "Do you mind sharing what's goes on inside of you as you listen to what I am saying?" (request for honesty)

Making Requests Grounded in Needs

AIM OF EXERCISE:

1. To train ourselves to focus on present needs before placing attention on strategies for problem-solving

2. To practice holding and cherishing our need, allowing requests or strategies to emerge from this process

INSTRUCTIONS FOR GUIDING AWARENESS EXERCISE: Read the following slowly, allowing time between each statement for the participant to engage in the process.

1. *Adjust your body so that you are sitting comfortably with your back straight.*

2. *Focus your attention inward by closing your eyes or gazing softly on the floor in front of you.*

3. *Bring your attention to your breathing.*

   a. *Listen to the breath entering and leaving your body and treasure your breathing.*

   b. *Feel your breath coming in and going out. Take time to cherish the gift of breath.*

   c. *Is there any request you might want to make to yourself regarding your breathing? For example, I might ask myself, "Am I willing to breathe more slowly?" "Am I willing to focus mindfully on my breath?" "Or do I need to breathe from lower down in my lungs?"*

4. *Ask yourself, "Is there anything in my life—or on Earth—that I feel angry, overwhelmed, discouraged, or unhappy about?"*

   a. *Be aware of thoughts as they arise in response to this question.*

   b. *Now ask yourself,*

   • *"What am I feeling emotionally? What are my feelings telling me about my present needs?"*

   • *"What is my body feeling? What needs might my body sensations be pointing to?"*

   c. *Be open to whatever messages come up for you.*

    d. If a need reveals itself and you sense a shift in your body, hold the need in your heart.

- *Ask yourself if you are willing to take some time to be present with that need. And if you are willing, take a moment to see it, feel it, hear it, and appreciate its preciousness.*

- *Treasure the need, cherish it, see its beauty, value it, knowing that this quality of connection you're establishing with the need is the first step toward fulfilling it.*

    e. If there are further ways you'd like to address the need, formulate a request in positive concrete language either to yourself or others. Say it out loud so you can hear yourself making this request: "Would you be willing to . . . ?"

SHARING CIRCLE:

- My name is _____ .

- This is how I would express my request: _____ .

REFERENCE: Chapter 6

ACTIVITY 8.2

Six Stepstones for Making Requests

PURPOSE OF ACTIVITY:

1. To practice clarifying our intention before making a request

2. To practice distinguishing between requests for connection and requests for action

3. To practice expressing requests

BRIEF DESCRIPTION: Participants work in pairs to practice articulating connecting requests and action requests.

MATERIALS NEEDED:

- ❑ General Learning Aid G3: Floor Map—"Honesty" portion
- ❑ Specific Learning Aid 8.2: Six Stepstones for Making Requests (consisting of six large cards for placement on the floor)
- ❑ Handout 8.2A: Six Stepstones for Making Requests
- ❑ Handout 8.2B or 8.2C: List of Scenarios (Choose either 8.2B—Prison, or 8.2C—General Community)

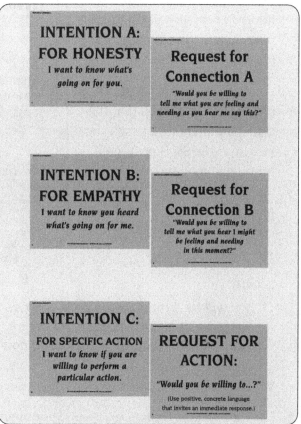

Six Stepstones for Making Requests

TIME REQUIRED: 45 minutes

GROUP SIZE: Flexible, as long as items placed on the floor are visible to everyone

SPACE REQUIRED: Floor space to lay out the Honesty portion of the Floor Map and the Six Stepstones, and for participants to work in pairs without mutual interference

LITERACY LEVEL REQUIRED:
Minimal

PROCEDURE:

Part I—Demonstrate the Six Stepstones for Making Requests

1. Position the Six Stepstones on the floor according to the diagram given in the accompanying Handout. Verify that all participants can see the cards on the floor; if necessary, encourage participants to either stand or to circle around you.

2. Lay out the Honesty portion of the Floor Map such that the last component ("request") is next to the Six Stepstones. Introduce "request" as the fourth component of the NVC model by pointing to its place on the Honesty Floor Map.

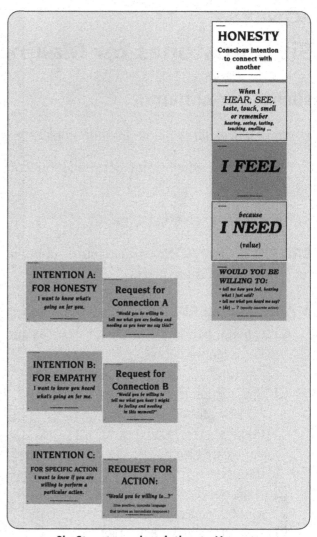

Six Stepstones in relation to Honesty portion of Floor Map

3. State the purpose of this activity:

> We will be distinguishing between two kinds of NVC requests: requests for connection and requests for action. The Six Stepstones help us decide which kind of request to make and how to express it.

4. Walk through the Six Stepstones using your own or the following example:

   a. *[Demonstrate intention for honesty]* Suppose my partner is going to a ballgame this evening. I have no plans, but realize I would like some companionship and relaxation. One choice I have to meet these needs would be to invite my brother to see the funny movie we'd all been talking about. When sharing this idea with my partner, I am aware that I want to know what goes on for him when he hears my plans. Thus the Stepstone I am using is Intention A. *[Stand on the card "Intention A for Honesty."]*

My intention here is to receive honesty from the other person: I want to know what is honestly going on for them in response to what I have to say.

b. *[Demonstrate request for honesty] With that intention in mind, I might express myself in the following way: "I would enjoy some relaxation and companionship tonight.*

   "I'm thinking of going to the new movie with my brother while you are at the game. [Stand on the card "Request for Connection A.] How would you feel about that?"

c. *[Demonstrate intention for empathy] Now suppose my partner replies, "Oh, please don't do that! I really want to see that movie with you and this is the only evening that I am not free." As I am about to answer my partner by honestly expressing myself, I realize that this time, I am wanting back empathy: I want to know that my partner understands what's going on for me. [Stand on the card "Intention B for Empathy."] I recognize that the intention behind the request I'm about to make is to know that I'm being heard and empathized with.*

d. *[Demonstrate request for empathy] With that intention in mind, I might express myself in the following way, "Hearing you ask me not to go to the movie, I feel frustrated because I am trying my best to figure out how to meet my needs for companionship and relaxation tonight. [Stand on the card "Request for Connection B."]* **Would you tell me what you hear is going on for me right now?"**

e. *[Demonstrate request for action] In addition to the above two ways of requesting for connection, we can also make "action requests" using positive, concrete language which invites an immediate response. In NVC we emphasize establishing trust in hearing each other's needs before we move into requests for action, i.e., strategies for problem-solving. In the earlier example with my partner, I would only make a request for action after I sense a mutual understanding of each other's needs. [Stand on the card "Intention C," and then step to the card "Request for Action."] To make a request for action of my partner, I might say:* **"If I don't like the movie enough to see it a second time, would you agree to go alone or see it with someone else?"**

Part II—Review

1. Review the two kinds of request.
    a. Requests for Connection:

       • *If my intention is to know what's going on in you, I would be standing here [Stand on card "Intention A"] and be expressing myself this way [Stand on "Request for Connection A" and read the words on the card.]*

- *If my intention is to know that I'm being heard and understood for what's going on for me, I would be standing here [Stand on card "Intention B"] and be expressing myself this way [Stand on "Request for Connection B" and read the words on the card.]*

    b. Request for Action:

> *If my intention is to know whether you are willing to do a specific task, I would be standing here [Stand on card "Intention C"] and be expressing myself this way [Stand on "Request for Action" and read the words on the card.]*

2. Invite responses from the group, using a different scenario.

> *Let's work with another scenario—suppose your cell gets searched because your cellmate had contraband. You're very annoyed and express your observation, feeling, and need.*

>   a. *After that, how would you make a connection request for empathy? [Sample response: "If you were in my shoes, how would you feel about what just happened?"]*

>   b. *Or, how would you make a connection request for honesty? [Sample response: "I wonder what goes on for you when you hear how I'm feeling right now."]*

>   c. *And how would you make an action request? But remember, action requests come only after connection has been established. Otherwise people are unlikely to hear requests with openness nor are they likely to respond willingly and honestly. Suppose you have now made a heart connection with your cellmate. What would be a specific action you might then request? [Sample response: "Would you be willing to agree, as long as I am in this cell, to keep it free of contraband?"]*

Part III—Partner Practice

1. Distribute the two Handouts provided with this exercise: (a) Six Stepstones for Making Requests and (b) List of Scenarios.

2. Request a volunteer to role-play a scenario with you to demonstrate the procedure. Use either your own scenario or one from the Handout.

3. State the scenario.

Example: "I am visiting my elderly mother who lives far away from me. Upon arrival, my sister informs me that last month Mother married a man named Simon. I have never heard of Simon or of Mother's relationship."

4. Ask the volunteer to role-play the other party to whom you express your observation, feeling, and need:

Example: "Mother, I just learned from Mimi that you got married last month to someone I had never heard of. I feel surprised as I would like to be included on important family affairs."

5. Before you complete your statement by articulating a request, clarify the intention behind the request. Demonstrate by stating the intention out loud.

   Examples:
   - "Here I want to know what goes on for Mother when she hears how I feel." (Intention A for Honesty)
   - "Here I want to know that she understands how I am feeling in this moment." (Intention B for Empathy)
   - "Here I want to know if she's willing to inform me about family matters that are important to her." (Intention C for Action)

6. Articulate the request.
   a. Example of request for Connection A—honesty: "What goes on for you when you hear me say this?"
   b. Example of request for Connection B—empathy: "What do you hear is being stirred up for me?"
   c. Example of request for action: "Would you agree to keep me posted on family matters that you consider to be significant?"

7. Continue to role-play, pausing each time to clarify your intention before making a request.

8. Invite participants to:
   a. find a partner.
   b. take a silent minute to either come up with a scenario to work with or to choose one from the List of Scenarios.
   c. role-play and practice formulating requests, using the Six Stepstones for Making Requests. Remind them to clarify the intention before articulating a request.

9. Inform the pairs that they have 30 minutes to practice, with each partner taking 15 minutes for their scenario. Signal participants at the halfway point.

DEBRIEF QUESTIONS:

1. Give an example from your own life of when you might make a request for connection and when you might make a request for action.

2. When you are making a request for connection, how would you determine whether to ask for honesty or to ask for empathy?

3. What have you learned from this activity, and what might you do to increase your confidence or skill in making requests?

SUGGESTION FOR PRACTICE IN DAILY LIFE: Practice clarifying your intention before making requests for connection and requests for action.

REFERENCES: Chapters 6, 7

Six Stepstones for Making Requests

INTENTION A
For Honesty

I want to know what's going on for you.

REQUEST FOR CONNECTION (A)

"Would you be willing to tell me what you are feeling and needing as you hear me say this?"

INTENTION B
For Empathy

I want to know you heard what's going on for me.

REQUEST FOR CONNECTION (B)

"Would you be willing to tell me what you hear I might be feeling and needing in this moment?"

INTENTION C
For Specific Action

I want to know if you are willing to perform a particular action.

REQUEST FOR ACTION

"Would you be willing to . . .?"
(Use positive, concrete language that invites immediate response.)

List of Scenarios: PRISON

1. The correctional officer just yelled at you for no apparent reason. It is the third time this week.

2. Your partner says to you, "I'm not coming back to visit you this month. I'm sick and tired of getting hassled every time I come through the gate and the metal detectors."

3. I just asked you for a cigarette and you said, "No, and quit bugging me for smokes all the time."

4. The officer handling your release plans tells you that they won't be able to get your report ready for the parole board in time for your scheduled hearing. They would like you to sign a waiver to delay your hearing for a month.

5. Your partner just announced that they are on a diet to lose weight. You are now seeing their hand reach out to take a third cookie to eat.

6. A fellow prisoner who committed to organizing an NVC workshop says to you, "I won't be able to do it; I'm swamped."

7. You miss seeing your partner who worked late every evening this week and thus has not come to visit you.

List of Scenarios: GENERAL COMMUNITY

1. You are greeting your elderly mother who lives far away in another city. You were just informed (while being picked up at the airport by your sister) that Mother had gotten married last month to someone you'd never heard of.

2. Your tenant, whom you suspect to be addicted to alcohol, says to you, "I know I am behind a month on rent. I'm short on cash, but I'll get it to you real soon, okay?"

3. You are about to meet a friend for tea when your disabled father calls asking you to pick up some groceries for him.

4. It is late at night. You and your partner are sitting at the kitchen table, deeply engrossed in discussion over an emotional issue. Suddenly your six-year-old appears at the door and declares: "I'm not sleepy. I want to know what you're talking about."

5. You and a friend have been in contact nearly daily. During the last week, however, this friend neither called nor returned your calls. You are shopping at the mall and spot your friend.

6. You are buying fish at the market and notice that salmon steaks cost considerably more than whole salmon. You would like a whole fish cut into steaks and to pay the same price as you would pay for the whole salmon.

7. You are exhausted and looking forward to the weekend. Your colleague approaches, asking you to cover for them this weekend because they just got invited to a large family celebration.

ACTIVITY 8.3
Making Requests in a Group

PURPOSE OF ACTIVITY: To practice making requests in a group in ways that increase the likelihood that our needs will be addressed

BRIEF DESCRIPTION: Participants make a statement which is likely to receive little or no visible response from anyone in a group situation. They then transform their statements into effective requests that provide an opportunity for their needs to be heard and addressed by the group.

MATERIALS NEEDED:

❑ Specific Learning Aid 8.3: Set of Eight Scenario Cards, one set per group. Each card has two sides:
- Front: statement that someone might make in a group
- Back: cues to transform the statement into a concrete request

> **3. I noticed that some people didn't raise their hands to vote.**
>
> NVC TOOLKIT FOR FACILITATORS • ©2008 Raj Gill, Lucy Leu, Judi M

> **CUES FOR MAKING A REQUEST IN A GROUP**
> a. Specify from whom you want a response, e.g. "I would like anyone who is willing to tell me…" "I'd like a couple of you to tell me…" "I would like to hear from anyone who would object to…." "I would like Shari and Abdul to tell me…"
> b. Specify the action you are requesting.
>   • Define it in concrete terms
>   • Use positive language
>   • Frame the request such that a listener can respond to it in that very moment
>   e.g. "Tell me what items on the agenda are most important to you." "Raise your hand if you are in agreement with what Keiko just proposed."
> c. Signal when your request has been addressed to your satisfaction, e.g. "I am finished." "Thanks; I am ready to move on."
>
> NVC TOOLKIT FOR FACILITATORS • ©2008 Raj Gill, Lucy Leu, Judi Morin

Scenario Card, front and back

TIME REQUIRED: 30 minutes

GROUP SIZE: Flexible: either one large group or several smaller groups of five to eight

SPACE REQUIRED: Adequate space for groups to work without mutual interference

LITERACY LEVEL REQUIRED: Ability to read sentences

PROCEDURE:

1. Begin this activity by making a statement such as, "It gets cold in this room when people leave the door open"—a statement which can apply in real time to the situation at hand. Use this statement to illustrate how easy it is for a group, not hearing a clear request, to proceed without ever addressing the speaker's needs.

2. Remind participants how to express a "doable" request in NVC:

    - Make it concrete

    - Use positive language

    - Frame the request such that a listener can respond to it in that very moment

    Ask participants to volunteer examples of NVC requests until you are confident that everyone is clear as to what constitutes an "NVC request."

3. Now demonstrate an NVC request (addressing a group) that also:

    (a) clarifies who is being asked to respond, and

    (b) signals completion when the request has been satisfactorily addressed.

    > Example: "I'm feeling cold and would like a show of hands from anyone who would object to my closing the door right now." To signal completion: "Thank you. I'm done." Or (if there are people objecting): "I see that some of you would like the door to remain open. I will go get a sweater. Please go on with the meeting."

4. Solicit further examples of statements that do not effectively convey a speaker's request. Work collectively to change these statements into effective requests.

5. Separate participants into small groups of five to eight and give each group a set of statement cards. Give the following instructions:

    - *Distribute the cards so that each person gets at least one card.*

    - *You will be taking turns.*

    - *Role-play a group situation. One person reads out loud the statement on the front of their card. Others role-play likely responses this speaker might receive after making such a statement.*

    - *Based on the statement they just read, the person will formulate an NVC request to the group. Remember to incorporate the two pieces we just demonstrated:*

a. *Specify from whom you are wanting a response.*

b. *Indicate when your request has been addressed to your satisfaction.*

- *Others in the group: please listen carefully to how the request is being formulated. Refer to the cues on the reverse side of your card. If you hear anything missing, support the speaker in rephrasing the request.*

- *When everyone in the group is satisfied with the request the speaker has made, move on to the next person.*

- *Please be aware that the purpose of this exercise is not to resolve conflicts that might arise for a group, but to practice making requests that can effectively generate an active response.*

DEBRIEF QUESTIONS:

1. What did you find to be the most challenging aspect of this practice?

2. As a listener in the group what differences did you experience between hearing the original statement and hearing it in the form of an NVC request?

REFERENCE: Chapter 6

First Four Scenarios

1. Everyone who is present at a meeting ought to have equal input, no matter how long they've been a member with us.

2. We don't have enough information on this issue to hold a meaningful discussion.

3. I noticed that some people didn't raise their hands to vote.

4. Why don't we alternate chairing these meetings?

Second Four Scenarios

7. It's important for us to start and end on time.

8. Nobody seems to remember the proposal we agreed to at the last meeting.

5. We never get anywhere with this subject.

6. Looks like some of us are starting to nod off.

ACTIVITY 8.4

The Request Behind a Statement

PURPOSE OF ACTIVITY:

1. To be aware of what I am requesting of my listener when I make a statement

2. To practice stating my need and request (rather than making a statement and expecting the listener to guess my request)

BRIEF DESCRIPTION: Facilitator illustrates how we often make statements without clear awareness of what we are needing and requesting. Participants brainstorm a list of such statements, and then in small groups practice articulating requests and identifying possible underlying needs.

MATERIALS NEEDED: None

TIME REQUIRED: 30 minutes

GROUP SIZE: Three or more

SPACE REQUIRED: Enough to work in groups of three

LITERACY LEVEL REQUIRED: One member of each small group needs to be able to read.

PROCEDURE:

Part I—Introduce the subject.

> *Marshall reminds us that when we speak, we are always saying either "please" or "thank you"—"thank you" when needs are met and "please" when we want them to be met. Frequently, however, when we speak, we ourselves are unclear as to what we are needing or requesting.*
>
> **Example 1:** *When you say, "Hello there," what are you requesting and what need are you trying to meet?*

Elicit responses from the group, and jot them down on the board.

> **Example 2:** *Suppose I say, "I am fed up with them telling me what to do." What might I be requesting of my listener? What need might I be trying to meet by making this statement?*

Once again, put the groups' responses on the board, emphasizing that in any situation, many different interpretations are possible.

Part II—Brainstorm

1. Give the following instructions:

   Please take a minute, working either alone or with a partner, to come up with statements you might make which carry an unspoken need and request. For example, I might say to my partner, "I thought you were going into town today." Or I might phone my counselor and say, "I was told you are going to be on vacation for four weeks."

2. After one minute, invite two or three participants to share their statements with the whole group. Write the statements on the board. After each statement, ask the speaker to name the request and need behind their statement. Fill the board with about ten statements.

Part III—Practice

1. Divide the room into groups of three. Ask groups to take their own statement and suggest possible requests and needs that the statement's speaker may not have been fully aware of.

2. Inform participants that they have approximately 15 minutes, after which the whole group will reconvene to share what they have learned.

   NOTE: This exercise develops awareness of unspoken requests and encourages participants to practice articulating requests overtly. It is important, however, to remind participants during debrief that the NVC request is not a stand-alone piece, but functions within the heart connection made through the vulnerable sharing of feelings and needs.

DEBRIEF QUESTIONS:

1. Share anything you learned about yourself or the way you talk.

2. What, if anything, would you like to take away from this exercise to apply in daily life?

SUGGESTIONS FOR PRACTICE IN DAILY LIFE:

1. When making a statement, ask yourself, "What need am I expressing and what am I requesting?"

2. When someone makes a statement, guess what they might be needing and requesting. If you are not sure, check it out with them.

REFERENCES: Chapters 6, 7

ACTIVITY 8.5

What Keeps Us From Making a Request?

PURPOSE OF ACTIVITY:

1. To develop awareness of what keeps us from making requests to meet our needs

2. To practice making difficult requests

BRIEF DESCRIPTION: After a review of the primary aspects of the NVC request, participants are invited to reflect on a situation where they had difficulty making a request of someone. Participants identify reasons (fears, beliefs, thinking) preventing them from making requests, and explore the underlying needs. Whole-group brainstorming, individual reflection, and small group sharing give participants opportunity to:

- understand the needs they meet by choosing not to make a request
- practice simultaneously holding two sets of needs
- formulate requests that are difficult to make

MATERIALS NEEDED:
- ❏ Board or flip chart
- ❏ Individual Handout: What Keeps Me from Making a Request?

TIME REQUIRED: 1 hour

GROUP SIZE: Any

SPACE REQUIRED: Adequate for groups of three to four to work without mutual interference

LITERACY LEVEL REQUIRED: Reading required; writing desirable

PROCEDURE:

1. Review "Request" as the fourth component of the NVC model (see Description of Concepts):

    a. *We use request as a strategy to meet a need*

    b. *Before requesting someone to take a particular action, we first make sure we are mutually connected. The two kinds of "connecting requests" are:*

        i. *"request for empathy," e.g., Would you be willing to tell me what you just heard me say?*

        ii. *"request for honesty," e.g., Would you be willing to tell me what you are feeling and needing in response to what I just said?*

   c. *We express our request in positive, concrete language and in such a way that the other party can*

        i. *respond verbally to our request for empathy or honesty,*

        ii. *take the particular action we ask for, or*

        iii. *agree to take a particular action in the future*

2. Present topic of what keeps people from making requests:

   a. Use a concrete example (ideally from your own life) to demonstrate the difficulty we sometimes have in making requests.

   b. Ask participants to silently recall a situation where they had (or still have) difficulty making a request.

       i. *What was the situation?*

       ii. *What action did you want the other person to take?*

       iii. *What prevented you from making the request?*

   c. Write the last question ("What prevented you from making the request?") on the board as you give participants a minute of silence to reflect. Then ask participants to volunteer their responses while you record them on the board.

   d. Read the list of responses out loud, asking participants to raise one hand if an item strikes a chord, and two hands if it is extra prominent for them.

   e. When complete, invite participants to expand the list by brainstorming together. Read the new items and once again, ask participants to raise 0, 1, or 2 hands, depending on the degree to which they resonate with an item.

3. Offer time for deeper reflection and integration.

   a. Distribute the handout "What Keeps Me From Making a Request?"

   b. Ask participants to take 10 minutes to read the handout and to reflect on the questions.

   c. Inform participants that they will be working on the handout in small groups, so they might want to jot down their responses to the questions if it would help them remember later on.

4. Divide participants into groups of three to four with each member taking 5 minutes to share their responses to the Handout questions.

5. Debrief, allotting at least 10 minutes for the whole group to address the debrief questions below.

DEBRIEF QUESTIONS:

1. What needs did you find preventing you from making requests?

2. Describe the experience of articulating your request to the group.

3. Share any physical sensations or shifts in energy you noticed during this activity.

4. What did you learn about yourself? How do you imagine applying this understanding to your everyday life?

SUGGESTIONS FOR PRACTICE IN DAILY LIFE: [NOTE: The two suggestions below are independent of each other.]

1. Identify a request you are having difficulty making in your life.

   a. Ask yourself:
      i. What action do I want the other person to take?
      ii. What is my need for requesting this action?
      iii. Is what I am considering an NVC request or a demand?
      iv. If it is a request, what need is holding me back from expressing it to the other party?
      v. What might I do or say to meet both sets of needs (i.e., the needs I wish to meet by requesting and the needs I wish to meet by not requesting)?

   b. If you intend to present a request to the other party, write it on paper first while holding both sets of needs in your consciousness.

   c. Approach the other party with clear intention to "connect first" before expressing your request. Be sure that you have clearly stated the need before making your request.

2. Without feeling compelled to "do something about it," simply pause each time you become aware of reluctance to make a request for what you want. Continue this practice over time. Notice if changes occur.

REFERENCES: Chapters 1, 6, 7

What Keeps Me From Making a Request?

Use the following to guide your exploration and sharing:

1. Bring to mind a situation where you would like (or wish you had been able) to make a request of someone.

2. Describe the situation, using NVC observations.

3. What would you want the other party to do or say?

4. What feelings come up when you think of making such a request to them?

5. What keeps you from making the request? Refer to the list of "Common Fears and Beliefs" below, and tick off those that resonate with you. Add your own reasons to the list.

6. For each item on the list that applies to you, ask yourself:
    a. What is my need here? (Jot down any needs underlying a particular fear, belief, or thought.)
    b. To what extent am I meeting (or not meeting) this need when I choose to refrain from making a request of the other person?
    c. Are there possible ways I can meet these needs other than refraining from making a request? (State concrete possibilities.)

7. When you choose not to make a request in the situation you describe, what needs are left unmet?

8. Take a silent moment to hold and value both sets of needs: the needs you hope to meet through making the request and the needs you choose to meet by refraining. Notice any physical sensations or shift in energy.

9. Take the following steps to practice making the request:
    a. Bring your attention inward and recall the situation once again.
    b. Formulate a request to the other party while being aware of how much you value both sets of needs.
    c. Express your request out loud, speaking to your group as if you were addressing the other party in the situation.

10. Share with your group:
    a. how you feel after verbalizing the request
    b. what would support you to make requests in the future.

COMMON FEARS AND BELIEFS

Which Keep Me From Making Requests

1. I fear the pain of hearing rejection.

2. I fear the pain of not being received or understood.

3. I fear the pain of not being able to express my request clearly.

4. I fear the pain of being triggered by past experiences.

5. I fear the pain of being hurt or angry if the other person says no to me.

6. I fear the pain of being viewed by others in ways I don't want to be viewed—for example, as being:

   a. "needy," "weak," "pitiful"

   b. "manipulative," "sleazy"

   c. "greedy," "grabby"

   d. "ignorant," "naïve," "uncool"

   e. "demanding," "aggressive"

   f. _____

7. I fear the pain of viewing myself in ways I disapprove, e.g., as "needy," "greedy," "aggressive," etc. (a–f, above).

8. I believe that I do not deserve what I am requesting.

9. I believe that a request is pointless since it will definitely be rejected.

10. I believe that the other party lacks the capacity to satisfy my request.

11. I believe that I should be self-reliant and able to cope without asking for help.

12. I believe that it is disrespectful or inconsiderate to put people in the potentially uncomfortable position of "having to say no."

13. I believe that the other person should know what I want without my having to ask for it.

14. _____

CONNECTING WITH SELF

9.1 Awareness Exercise: Self-Empathy

9.2 Awareness Exercise: Resolving Inner Conflict

9.3 Activity: Freeing Ourselves of Self-Violence

9.4 Activity: Freeing Ourselves of Self-Demands

9.5 Activity: I see, I think, I feel, I sense, I value

KEY CONCEPT 9:

Connecting With Self

Description: Our ability to apply NVC effectively in our relationships with others depends on our ability to relate to ourselves with NVC consciousness. We are called to feel our feelings from moment to moment and to be aware of the current need that is generating the feelings. "Connecting with self" may take several forms. It may entail a self-dialogue to translate judgments (of myself or others) into an awareness of my own needs. Or it may involve focusing inwardly to actually experience this moment's physical and emotional feelings. We also "connect with self" when we take the inner-witness stance, cultivating mindfulness of this moment's experience, being aware that we are thinking or feeling, judging or observing, sitting or standing.

Toolkit exercises in this section focus on self-awareness and the ability to connect with our own feelings and needs. They provide practice in noticing our thoughts, self-judgments, and self-demands and in transforming them into awareness of feelings and needs.

Tips for Facilitators: Because we communicate through words and often think through words, we naturally tend to rely on words when we study, learn, or practice NVC. However, it may be helpful to emphasize that words comprise only one means by which we create connection (or disconnection!). Our intention is not to suppress thoughts, but to be able to recognize them with awareness. Awareness is nurtured by stillness. When facilitating, we can experiment with ways to support stillness. This is especially helpful during practices that focus on self-connection, so that participants can experience this important aspect of NVC beyond the arena of speech.

AWARENESS EXERCISE 9.1

Self-Empathy

AIM OF EXERCISE:

1. To experience how, in offering ourselves our own full presence, we restore a sense of well-being and connectedness

2. To practice:

   - recognizing thoughts as thoughts

   - opening deeply to our feelings

   - connecting to the energy of needs

   - fully accepting the experience in this moment without trying to change it or to get somewhere else

BRIEF DESCRIPTION: This exercise guides individuals through a process of connecting silently with painful feelings and their underlying needs. It is designed for people who are familiar with the various NVC components and who already have experience applying the NVC model to their lives. The process calls for 15–20 minutes of silent inner focus and is best undertaken when participants are rested and alert.

Note to facilitator: Experience this process on your own at least once before introducing it to others. (You might ask a friend to read the instructions so you can follow the process or audio-record your own voice to play back.)

MATERIALS NEEDED:
   - ❑ A timer or watch with second hand for the facilitator
   - ❑ Optional: Individual Handout 9.1: Self-Empathy Meditation for participants wishing to sustain a home practice

TIME REQUIRED: 35 minutes (15–20 minute guided silence followed by a debrief of about the same length)

GROUP SIZE: Any

SPACE REQUIRED: Enough for each person to be seated comfortably with a sense of privacy

LITERACY LEVEL REQUIRED: None

PROCEDURE:

Facilitator, take a moment to be fully present in the moment before inviting participants into this silent self-empathy process. Specify the purpose of this activity to groups unfamiliar with meditation practices (see above, "Aim of Exercise").

Introduce the subject:

> *Self-empathy is a process of opening myself fully to life (what is alive, what is happening for me) in this moment. Often, when we experience unpleasant feelings, we have the urge to resolve the unsatisfying situation associated with the feeling in order to arrive at a different, more pleasant feeling. This very desire to "get someplace" keeps me from fully accepting the present moment, fully accepting my experience, fully accepting myself. . . . By resisting what I am experiencing and feeling, I am cutting off—separating—part of me from myself. Separation is the source of pain. Is it possible to be present to all my experience—including feelings of resistance or urgency—without acting them out? When I apply NVC (or any other approach) with the goal of skirting or overcoming pain rather than opening up to whatever is present, I contribute to further self-alienation. When we practice deep self- empathy and embrace this moment's experience fully, we are in fact embracing ourselves and giving ourselves the love and connectedness we so often seek from others.*

Read the following instructions slowly, allowing time between words for participants to follow the directions. Suggested time is given in parentheses. Where there is a succession of dots, each dot represents about 1 second.

A. Introduction and Grounding [2 minutes]

1. *I would like to guide us through a silent self-empathy process. . . .*

2. *First, identify a painful moment . . . memory . . . feeling. . . . Is there a part of yourself that's unhappy toward which you would like to extend empathic presence? . . .*

3. *Now establish clarity as to what stimulated this pain. What did someone (or you yourself) say or do that triggered this pain? State the observation to yourself. [30 seconds] (NOTE: If you sense any confusion in the room, break silence by asking, "Does anyone need help getting clear on what they are observing free of evaluation?" Verify that everyone can clearly state their particular stimulus before returning to the guided silence.)*

4. *Let's take a moment to gather ourselves. Try settling into a stable seated position . . . upright and alert but still relaxed. . . .*

5. *If you feel safe and comfortable doing so, let your eyes close. Otherwise, lower your gaze to focus your attention inward. . . .*

6. *Feel yourself seated here, body resting, supported by the chair, floor, earth. . . .*

7. *Take a few conscious breaths, noticing what it feels like right now . . . to be breathing . . . to be alive and breathing . . . right now . . . in this moment. . . .*

B. Staying Seated to Watch the Movie [8 minutes]

1. *Now bring your attention to that part of your body where you are most able to experience the sensation of breathing. For many of us, this could be the rising and falling of the belly. . . . Or perhaps it's the sensation of air moving in and out at the nostrils. . . . Breathe naturally and notice where you experience the breath most acutely. Is it in the rise and fall of the chest? . . . Once you decide, rest your attention here for a few breaths. . . . Notice the sensation of inhaling . . . of exhaling. . . . Notice the pause, if any, between breaths. . . . Let's take a few moments here . . . breathing naturally . . . being present to this moment's experience of our body breathing. . . . [15 seconds]*

2. *Now open your awareness to encompass your total experience of life in this moment.*

   a. *Notice, for example, that you are hearing in this moment . . . hearing my voice and perhaps other sounds. Continue breathing.*

   b. *Notice if there is thinking going on in you. Simply recognize thoughts as they come and go. For example, there might be a thought, "Gee, I don't know what I am doing," or "This is weird," or "I forgot to bring my keys," or "I wonder what we're having for lunch." There's no need to judge thoughts as they arise. You don't need to believe them, you don't need to resist them, you don't need to analyze or pursue them in any way. Just notice that you are thinking, and recognize thoughts as they appear and fade away. . . .*

   c. *Notice any feeling or physical sensation in the body. Where is it? . . . Feel the feeling without having to give it a name.*

   d. *Hearing, thinking, smelling, feeling . . . Just notice the experience of each moment and let it pass. [10 seconds]*

3. *Now bring to mind the stimulus that you clarified earlier for yourself. Repeat the observation silently to yourself. . . . As you continue breathing, imagine yourself seated, facing a movie screen. On this screen, you'll be witnessing the contents of your mind play out in the form of thoughts, images, stories. . . . Continue to breathe. . . . Direct your attention to the screen to see if any thoughts or images*

are showing up in response to the stimulus you just recalled. Take a moment to watch or hear your own thoughts as if watching a movie. Continue to breathe as you watch the display of thoughts and images on the screen. *[10 seconds]*

4. Interrupt the show briefly to bring your attention back to the body. Notice yourself breathing. Come back inside your body. See if you notice any feelings or sensations in the body. . . . Feelings may be confusion, sadness, agitation, peacefulness. . . . Sensations may be a tightness somewhere . . . or tingling . . . palpitation . . . warmth . . . pressure. *[5 seconds]*

5. Return your attention to the screen if thoughts are coming up for you. Be receptive to hearing the thoughts and seeing the images that are arising in your mind as they appear on the screen. . . . Consciously receive them on the screen in front of you . . . Continue to breathe as you . . . watch the spectacle. *[5 seconds]*

6. Challenge yourself to stay focused for the next 2 minutes, alternating between watching the movie and feeling your feelings. Consider giving your thoughts and feelings equal time. Remember to keep breathing as you switch your attention back and forth. *[Allow 2 minutes between here and the next part. To support participants in staying focused, intermittently read one of the following brief reminders.]*

   a. Continuing to breathe . . .

   b. Feeling the feelings in the body . . .

   c. Watching the thoughts and images on the screen . . .

   d. Being present to myself . . .

C. **Connecting to My Needs** |5 minutes|

1. As you continue to move your attention back and forth between the contents of the mind being displayed on the screen and the awareness of what you are feeling in this moment, pause at any point and ask, "What is my need here?" "What need or value is wishing to be met?" Allow these questions to percolate as you move back and forth . . . now watching your thoughts on the screen, now feeling your feelings in the body. . . . Continue to breathe . . . asking "What is my need here?" . . .

2. There may be more than one need. . . . There may be deeper layers of needs underneath more apparent needs . . . Sometimes there is the deep need to know that I count . . . people count . . . I matter . . . people matter. . . . I belong . . . everyone has a place at the table. . . . Keep breathing . . . feeling . . . watching whatever thoughts show up . . . asking yourself, "What is my need here?" "What do I value here?" *[10 seconds]*

3. If you connected with more than one need, which one seems most poignant, most alive in this moment? . . . Focus your attention on one need that is stirring deeply in you right now.

4. Imagine taking this need and placing it in the center of your heart. Feel how important it is . . . how much you value it . . . how much you want to nurture, protect, and cherish this quality. . . . Continue to breathe. . . .

5. Connect deeply with this need. . . . What does it look like? . . . Feel like? . . . Smell, taste, sound like? . . . What is this need?

6. Allow yourself to feel the longing, the desire for this need to manifest, to take root, to blossom. . . . What is this longing? . . . Is there someplace inside where you can experience the longing for this need which you so value? What does that yearning feel like? . . . Where is it in your body? . . . What do you notice? . . . Is it cool? Warm? Tight? Spacious? Agitated? Calm? . . . You may not have words; simply feel . . . feel the longing. . . .

7. What would life be like right now in this moment with this need deeply met in all its beauty? . . . Hold that feeling in your heart. . . . (repeat Line #7)

D. Resting in the Universality of My Need [3 minutes]

1. Feel how much you cherish this need for yourself and for everyone you care about. . . . See if you treasure this need for yourself and for everyone in the world. Experience how strongly this need exists in your own heart right now. . . . Let it fill your heart. . . . Feel what life feels like right now, right here, with this need so deeply cherished in your heart. . . .

2. Breathe in this feeling. . . . Breathe into your heart. . . . Imagine breathing in the fulfillment of this need right into your heart. . . . [10 seconds]

3. On your next out-breath, send this precious need, which is right now enfolded in your heart, to someone sitting near to you. . . . Imagine saying this need, repeating the word, whispering it into their heart. . . .

4. As you continue breathing in the fullness of the need you are holding, spread it further and further out with each exhalation . . . out to everyone in this room . . . out to everyone you love. . . .

5. Keep breathing . . . in and out . . . out to every life you touch . . . out to all people everywhere and out to any creatures who might have this need which is being honored and held in your heart and by your being in this very moment. . . . Continue breathing, offering the blessing of this need to be fulfilled for all living beings everywhere. . . . [5 seconds]

6. *As we close this process, take a few more breaths . . . being present in your body, . . . coming home to yourself. . . . Now gently bring your attention back to the room and when you are ready, open your eyes if they've been closed. . . .*

DEBRIEF QUESTIONS:

Notes to facilitator: It is important to share with participants during the debrief that the self-empathy process being presented is not a linear procedure. The instructions in this guided exercise are sequenced to give participants a general sense of the various elements that come into play, and how to approach them. The whole process might take a split second, several hours, or, to the degree we are able to maintain focus, a whole lifetime.

Start the debrief session by checking to see if anyone is feeling stress or an urgency to be heard. The process of self-empathy can trigger a lot of feelings, whether happy or distressing, so take time for empathy where needed.

Use any of the following questions to generate further learning and discussion.

1. What body sensations did you notice?

2. What emotion did you connect with? How (and where) did you experience it?

3. Were you able to see your thoughts without identifying or getting lost in them (i.e., watch the movie without hopping into the screen)? In what ways was this easy or difficult?

4. Were there judgments and opinions regarding this process that came up for you? Were you aware that you were thinking when these thoughts emerged? What did you do with the thoughts? What were you feeling?

5. What was it like to move back and forth between thinking and feeling?

6. Were you connected to your needs? What helped you in or deterred you from connecting with your needs?

7. How many needs were you aware of? Which needs were on the surface and easy to access? Which needs were you able to connect with only after some time? What was the most poignant need?

8. What was it like to hold the need in your heart while breathing in?

9. Did you experience yearning or longing for the need to be met? Describe how that felt.

10. Was it difficult to stay focused? What part was most difficult? What would have helped you stay focused?

11. How did you experience breathing out the need you were holding in your heart to others in the room and beyond?

12. What differences, if any, do you notice now—either in the way you feel about yourself or about the stimulus—compared to when we started the exercise?

13. What did you learn about yourself during this process?

14. What do you wish to take away from our practice today?

SUGGESTIONS FOR PRACTICE IN DAILY LIFE: Consider setting aside 15–20 minutes a day to practice this process of self-empathy. The more we practice, the more skillfully and effectively we can self-empathize on the spot when life presents us with a difficult moment. During daily practice, if no stimulus comes to mind, simply be present during the allotted time to whatever comes up in the form of thoughts, emotions, sensations, and needs. (Facilitator: provide optional Handout 9.1 that outlines this process to those who wish to experiment with a daily practice.)

REFERENCES: Chapters 9, 13

Self-Empathy Meditation

(15–20 minutes) Begin by connecting with your intention to be fully present to yourself. Identify a painful experience for which you would like to practice self-empathy. Clarify the stimulus and state (or write) it in the form of an NVC observation.

A. GROUNDING

Settle into a stable seated position.

B. STAYING SEATED TO WATCH THE MOVIE

1. Establish the breath as your ongoing anchor.

2. Open to present-moment thoughts, feelings, and body sensations.

3. Bring to mind the stimulus that was identified earlier. Notice what thoughts and images come up for you in the presence of this stimulus.

4. Feel what comes up, both physically and emotionally.

5. Return to watch the thoughts and images as if they were being projected onto a movie screen.

6. Alternate your attention between (a) the thoughts and images on the screen and (b) the physical and emotional feelings present in the body.

C. CONNECTING TO MY NEED

1. Ask "What is my need here?" as you continue #6 above.

2. Allow for the possibility of many needs or several layers of needs.

3. Choose the most poignant need and hold it in your heart.

4. Move close to and connect deeply with this need.

5. Feel the yearning and cherishing this need brings up.

D. RESTING IN THE UNIVERSALITY OF MY NEED

1. With each inhalation, take the need more deeply into your heart.

2. With each exhalation, spread it further and further to more people and living beings.

   Close by celebrating your intention and efforts to cultivate deep self-empathy—bringing compassionate presence and awareness into the world.

AWARENESS EXERCISE 9.2

Resolving Inner Conflict

AIM OF EXERCISE: Practice resolving an inner conflict

INSTRUCTIONS FOR GUIDING AWARENESS EXERCISE: Read the following slowly, leaving space between each statement for the participant to engage in the guided process.

1. *Sit comfortably. Straighten your spine. Make any necessary adjustments.*

2. *Focus your attention inward by either closing your eyes or gazing softly on the floor in front of you.*

3. *Focus your attention on your breathing.*

4. *Simply notice your breath as you breathe in and out.*

5. *Look at your current life and see if you can find any "should messages"— anything you tell yourself that you should or should not be doing. Pick one of your "should-thoughts" to focus on.*

    • *Now listen to the part of you that is saying, "You should . . ." or "You should not . . ."*
    — *What does this voice value or need?*
    — *Take this value. Connect with how precious this value is to you. Hold it tenderly in your right hand.*

    • *Now listen to the part of you that is resisting the voice that is telling you what you should or should not be doing—the part of you that is resisting the "shoulding-voice."*
    — *What is this voice valuing or needing?*
    — *When you connect with the value that this voice is expressing, place it in your left hand and hold it tenderly.*

    • *You are now holding two values: one in your right hand and one in your left. Simply hold them until you experience how much you cherish both.*

6. *When you are ready, open your eyes. Look around the circle with the awareness that we are each holding two values that we cherish.*

SHARING CIRCLE:

• My name is _____ .

• I am holding _____ in my right hand and _____ in my left hand.

REFERENCES: Chapters 5, 9

ACTIVITY 9.3

Freeing Ourselves of Self-Violence

PURPOSE OF ACTIVITY:

1. To become more aware of the judgments and demands we make of ourselves

2. To translate such self-judgments into needs and to explore requests (strategies) to meet the needs

BRIEF DESCRIPTION: Participants brainstorm violent statements they make about themselves and then use a worksheet to:

- Become aware of and acknowledge their violent self-talk

- Make clear observations of what is triggering the violent self-talk

- Connect to the underlying feelings and unmet needs

- Explore and freely choose strategies that would meet those needs

MATERIALS NEEDED:
- ❑ Individual Handout: Freeing Myself of Self-Violence

TIME REQUIRED: 40 minutes

GROUP SIZE: Any

SPACE REQUIRED: Enough for participants to be seated

LITERACY LEVEL REQUIRED: Able to write

PROCEDURE:

1. Introduce the concept of "self-violence" as behavior that causes damage to our physical and emotional well-being, including the use of:

   a. language that blames and judges ourselves: DIAGNOSES,

   b. language that implies that we DESERVE punishment, and

   c. language that DEMANDS that we "must," "should," "have to," "ought to."

2. Invite participants to think of violent self-talk in the above three categories.

3. Ask someone to volunteer a piece of violent self-talk. Encourage them to "translate" the statement into observations, feelings, and needs. Then invite them to generate strategies which would address the unmet need(s) they identified.

Example:

- Violent self-talk: "I am a useless piece of trash."

- Translation into observation, feeling, and need: "When I hear that my children are approaching strangers for help, I feel distressed and ashamed. I really value being able to support my family."

- Possible requests of myself (strategies to meet need):
  a. "I will make an appointment on Monday to speak to a counselor about job training."
  b. "I will take 1 minute every day this week to hold the awareness of how much I truly cherish my family and how much I value supporting and contributing to those I love."
  c. "I will sign up for the carpentry training and each time I complete a module I will write my family to let them know."
  d. "When I realize that I haven't empathized with my children during a conversation, I will write down what I had said. Then I will find an opportunity to share this with them."

4. Distribute the Handout. Give participants 10 minutes to work silently on their own using the following instructions:
   a. Brainstorm for D-D-D (Diagnose, Deserve, Demand) statements.
   b. Choose one statement you would like to work with.
   c. Use the Learning Guide to help connect with your feelings and needs.
   d. Identify a concrete strategy for meeting your need(s) that you feel free and willing to pursue.
   e. If you have extra time, choose another D-D-D statement and repeat Steps (b), (c), and (d), above.

5. Invite participants to work in two's and three's, taking turns sharing:
   a. a self-violent statement,
   b. its translation into feelings and needs, and
   c. a concrete request or strategy.

   Inform them that they may either share what they wrote on the handout or come up with a different statement.

6. After 10 minutes, reconvene the whole group and ask participants to volunteer one or more additional examples of how they moved from violent self-talk to feelings, needs, and self-requests.

SUGGESTION FOR PRACTICE IN DAILY LIFE: Every day for one week, take a D-D-D statement you have made to yourself and translate into feelings, needs and a strategy.

REFERENCE: Chapter 9

Freeing Myself of Self-Violence

Write down violent statements you make to yourself:

1. Statements that shame, blame, judge, label, criticize, and DIAGNOSE what's wrong with me: _____

   _____

   _____

2. Statements implying that I DESERVE punishment: _____

   _____

   _____

3. Statements that DEMAND that I "must," "should," "have to," "ought to":

   _____

   _____

Pick one violent statement and translate it into the four components of Nonviolent Communication:

1. OBSERVATION: When I see or hear (observable fact)_____

   _____

   _____

2. FEELING: I feel _____

   _____

   _____

3. NEED: Because I need (or value) _____

   _____

   _____

4. REQUEST (strategy): In order to meet my need I choose (ask myself) to do the following: _____

   _____

ACTIVITY 9.4

Freeing Ourselves of Self-Demands

PURPOSE OF ACTIVITY:

1. To become aware of the demands we make of ourselves

2. To become aware of the "demand-resistance cycle" brought on by self-demands

3. To translate demands into requests so we can make free choices

BRIEF DESCRIPTION: In this activity participants brainstorm and list demands they make of themselves. They are encouraged to notice the effects of self-demands, and to imagine how they would react if the demands were coming from another source. Working solo or in groups of three, they practice translating self-demands into needs and self-requests—strategies freely chosen to meet specific needs. A worksheet is available to help guide those who prefer to work privately.

MATERIALS NEEDED:
- ❑ Individual Handout: Freeing Myself of Self-Demands
- ❑ Paper and pen (or marker) for each group of three

TIME REQUIRED: 60 (or 80, 100 minutes, depending on whether small groups will work with one, two, or all three members' personal situation)

GROUP SIZE: Any

SPACE REQUIRED: Enough for groups of three to work comfortably

LITERACY LEVEL REQUIRED: Ability to read and write

PROCEDURE:

1. **Introduce** the subject of "Self-Demand," defining it as self-talk that contains "shoulds, musts, ought to's, 'gotta's,' have to's, etc."

    a. Invite the participants to think of demands they make of themselves—especially those that they have difficulty complying with. Ask the group to volunteer a few examples out loud.

    b. Have participants take 5 minutes to silently brainstorm and list their self-demands in writing. Ask them to pick one or two which are most alive for them.

2. **Demonstrate** the activity.
   a. Ask for three volunteers:
      i. A, who will be working with a self-demand
      ii. B, who will role-play A's demanding internal voice
      iii. C, who will be writing on the board

   b. Ask A to read their self-demand out loud to the group while C records it, using the top left quarter of the board.

   c. Ask A to focus inside for a few seconds and to become aware of this moment's feelings and body sensations.

   d. Ask A and B to face each other. Give the following instructions:

      i. *B, you are role-playing A's self-demanding voice. Please state the demand out loud now as you look into A's face.*

      ii. *A, go inside and notice your feelings and physical sensations. Are there changes in body temperature anywhere? Any tightness or constriction? Any resistance? Just notice what is going on for you inside. [15 seconds] Now please tell B the body sensations you are experiencing—to the degree that you are able to verbalize them.*

      iii. *B, repeat the demand to A, this time using as much force in your body and voice as you guess A might be applying to themselves.*

      iv. *A, once again take a few silent moments to go inside and notice the physical sensations which are present. When you are ready, tell B what you notice.*

   e. Have A and B repeat this exchange until A is able to communicate to B the physical effects they experience hearing the demand. (If, after repeated exchanges, A seems unaware of any physical sensations resulting from hearing the self-demand, simply acknowledge this and move on to the next part.)

   f. Provide guidance in translating self-demands into unmet needs, using the following instructions:

      i. *A and B, what do you think are the needs that A might be trying to meet by making this self-demand? C, please record these needs in a single column on the board beneath A's self-demand.*

      ii. *A, which of these needs most resonate with you in the context of this self-demand? C, please circle it on the board.*

      iii. *A, would you be willing to reflect and let us know whether this is a need which you frequently ignore or are reluctant to embrace?*

      iv. *A, focus attention on the part of you that is resisting the demand.*

What need(s) are you trying to meet by not complying with this demand? C, please make a heading on the right side of the board that reads, "My Noncomplying Self," and record A's needs underneath it.

v. *A, take a look at the needs that your Noncomplying Self holds dear. Which one is most alive, poignant, or relevant for you? C, please circle the need A identifies.*

g. Invite participants to look at the two sets of needs, one belonging to the part of A making the demand and the other to the part of A resisting the demand.

h. Ask everyone in the room, including A, B, and C, to acknowledge both sets of needs, using the following instructions:

Let's take a few moments to hold both these needs (or both sets of needs) in our heart. See if we can connect with the needs of the one making the demand and the needs of the one resisting the demand. Can we appreciate the importance of both needs and value both in our heart?

i. **Optional demonstration on exploring strategies**

NOTE: Based on availability of time, number of participants, group size, and other priorities, decide whether or not to include this piece in the demonstration. It may involve discussion of personal and practical details that do not contribute to everyone's learning. It may also not be possible to generate satisfactory strategies within the time allotted.

- Ask A to explore strategies that would address both the needs behind the demand and the needs behind the resistance.
- Invite B and C to brainstorm with A for concrete strategies.
- Ask C to record this on the board using the following format, "To meet my need for _____ , I choose to _____ (name the specific strategy)."

3. **Participant Practice**

a. Give participants the option of either working privately or in groups of three.

b. Offer the Handout, "Freeing Myself From Self-Demands," to help guide those who are working by themselves.

c. Ask those in groups to determine who is to take role A, B, and C.

d. Allow 20 minutes for participants to work through one self-demand, using the process as demonstrated. Inform groups as to how much time they have, and remind them to switch roles every 20 minutes.

NOTE: When you reconvene for the debrief, offer everyone a handout as a resource to encourage them to continue working with self-demands.

DEBRIEF QUESTIONS:

1. What did you learn about yourself in this activity?

2. What was the most difficult part of the process:

    a. recognizing self-demands,

    b. identifying the needs behind your demand,

    c. experiencing the physical sensations associated with resistance,

    d. identifying the needs behind your resistance,

    e. valuing both sets of needs, or

    f. generating strategies to meet both needs?

3. How do you see yourself applying what you learned in this exercise?

SUGGESTIONS FOR PRACTICE IN DAILY LIFE: Be alert to the tone you use when speaking to yourself. Notice when you are making a demand. Pause, go inside and get in touch with the need you want to meet. Then, make space for the part of you that is reluctant to comply: take a few moments of silence to feel the feelings and physical sensations inside of you that signal your resistance. Ask yourself, "What need am I trying to meet through this resistance?" Honor both needs. Afterward, explore choices that would meet both needs.

REFERENCE: Chapter 9

Freeing Myself of Self-Demands

1. List below statements you make to yourself using the words "should," "must," "ought to," "got to," "have to," "can't," etc. (e.g., "I can't keep gaining weight like this." "I ought to attend the meeting." "I've got to do better.")

   _____

   _____

2. Pick one statement and repeat it to yourself. What need(s) is this voice wanting to meet by making this demand? _____

   _____

3. Now imagine someone else making this demand of you. Go inside and notice the feelings and physical sensations that come up for you. Write them down:

   _____

   _____

4. Ask yourself, "This part of me that is resisting the demand—what need(s) does it value? What need(s) is it wanting to protect?" _____

   _____

5. Look at the need words you listed under #2 and #4, above. Write down those needs which carry the most energy or meaning for you right now.

   _____

   _____

6. Hold the needs which you circled and cherish them for a few moments. Notice how much you appreciate these needs. Over the course of the next 24 hours, return periodically to acknowledging and valuing these needs while allowing possible strategies to manifest themselves. Record strategies here.

   _____

   _____

7. Pick one strategy and decide whether you wish to actively commit to following through on it. If so, fill in the statement, "To meet my need for _____

   I choose to _____ ."

ACTIVITY 9.5

I see, I think, I feel, I sense, I value

PURPOSE OF ACTIVITY:

1. To distinguish observation from interpretation (evaluation, thought)

2. To distinguish thought from feelings and physical sensations

3. To identify the need behind a feeling

BRIEF DESCRIPTION:

1. Participants work in pairs or small groups, using pictures to make observations.

2. Participants then state the thoughts (interpretations and evaluations) about what they see in the picture they have selected.

3. Next they connect to the feelings and physical sensations triggered by their observation and interpretation.

4. Finally, participants identify the need (or value) behind their feeling(s).

   This exercise offers an opportunity to experience how the same image can generate different observations, thoughts, feelings, and needs.

MATERIALS NEEDED:

- ❑ A stack of pictures, at least one for each participant. See General Learning Aid G9: Guidelines for Assembling a Set of Pictures.
- ❑ One large photo that is visible to the whole group for use in the initial demonstration of the exercise.
- ❑ Group Handout: For each pair or small group, a cue sheet with the following words in large letters: I *see*, I *think*, I *feel*, I *sense*, I *value*

TIME REQUIRED: 30–60 minutes

GROUP SIZE: Any size, divided up into small groups of two to four

SPACE REQUIRED: Enough space to allow groups to work without mutual interference

LITERACY LEVEL REQUIRED: None

PROCEDURE:

1. Demonstrate the exercise, using a large photo.

2. Ask for a volunteer to offer an observation free of evaluation by starting their statement with the words, "I see. . . ."

3. Ask the group, **Does everyone observe what [the volunteer] just described?** If anyone hears an interpretation, use this opportunity to explore the concept of "observation free of evaluation."

   [NOTE: Be sure to emphasize there is no right or wrong. In fact, the only things our eyes can actually see or observe are shapes and colors. For example, when we see something of a certain shape and size situated at a certain place in a certain way, we might say that we "see" a house. In fact, our mind is interpreting the visual data to conclude that this image fits its concept of "house." While not every human being on the planet might see "house" when looking at the same object, there is usually a consensual reality that we all generally accept. Within this reality, we are training ourselves to distinguish what is an "objective" observation and a "subjective" evaluation. Our ability to perceive our thoughts as subjective evaluation gives us freedom to choose how to relate to our thoughts rather than be controlled by them. It also allows us to dialogue with another person starting from a shared common standpoint ("the facts" or "objective observation").]

4. Continue by asking the same participant who had volunteered, **When you see** [what was just stated], **what thoughts come up?** [You might add for clarity: "What is your interpretation of that? What meaning do you give it?"] **Start your sentence using the words, "I think. . . "**

5. Continue by asking the same volunteer, **And when you see and think what you just shared, what do you feel? Start your sentence using the words, "I feel. . . "**

6. Continue with the same volunteer: **Now I'd like to suggest that you close your eyes and turn your attention inward to connect with the feeling. Feel what it actually feels like. Where do you notice physical sensations? Warmth, pressure, tightness, tingling . . . ? You may not have words for them, but just take a moment to open up to what you are noticing inside as you recall your thoughts and feelings about the picture. If you wish to use words, start your sentence by saying, "I sense . . ."**

7. Continue with the same volunteer: **And now tell us the need—either met or unmet —causing those feelings. Begin your sentence with the words, "I value . . ."**

8. Thank the volunteer and check for questions among the group. Now use the

same picture and offer your own observation, followed by thought, feeling, sensation, and value. This illustrates how the same image can generate very different responses.

9. Pass out one picture to each participant. Form groups of three or four.

10. Give each small group a copy of the Group Handout (sheet of cues).

11. Instruct the groups: **Give each person in your group an opportunity to work through the entire sequence (I see, I think, I feel, I sense, I value) before offering feedback to them. After each person has completed a sequence switch pictures and go a second round.**

12. Invite the participants back to the large circle to share one thing they learned from this exercise.

SUGGESTIONS FOR PRACTICE IN DAILY LIFE:

1. When you experience an unpleasant feeling related to someone or something around you, stop and ask, "What am I actually observing that I am reacting to here?" "How am I interpreting what I am observing?" "Am I absolutely certain that my interpretation is accurate?" After you have distinguished between your observation and interpretation, always connect with the unmet need(s) in the situation.

2. Watch a TV drama with the sound turned off. Describe what your eyes are actually seeing. List the interpretations that your mind is making.

REFERENCES: Chapters 1, 3, 4, 5

Cue Sheet

I see... (observation)

I think... (interpretation)

I feel... (emotion)

I sense... (physical sensation)

I value... (universal need)

HONESTY

10.1   Awareness Exercise: Honesty
With Ourselves

10.2   Activity: Building Blocks of
Honesty

10.3   Activity: Feedback to Feed
Growth

10.4   Activity: Components Practice

KEY CONCEPT 10:

Honesty

Description: "Honesty" in NVC is expression grounded in awareness of the four basic components of the NVC model: what I am observing, feeling, needing, and requesting in this moment. In the beginning, when we practice expressing NVC honesty, it is helpful to articulate all four components using the cues, "When I see/hear . . ., I feel . . . because I need. . . . And would you be willing . . .?" Speech based on this formula is sometimes referred to as "classical NVC." While NVC honesty always calls for clear awareness of these four components, most of us eventually learn to speak "colloquial NVC"—consciously choosing words most likely to enhance heart connection given a particular relationship, circumstance, time, place, cultural context, etc.

Toolkit exercises in this section provide practice in learning the four components of the NVC model and in expressing honesty, especially where it may be difficult to do so.

Tips for Facilitators: Participants sometimes express misgivings about NVC when they assume that it consists of a formulaic way of speaking the four components. Facilitators can empathize by demonstrating understanding of needs that underlie such misgivings. For example, participants may have a need for authenticity—to express themselves the way that seems natural to them rather than through someone's idea of how to talk; they may have a need to trust that they are putting their time and effort into learning something that will truly be effective in enhancing their lives; they may have a need for acceptance—for communicating in ways that won't be judged by those around them; they may have a need for creativity—to use language in lively, poetic ways. . . . After participants receive understanding for their misgivings, facilitators can explain that the formula for NVC honesty, much like training wheels for bike-riding, guides us in mastering the basic skills. Worldwide NVC practitioners come from a diversity of backgrounds and continue to speak in diverse ways; what they share in common is speech grounded in the intention to connect and an ongoing awareness of observations, feelings, needs, and requests.

Honesty With Ourselves

AIM OF EXERCISE: In order to express ourselves honestly to others, we need to open honestly to our own experience. This awareness exercise invites us to touch the truth of our own experience in the moment, and to then imagine expressing it to a compassionate listener.

INSTRUCTIONS FOR GUIDING AWARENESS EXERCISE: Read slowly, allowing time between statements for the participant to engage with each step:

1. *During this Awareness Exercise, you will be invited to jot down thoughts that may come up for you. If you would like to do this, have some paper and pen on hand.*

2. *Adjust your posture so that you are sitting comfortably with your back straight.*

3. *Either close your eyes or drop your gaze softly to the floor in front of you.*

4. *Bring your attention to the breath: inhale, receiving, exhale, letting go. Take a few conscious breaths here, inhale, receiving, exhale, letting go.*

5. *Now focus your attention on your body and notice any physical sensations: tightness in the shoulders, shallowness of breath, heat, coolness, constriction, vibration. . . . Give yourself space to feel whatever body sensation is present in this moment.*

6. *As you focus inward, notice any emotions currently alive in you. Are you feeling anxious, delighted, resentful, joyful, bored, peaceful . . .? Allow yourself to fully feel whatever emotion is present for you right now.*

7. *As you sustain awareness of this moment's body sensation or emotion, notice any thoughts you are thinking that might be generating these feelings. If you wish, write down what you are saying to yourself. We'll take 2 minutes to do this, going back and forth between feeling our feelings and hearing the thoughts associated with these feelings.*
   [Allow for 2 minutes of silence.]

8. *As you rest your attention on your feelings and thoughts, ask yourself, "Are my feelings and thoughts inviting me to notice needs I may not be fully conscious of?"*

9. *Take some time to connect with whatever needs come up for you. Acknowledge the need, embrace its value, appreciate its beauty. Take a few moments to be present to this important need.*

10. *Now ask yourself, "Are there deeper needs underneath this one? Are there other needs wanting to be known?" If you encounter another need or a deeper need, pause and once again, give yourself time to welcome and appreciate it. Then ask yourself, "Is there another need beneath this one?" Continue in this way until you touch a need that generates a physical shift or a letting go in your body. Hold this need in your heart and cherish it, knowing that the power is within you to both recognize this need and to fulfill it.*

11. *Spend the next couple of minutes acknowledging the value of this need and, if you wish, imagining strategies for addressing this need.*

12. *Having listened fully to yourself, imagine now expressing your truth to another person. In your mind's eye, invite a Compassionate Being to come into your space and tell them:*

    - *what you were feeling, thinking, needing,*

    - *how you might like to fulfill the need(s), and*

    - *how you are feeling right now. [Restate these three bulleted items above. Then allow a minute of silence.]*

13. *When you are ready, slowly open your eyes and look around the room. Receive each person with the awareness that, like yourself, they have just spent the last 10 minutes opening with honesty to their own truth.*

SHARING CIRCLE:

- My name is _____ .

- A feeling or need I honestly experienced during this exercise was _____ .

SUGGESTION FOR PRACTICE IN DAILY LIFE: Before you approach another person to share something significant for you, first ground yourself in self-honesty through the process we just used.

REFERENCES: Chapters 5, 9, 13

ACTIVITY 10.2

Building Blocks of Honesty

PURPOSE OF ACTIVITY:

1. To learn to identify and distinguish each of the four NVC components

2. To practice creating phrases that reflect each of the four components

3. To practice integrating the components into a complete NVC expression of honesty

BRIEF DESCRIPTION: This is a highly interactive hands-on activity using colorful materials to support participants in grasping the structure and four components of the NVC model. There are two levels of activity:

- **Level I:** Participants take turns selecting ready-made phrases from a set of cards to create a complete and meaningful NVC expression. This level of the activity is immensely effective in helping new practitioners solidify their awareness of the four components. For more experienced practitioners, it is a fun review and a preview for the next level.
- **Level II:** Participants translate a statement into NVC honesty, taking turns creating a phrase that reflects one of the four components. This level of the activity challenges both new and experienced practitioners to apply the concepts they've recently learned or reviewed.

NOTE: The materials (learning aids) for this activity require a substantial chunk of time to produce. However, once constructed, they are simple and enjoyable for the participants and may be used over and over again by the facilitator. Please watch the **Instructional Video** demonstration to gain a clear picture of this activity before you begin to produce the materials.

MATERIALS NEEDED: For each group of four to five participants
- ❏ A laminated strip charting the four (color-coded) components
- ❏ Four labeled and color-coded envelopes, each holding:
  - A set of (eight to ten) small cards (dialogue cards): each card contains a phrase that demonstrates a particular component
  - A set of (two to five) big cards (cue cards): each card is a reminder of an important aspect of a component
- ❏ For Level II only: A set of five Scenario Envelopes, each with a statement on the face of the envelope. Participants will translate these statements using the four NVC components. Each envelope contains four blank inserts labeled by component for participants to fill in.

See Specific Learning Aid 10.2 to produce these materials.

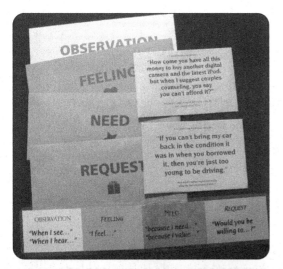

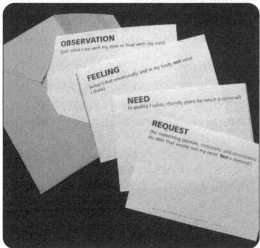

Complete set of materials, consisting of:
(A) four color-coded long envelopes,
(B) five scenario envelopes, and
(C) one laminated strip

TIME REQUIRED: 20 minutes for Level I, 45–75 minutes for Level II

GROUP SIZE: Small groups of four to five

SPACE REQUIRED: Adequate for groups to work without mutual interference.
NOTE: A working surface such as a table or floor would be ideal, but not necessary.

LITERACY REQUIRED: Ability to read and write sentences

PROCEDURE:

Level I Activity: Give the following instructions, using four volunteers to demonstrate the procedure you are describing:

1. *We will be working in groups of four or five. Each group will get one of these laminated strips and a set of four colored envelopes, one for each component. Notice there are words on both sides of the laminated strip. There are two parts to this activity. For the first part, use the side of the*

strip that shows only the four words "Observation," "Feeling," "Need," and "Request."

2. Each person takes one of the envelopes—be sure to keep to this order: first person takes "Observation," second "Feeling," then "Need," and finally "Request." If there is a fifth person in the group, that person will hold the strip so that it is visible to everyone. If there are only four people in your group, place the laminated strip on a surface in such a way that you can all read it easily.

3. You will find a set of big cue cards and a set of small dialogue cards in each envelope. In this first part of the exercise, we use only the small cards. Flip through your set of small cards to familiarize yourself with them.

4. The person with the "Observation" envelope, please begin by attaching one of your cards to the laminated strip where it is labeled "Observation." Then each person will follow by adding the feeling, need, and request to create a meaningful and complete NVC expression.

5. Each time you add your own card to the chart-strip, read out loud what is already on the chart-strip, and then read the words on your own card so everyone can hear, as well as see, the component pieces being added to complete the model. I believe our learning is reinforced when we take time to say each piece and then also to hear it and read it.

6. When all four components have been placed on the strip, check to see if everyone in the group is satisfied with the NVC expression your group has assembled.

7. When you have completed this round, return all the cards to their original envelopes except for the "Observation" card. Leave that card out as you will not be using it again.

8. To start the next round, pass the envelopes clockwise. Always begin with the person holding the "Observation" envelope and keep the four envelopes in their original order. There are enough Observation cards for eight rounds altogether.

Divide into groups of four or five and give each group a laminated strip and a set of four color-coded envelopes. Inform participants that they have 20 minutes for this part of the activity.

Level II Activity: After 20 minutes, pass out a set of five Scenario Envelopes to each group and give the following instructions:

1. After you have completed Level I and feel confident in proceeding, flip the laminated strip over to the other side: this side offers some phrases to use in expressing each component. Instead of relying on the ready-made phrases on the small cards you used in Level I, here in Level II, you will be creating your own expressions for the four NVC components.

2. Take a look at the five Scenario Envelopes I just passed out to each group. There is a statement on each envelope. Your task will be to translate this statement into the four NVC components.

3. Again, distribute the color-coded envelopes. Take some quiet time for everyone to read the set of large cue cards in their envelope. These are reminders of what to pay attention to when expressing a particular component. The "Request" envelope has the most cards and takes the longest time to read. Therefore, allow the person holding the "Request" envelope to take the lead in checking to see if everyone is ready to begin.

4. Once ready, pick a Scenario Envelope and read the statement that is to be translated into "observation," "feeling," "need," and "request." Inside the envelope are four blank sheets of paper labeled by component. Pass them out so that each person will be able to jot down their phrase when their turn comes.

5. The person holding the "Observation" envelope will begin. Use the cue on the laminated strip —"When I see . . . When I hear . . ."—to create an observation that the speaker of the statement might have had in mind when they made the statement. Please remember that everyone will be repeating all the pieces after you, so keep your observation short—ten words or so.

   With the group's help, check that the observation is free of evaluation. Then write it down and clip it to the laminated strip.

6. Next, the person with the red ("Feeling") envelope will add their piece. Always read out loud what's already on the strip when you are about to add another piece to it.

7. Continue until the statement is complete and contains all four components.

8. Check among yourselves to verify that everyone is satisfied with your completed expression of NVC honesty. You will be sharing it with the larger group at the end of this activity.

9. Begin a new round by passing your envelopes clockwise. Remember to take some quiet time to read the large cue cards before you start each new round.

DEBRIEF: Ask each group to pick one of the Scenario Envelopes and share their expression of NVC honesty with the whole group. Ask one member of the group to read the original statement out loud and another to read the group's translation of it into the four components. Invite participants to offer feedback. Ask the group to identify the most challenging aspect of the work they did together.

REFERENCES: Chapters 1, 3, 4, 5, 6

ACTIVITY 10.3

Feedback to Feed Growth

PURPOSE OF ACTIVITY:

1. To practice offering honesty to someone whose actions or words are not meeting our needs as well as they might

2. To practice offering feedback to someone with the clear intention of supporting their growth

3. To practice receiving feedback as an opportunity for growth

4. To develop trust in one's ability to offer and receive honesty in ways that can contribute to personal growth

BRIEF DESCRIPTION: This activity is designed for participants with experience in NVC who would like to practice offering each other feedback in real time within a supportive structure. It is especially beneficial for those who are interested in sharing NVC with others. Consider introducing this activity toward the end of a training period after participants have had many interactions and have developed a degree of mutual trust and understanding.

MATERIALS NEEDED: None

TIME REQUIRED: Flexible, but allow for at least 45 minutes

GROUP SIZE: Any

SPACE REQUIRED: Chairs are to be arranged in a horseshoe formation (U-shape, with an open space at one end). If necessary, double the rows within the horseshoe.

PROCEDURE:

1. Introduce the activity and explain its purpose.

> *All of us need feedback from the outside world to know how our words and actions affect others. Even if we have a conscious intention, and are behaving and speaking out of that intention, it is often only through other people's honest feedback that we can verify whether our intention was met. The inability to offer and receive feedback based on fear of judging, being judged, hurting, or being hurt deprives us of the vast and rich source of learning that we can be for one another. We can take advantage of the community of NVC practitioners to develop our skills and deepen our trust that we are able to give and receive feedback that nurtures growth.*

The following activity is called "Feedback to Feed Growth" and the practice is done in "real time." This means we will be offering one another. honest feedback regarding things being said or done in this room (in this training) that have not met (or are not meeting) our needs. (Feedback for needs met is covered under Key Concept 15: Appreciation and Celebration. In the present activity, we are practicing honesty regarding needs that have not been met.) Take a breath, go inside and see what you are feeling and needing as you hear me say this. [Pause]

2. Allow expressions of tension to surface. Take time to allow the group to connect to their difficult feelings (e.g., anxiety, fear, reluctance) and the needs behind the feelings (e.g., emotional safety, harmony, respect, etc.). After a while, check to see if there are other (nonstressful) feelings (such as curiosity, anticipation) and explore the needs behind those as well.

3. Arrange seats in a horseshoe. Then place one comfortable chair in the open space (on top of the U) facing everyone else. Give the instructions, and let the group know that you will be repeating them as needed along the way.

   a. Instructions for the Person in the Chair: **Anyone may step up with a request for feedback by taking this chair.** (NOTE: Consider being the first person to take the Chair, to demonstrate and model this role.)

      Before doing so, however, please ask yourself: "What need(s) am I trying to meet by doing so?" Once you sit in the chair, express your feelings and needs to the group and request feedback.

      For example: "I'm kind of nervous right now, my need is for acceptance. I also feel excited because I value learning. Here is my request: I'd like to know what I did or said that affected you in a way you didn't completely enjoy, what your need was, and at least one possibility of what you would have preferred to have seen or heard instead."

      Another example: "I'm eager to have this opportunity to receive honest feedback because my desire is to share NVC as effectively as I can. Yesterday when I gave the instructions to the activity I led, did any of you get lost or confused? Do you have suggestions as to how I might have done that more effectively?"

   b. Instructions for those in the horseshoe: **Anyone in the horseshoe may speak.** (NOTE: This activity is not designed for participants to address long-standing conflicts, which are best served by more time and a different structure.) **Before doing so, ask yourself, "What is my intention? Am I trying to meet my need for contribution? For connection? Am I upset about something that happened and would like to be heard and understood?" Begin by sharing your intention,** *feeling, and need to the **Person in the Chair.** For example, "I feel a tad anxious as I need to trust that I can express myself in a way that can be accurately understood without being judged. My intention is to offer my honesty in a way that you might find useful. Would you be willing to hear feedback on something you did (or said) that stimulated (name the feeling) in me?"*

c. Instructions for proceeding:

i. Invite the Person in the Chair to answer yes or no in NVC (stating feelings and needs) as to whether they wish to receive the feedback being offered. If no, wait for someone else in the Horseshoe to speak up.

ii. If yes, ask the individual in the Horseshoe to offer feedback using all four components in this way:
   — What I observed or heard
   — My feelings when I observed or heard the above
   — My unmet needs
   — One possibility of what I would have liked to have seen or heard instead

iii. After the Person in the Chair has heard the feedback, encourage them to take a silent moment to go inside and check out what's going on—to carefully notice any fear, anger, discouragement, to notice any impulse to defend, explain, attack. . . . Ask the Person in the Chair to experiment with holding these feelings and impulses with awareness. Encourage them to connect with sensations in the body if strong feelings come up.

iv. When the Person in the Chair seems ready, ask them to simply reflect back the observation, feeling, need, and suggestion that the feedback person just offered. Discourage them from adding their own comments to this reflection, and remind them to stop and experience whatever impulses are present.
   If needed: allow the Person in the Chair time to self-empathize silently. Ask everyone in the Horseshoe to extend silent empathy to what they sense might be the person's feelings and needs. Ask the Person in the Chair to signal when ready to continue and receive someone else's feedback.

v. Let the Chair know that they can decide when to step out and return to the Horseshoe. Tell them that before returning to the Horsehoe, they have an opportunity to:

(1) Express their feelings and needs regarding each feedback. Examples:

- "I feel sad hearing Emma's feedback because I was wanting to contribute by bringing humor to our group."
- "I'm confused hearing Rashid's feedback and would have liked more clarity."
- "I feel frustrated hearing Juanita's feedback because I want for the situation to be correctly understood."

(2) Share how they experienced this process and what, if anything, they have learned.

vi. Before moving on to the next round (with another volunteer in the Chair), offer any appreciation you genuinely feel for the individual who has been receiving feedback in the Chair. Remind them that we always have choice regarding what we do with feedback we receive: Some feedback we apply immediately, some we hear and allow to percolate, some we discard as irrelevant or maybe just too painful to consider in this moment. We are honing our ability to fully receive feedback, but it's always our choice as to how to use it.

d. Continue the activity as long as someone wishes to take the Chair.

4. When there are no more volunteers to take the Chair, ask that seats be returned to their original formation (ideally a circle).

a. Introduce the closing segment by acknowledging the work that was done together.

As we close, let's take a moment to acknowledge the work we have done and whatever difficulty we've encountered in both offering and receiving honest feedback. Can we appreciate how practicing these skills deepens our trust in our capacity to be more open and vulnerable? Can we appreciate the strength this brings not only to ourselves but to our whole community?

b. Ask if there is anyone who wishes to express honesty in the form of NVC appreciation before moving on to the debrief.

DEBRIEF QUESTIONS:

1. What was difficult for you in either giving or receiving, or witnessing the giving and receiving of feedback?

2. What would make it easier?

3. What was the experience of listening without immediately responding?

4. Did anyone notice any difference between:

   - Offering feedback with a clear intention to contribute to the other's growth versus

   - Offering feedback from a place of wanting to be heard for some pain we experience?

   (Facilitator: make sure there is no judgment of one being "better" than the other. The point is simply to heighten awareness regarding our motive.)

5. Imagine a world where nearly everyone felt at ease and safe offering and receiving feedback for choices made that did not meet one's own or the other person's needs. What would that world look like?

SUGGESTIONS FOR PRACTICE IN DAILY LIFE:

1. When your heart is feeling strong and loving, approach someone you care about who is important to you and ask, "I wish to grow by receiving feedback about how my words and actions affect the people who are close to me. Are there ways I have behaved (or am behaving) that you wish were different?"

2. Make a request (not demand) of someone to whom you want to give feedback regarding something they did or said that did not contribute to your well being. Share the feelings and need behind your request, and ask for their agreement before proceeding. You might want to acknowledge how they might be feeling in that moment.

   NOTE: When making a request to either offer or receive feedback, check to see that both parties feel connected before starting and concluding the dialogue. At the end, take time to appreciate the honest exchange.

REFERENCE: Chapter 13

Components Practice

PURPOSE OF ACTIVITY:

1. To clarify the four NVC components: observation, feeling, need, request

2. To increase skill in identifying each component

3. To understand how different interpretations of the same stimulus (observation) may generate different feelings, needs, and requests

BRIEF DESCRIPTION: Participants take turns expressing the four components in sequence: observation, feeling, need, and request. The exercise may be done in small groups of five, as well as in pairs or individually.

MATERIALS NEEDED:

☐ Sets of five color-coded practice strips, one per group, per pair, or per individual (depending on how the activity is to be conducted). See Specific Learning Aid 10.4: Component Practice Strips

☐ Definitions (see below) of *Observation, Thought, Feeling, Need, Request* ready to be posted or written on the board before group gathers

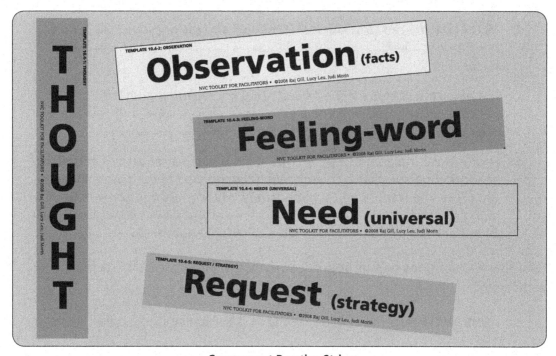

Component Practice Strips

TIME REQUIRED: 30–40 minutes

GROUP SIZE: Any

SPACE REQUIRED: If working in groups: adequate space for groups of five to sit in circles without mutual interference

LITERACY LEVEL REQUIRED: Able to read the five key words or their corresponding symbols

PROCEDURE:

Demonstrate use of Component Practice Strips

1. *First I take a moment to go inside. [Close eyes and be silent for a few seconds] I open to any feelings that may be brewing inside of myself right now . . . and see if there is one I can clearly identify. Yes, here it is: I am feeling* _____ . *[Name a feeling you are experiencing, e.g., "anxious."]*

2. *I hold the yellow strip which is labeled "Observation," and name the stimulus for my feeling:* _____ . *[Example: "I am standing in the front of the room talking to fifty people."]*

3. *I then take the orange strip labeled "Thought," and say what I am thinking in relationship to that stimulus:* _____ . *[Example: "I always fumble in front of large groups."]*

4. *Next I take the red strip labeled "Feeling," and say out loud, "As I think this thought I feel* _____ ." *[Use the feeling word you had named earlier, e.g., anxious.]*

5. *The blue strip stands for the "Need" that my feeling is pointing to. In this case, what I need or value is* _____ . *[Example: "effectiveness—to be able to effectively convey this information in a way that is clearly understood."]*

6. *Finally I take the green strip, "Request," and make a request of myself or another person that is (1) concrete, (2) expressed in positive language, and (3) can be responded to immediately. My request right now may sound like this:* _____ . *[Example: "Would you be willing to raise your hand if you have understood this demonstration of how Component Practice Strips are to be used?"]*

Post these definitions on the board: (either beforehand or while participants are getting settled into groups)

- **OBSERVATION:** what I am observing that is stimulating thoughts, feelings, and needs

- **THOUGHT:** what I am telling myself in relationship to what I am observing

- **FEELING:** emotion or body sensation associated with these thoughts

- **NEED:** universal need or value—met or unmet—which my feeling is pointing to

- **REQUEST:** strategy (in the form of a specific, positive, and immediately do-able action) that I might suggest of myself or others in order to address a need

Give instructions to groups of five:

Sit in a circle and distribute the Component Practice Strips clockwise in this order: Observation, Thought, Feeling, Need, Request.

The person holding the Observation strip, please begin by making an observation. Then the rest of you, follow in sequence: name a possible thought related to the stimulus, then a feeling, then the need which the feeling is pointing to, and finally, the last person will voice a request or strategy.

When the round is complete, pass your strip to the person on your left, and begin a new round.

NOTE: If there are six people in a group, ask members to take turns being a "coach" for those who would enjoy support.

Give instructions to individuals or pairs

- *Take a moment to check in with yourself and connect with your own feelings in this moment. Is there a feeling that you can clearly identify? If you are not connecting with a clear feeling right now, please recall a moment when you had a strong feeling. Use that situation to proceed with this exercise.*

- *Take the five strips and go through them step by step. If you are working alone, write down your response at each step. If you are working in pairs, say each piece out loud to your partner.*

DEBRIEF QUESTION: What is one specific thing you learned through this exercise?

REFERENCES: Chapters 1, 6

NOTE: This exercise may also be used as a review after all four components have been covered, i.e., upon completion of Chapters 3, 4, 5, 6.

EMPATHY

11.1 Awareness Exercise: Living in the Flow of Giving and Receiving

11.2 Activity: Reflecting Back Empathically

11.3 Activity: Practicing Empathy as Connecting Presence

11.4 Activity: Empathy Poker

11.5 Activity: Empathy Mill

KEY CONCEPT 11:

Empathy

Description: Empathy is a quality of attention in the presence of which connection, healing, and understanding naturally thrive. To be empathic, we need to empty our minds and offer someone the full attention of our being. Instead of simply hearing the person's words or the contents of their mind, empathy hears and receives their whole being. This happens only when we ourselves can bring forth our whole being—unencumbered by ideas, expectations, desires, and unresolved feelings.

In NVC we practice empathy by focusing our attention on the other party's feelings and needs. While empathy is an energetic presence that does not depend on speech, we can practice directing our attention by verbally reflecting back what we sense to be the other person's feelings and needs. Sometimes Empathy and Honesty (see Key Concept 10) are presented as the two parts of the NVC model. While "Honesty" consists of expressing one's own observation, feeling, need, and request, "Empathy" consists of hearing or receiving the other person's observation, feeling, need, and request.

Toolkit exercises in this section emphasize hearing and identifying feelings and needs behind other people's words, developing fluency in reflecting back verbally, practicing listening with full attention to another's being, and distinguishing empathy from its verbal expression.

Tips for Facilitators: When practicing empathy using the cue, "Are you feeling . . . because you are needing . . .?" remind participants that this is a question to connect with the listener and to help the listener connect with their own heart. As we are not telling the listener what they are feeling and needing, we pay attention that the tone of our voice conveys our intention to connect rather than to inform or interrogate.

When practicing empathy for the first time, some participants may balk at what they experience as formulaic and insincere speech. Please review the "Tips for Facilitators" under #10 Honesty should you encounter this issue.

While there are four components to the NVC model (observation, feeling, need, request), most practice on empathy centers on only two components—feeling and need. While we want to be clear about the other person's observation that stimulated their feelings and needs, it is unnecessary to repeatedly state the observation during the course of a dialogue. As to the fourth component—request—we want to make sure that we have successfully established a mutual heart connection before directing attention to solutions. Thus when we extend empathy in the form of verbally reflecting back, we may not reflect back requests until the end of the dialogue.

Sample Dialogue:

Little sister: Mommy, Mommy, guess what Big Brother just did! He just . . .

Big brother: SHUT UP, *you brat!*

Mother (empathizing with older brother by reflecting back what he might be observing, feeling, and needing): (O) *When you see your little sister about to tell me something you just did,* (F) *do you feel annoyed* (N) *because you'd like some choice as to what you share about yourself?*

NOTE: Mother does not reflect back Big Brother's original "request" (which is for Little Sister to "shut up") because she trusts that once heart connection has been reestablished between the two, he may choose another request that would meet both his and his sister's needs.

Mother's empathy with the Little Sister might sound like this: (O) *When you hear him say "Shut up!" like that,* (F) *are you upset and* (N) *wanting a bit more respect?"* [Similarly, she does not reflect back Little Sister's "request," which in this moment might be for Big Brother to apologize or for Mother to reprimand or punish him. Instead, Mother wisely empathizes with both brother and sister and waits for heart connection to be re-established, by which time, the requests (strategies) will be very different from what they might be in this moment.]

AWARENESS EXERCISE 11.1

Living in the Flow of Giving and Receiving

AIM OF EXERCISE:

1. To be aware of an experience of mutual giving and receiving

2. To cultivate being fully present to others as they give to me and receive from me

INSTRUCTIONS FOR GUIDING AWARENESS EXERCISE: Read the following slowly, allowing time between each statement for the participant to engage.

1. *Adjust your body so that you are sitting comfortably with your back straight.*

2. *Bring your attention inward by either closing your eyes or lowering your gaze.*

3. *Place your attention on your breathing.*

4. *First notice the in-breath.*

5. *Each time you breathe in, be conscious of yourself receiving. Notice how you feel as you receive.*

6. *As you breathe in, you are breathing in air purified by plants.*

    *   *Imagine a particular plant or tree, or a cluster of plants or trees.*
    *   *Hold them in your consciousness as you receive the air they have purified for you.*
    *   *Sustain this awareness for a few moments.*

7. *Now focus your attention on the out-breath.*

8. *Each time you breathe out, be conscious of yourself giving. Notice what you are feeling.*

9. *As you breathe out, bring to mind the plants or trees you are feeding with your out-breath.*

10. *Hold them in your consciousness as you offer the nourishment they need to flourish.*

11. *Sustain this awareness for a few moments.*

SHARING CIRCLE:

*   My name is _____ .

*   One thing I noticed during this exercise was: _____ .

REFERENCES: Chapters 1, 7, 8

ACTIVITY 11.2
Reflecting Back Empathically

PURPOSE OF ACTIVITY:

1. To practice receiving the four components:

    a. Hearing the other's OBSERVATIONS

    b. Hearing the other's FEELINGS

    c. Hearing the other's NEEDS

    d. Hearing the other's REQUESTS

2. To understand how each component fits into the overall NVC model

BRIEF DESCRIPTION: This activity consists of four parts, giving participants practice in hearing and reflecting back each component separately.

MATERIALS NEEDED:
- ❑ General Learning Aid G1: Learning Guide
- ❑ General Learning Aid G3: Floormap—Empathy and Honesty portions
- ❑ Pen and paper or Empathy Mill cards (see Activity 11.5)

TIME REQUIRED: 60 minutes

GROUP SIZE: Any size

SPACE REQUIRED: Space for people to work in triads without mutual interference

LITERACY LEVEL REQUIRED: Ability to read and write sentences

PROCEDURE:

1. Review the meaning of "empathy." Emphasize that empathy is a quality of presence. We will be practicing listening and then reflecting back verbally what we hear. Such verbal reflections express our intention to empathize. However, they do not by themselves constitute empathy.

    > *Empathy is a quality of presence. It is a quality of openness and receptivity to another person's life energy, to what is alive in their heart—to their feelings and needs. Empathy does not depend on words—either theirs or ours. We can be fully empathic with a person speaking a foreign language. Empathy is about listening and understanding, not about agreement.*

2. Review the Floor Map: Honesty and Empathy. Explain that this activity focuses on the four components listed under the Floor Map heading "Empathy." Participants will practice hearing and then reflecting back to the speaker each of the four components:

- Hearing and reflecting back what the other might be observing (What facts are they seeing and referring to?)

- Hearing and reflecting back what the other might be feeling

- Hearing and reflecting back what the other might be needing

- Hearing and reflecting back what the other might be requesting

In this activity, we are training ourselves to listen and practice reflecting back so that we can be fully receptive to the other's presence—which is the essence of empathy.

3. Decide whether to use the ready-made Empathy Mill cards or to have participants create their own "difficult-to-hear messages." To have them create their own, ask participants to work in triads and give each group half a dozen pieces of paper. Ask them to recall messages that were hard for them to hear and print each on a piece of paper. Fold each paper in half and on the outside, write down who made this statement (teenage daughter? parole officer? boss?) Collect all the papers, mix them up, and pass them out. Each participant is to receive two "difficult-to-hear messages" (either two pieces of paper or two Empathy Mill cards).

Part A—Hearing and reflecting back the speaker's OBSERVATIONS

1. Invite two volunteers to demonstrate this part of the activity.

   a. First volunteer reads a "difficult-to-hear message" to the other, e.g., "Will you stop picking on your little brother?"

   b. Second volunteer listens carefully and reflects back what the other might have observed. For example, "Are you referring to my yelling just now at Tommy to go to his room?"

   Second example: Parole Officer says: "You have made no progress since you arrived here." Possible reflection of what was observed: "Are you referring to the fact that I missed three out of ten of the cognitive thinking sessions?"

2. Engage additional pairs of volunteers to demonstrate this until everyone is clear on how to listen for and reflect back a possible observation.

3. Ask participants to work in triads, taking turns reading their "difficult-to-hear messages" while another person listens and reflects back an observation.

4. After 10–15 minutes (or when most triads have completed the work), reconvene the group and invite participants to share questions or learning.

5. Point to the Floor Map and explain how this part fits in the NVC model.

We have just practiced listening for the speaker's observation and reflecting it back to them. In real life, we want to know how to listen for observations, and if we are unsure about our guess, we have the choice of reflecting back verbally as a way to check in with the speaker and better understand what they are observing. In the next part of this activity, we will practice listening for and reflecting back the second component of NVC: feelings.

Part B—Hearing and reflecting back the speaker's FEELINGS

1. Invite two volunteers to demonstrate this part of the activity.

   a. First volunteer reads a "difficult-to-hear message" to the other, e.g., "Will you stop picking on your little brother?"

   b. Second volunteer listens carefully and reflects back what the speaker might be feeling. For example, "Are you feeling frustrated?"

   Second example: Parole Officer says: "You have made no progress since you arrived here." Reflection of possible feeling: "Do you feel disappointed?"

2. Engage additional pairs of volunteers to demonstrate this until everyone is clear on how to listen for and reflect back a possible feeling.

3. Ask participants to work in triads, taking turns reading their "difficult-to-hear messages" while another person listens and reflects back a feeling.

4. After 10 minutes (or when most triads have completed the work), reconvene the group and invite participants to share questions or learning.

5. Point to the Floor Map and explain how this part fits in the NVC model.

We have just practiced listening for the speaker's feelings. In real life, we want to know how to listen for feelings underneath the speaker's words. We can reflect them back verbally either as a way to reassure the speaker that we have understood them or as a way to check that we have heard their feelings accurately. In the next part of this activity, we will practice listening for and reflecting back the third component of NVC: needs.

Part C—Hearing and reflecting back the speaker's NEEDS

1. Invite two volunteers to demonstrate this part of the activity.

a. First volunteer reads a "difficult-to-hear message" to the other, e.g., "Will you stop picking on your little brother?"

b. Second volunteer listens carefully and reflects back what the speaker might be needing. For example, "Do you need peace in the family?" or "Are you wanting everyone to get along?"

   Second example: Parole Officer says: "You have made no progress since you arrived here." Reflection of what the speaker might need: "Do you want to trust people doing what they say they would?" or "Are you longing to see growth in those you work with?"

2. Engage additional pairs of volunteers to demonstrate this until everyone is clear on how to listen for and reflect back a possible need.

3. Ask participants to work in triads, taking turns reading their "difficult-to-hear messages" while another person listens and reflects back a need.

4. After 10 minutes (or when most triads have completed the work), reconvene the group and invite participants to share questions or learning.

5. Point to the Floor Map and explain how this part fits in the NVC model.

> *We have just practiced listening for the other's needs. In real life, we listen for needs underneath the speaker's words. We may reflect them back verbally either as a way to reassure the speaker that we have understood or as a way to check whether we have heard their needs accurately.*
>
> *In the next part of this activity, we will practice listening for and reflecting back the fourth component of NVC: requests.*

Part D—Hearing and reflecting back the speaker's REQUESTS

1. Invite two volunteers to demonstrate this part of the activity.

   a. First volunteer reads a "difficult-to-hear message" to the other, e.g., "Will you stop picking on your little brother?"

   b. Second volunteer listens carefully and reflects back what the other might be requesting. For example, "Are you asking me to tell Tommy what I'm feeling and needing when he comes in and takes my stuff?"

      Second example: Parole Officer says: "You have made no progress since you arrived here." Possible reflection of what is being requested: "Are you requesting that I tell you ahead of time if I plan to miss class and also to let you know my reason?"

2. Engage additional pairs of volunteers to demonstrate this until everyone is clear on how to listen for and reflect back a possible request.

3. Ask participants to work in triads, taking turns reading their "difficult-to-hear messages" while another person listens and reflects back a request.

4. After 15 minutes (or when most triads have completed the work), reconvene the group and invite participants to share questions or learning.

5. Point to the Floor Map and explain how this part fits in the NVC model.

> *We have just practiced listening for the other's request. In this activity we focused on hearing each of the four components separately. Please remember, however, that each component is only one piece of the whole NVC process. As we practice the "NVC dance," we will come to understand how the components work together and why we would not independently reflect back a request without having first connected on the heart level.*

Part E—Summary

Point to the Floor Map and summarize the four components under the heading, "Empathy":

- Hearing the speaker's observations
- Hearing the speaker's feelings
- Hearing the speaker's needs
- Hearing the speaker's requests

SUGGESTION FOR PRACTICE IN DAILY LIFE: When someone speaks to you, guess silently what that person might be observing, feeling, needing, or requesting. You might practice this in any situation where you notice people expressing themselves. Try it when you are waiting in line, reading an editorial, watching TV, etc.

REFERENCES: Chapters 7, 8

ACTIVITY 11.3

Practicing Empathy as Connecting Presence

PURPOSE OF ACTIVITY:

1. To distinguish empathy from its verbal expression

2. To practice listening with full attention to another's being

3. To experience empathy as a quality of presence

4. To cultivate being present in each moment, either to oneself or to the other

5. To develop awareness of our own patterns of thinking and habitual reactions when we are engaged in conversation

BRIEF DESCRIPTION: This activity consists of a sequence of ten short interactions for partners working in pairs to practice mutual empathy. A facilitator keeps time, offers instructions for each interaction, and leads the partners through the series.

NOTE: Instructions for an abbreviated 10-minute version of this activity are given at the end. This version may be used frequently, especially after practitioners have had the longer experience.

MATERIALS NEEDED:

- ❏ A bell that can be controlled to deliver a single tone (to be used to signal the beginning and ending of each interaction)
- ❏ A timer
- ❏ A second bell or instrument that can deliver an audio signal easily distinguishable from the first bell. The sound needs to be clear and short.

TIME REQUIRED: 1 hour

GROUP SIZE: Any even-numbered group

SPACE REQUIRED: Adequate space for each pair seated facing each other to be able to hear themselves without excessive distraction from the voices of those around them.

LITERACY LEVEL REQUIRED: None

PROCEDURE:

- • After introducing the concept of empathy as connecting presence, invite participants to pair up and find a space in the room to sit facing each other where they can hear each other without straining. Have each pair designate who will be A and who will be B. Inform them that you will be guiding them through a series of interactions, taking altogether about 45 minutes.

- After everyone is settled in pairs, ask Partners A to raise their hands so each pair is clear who is A and who is B. Explain that you will be giving specific instructions for each interaction segment. Ask participants to raise their hand at any time during the activity if they would like to hear instructions repeated. Reassure them that you will be scanning the room constantly for raised hands even if you don't stop to address anyone personally. Ask if there are any concerns or questions before the activity begins and remind participants that they may raise their hand and keep it raised until they have fully understood the directions at the beginning of each interaction segment.

NOTE: You might begin this activity with a favorite poem, quote, or song that captures for you the essence of empathy, presence, or the art of listening. Be sure to check your own quality of presence when delivering the instructions below. The italicized words may be read verbatim.

INTERACTION 1:

15 seconds. Both parties are silent. If you sense that participants are relatively comfortable with silence, start with 30 seconds.

When I give the signal to begin, please connect silently with your partner—extending your whole being to their whole being. Try using "soft eyes" by maintaining your gaze without staring one-pointedly at the other person. Research indicates that young children often maintain "soft eyes"—where their gaze radiates out to cover about a thirty-degree angle." [Show this with your hands.]

Some of you might experience some discomfort during this exercise: we are so used to communicating with words or gestures when we're with another person. Please allow space for whatever discomfort to arise but continue trying to connect without resorting to words or gestures. You'll have 15 (or 30) seconds for this connection."

Before we begin, I'd like to invite those of you who feel comfortable to close your eyes. Otherwise simply lower your gaze to bring your attention inward. [For prison workshops: acknowledge how our need for safety may depend on our being visually alert.]

Take a moment to come home to yourself. Are you aware of any feelings going on inside right now after hearing what I just said? [Pause] Any body sensations? [Pause] Any thoughts getting triggered? [Pause] Any needs met or unmet? [A few moments of silence]

Please see if you can be aware of whatever feelings, sensations, thoughts, or needs are showing up without either judging them or getting caught up in them. [Pause]

When you hear the bell, please open your eyes and allow yourself to be fully present to the human being in front of you. [Ring bell]

GROUP DEBRIEF: After you ring the bell to signal the end of Interaction One, ask the group, "How was that for you?" Encourage any expressions of discomfort.

INTERACTION 2:

30 seconds. Both parties are silent. (If you started with 30 seconds for the first interaction, then increase here to a minute.) NOTE: Before you give the signal to begin, tell them how much time they will have for this interaction.

COME HOME: After you give the signal to stop, invite participants to close their eyes and come home, encouraging them once again to notice any feelings, sensations, thoughts, and needs that are met or unmet:

Are you aware of any feelings going on inside right now? [Pause] Any body sensations? [Pause] Any thoughts getting triggered? [Pause] Any needs met or unmet? [A few moments of silence] Please notice whatever feelings, sensations, thoughts, or needs are stirring in you without either judging them or getting caught up in them." [Pause]

NOTE: From here on, include the above "Come Home" instructions after the completion of each interaction. You might remind participants to take a breath and re-center as well as to connect with their feelings, sensations, thinking, and needs. Explain that you are not asking them to examine what they are thinking, but to simply be aware that thoughts are going on. There may be thoughts such as, "This is boring." "I don't know what I'm doing." "Oh, no, someone is crying." Invite participants to challenge themselves by noticing their thoughts without having to either believe or disbelieve them.

INTERACTION 3:

1 minute. Person A speaks. Person B is silent.

When I give the signal to begin, please open your eyes and again, connect silently. Then Person A, at any time, please begin speaking. You may say anything that comes up for you. You'll have 1 minute.

[Come Home]

INTERACTION 4:

1 minute. Person B speaks. Person A is silent. Use same instructions as Interaction Three, but replace Person A with Person B.

[Come Home]

INTERACTION 5:

2 minutes. Person A starts. Person B responds after being cued.

This time, after you open your eyes and connect silently, Person A will begin speaking, while Person B listens with their full presence. After 30 seconds, I will give you the following signal [demonstrate signal you will give, using the second bell or a different sound-maker]. Person A, as you continue speaking, please find a natural place to pause and say the words, "You know what I mean?" Person B, use this as a cue to respond with verbal empathy; try reflecting back what you hear Person A to be feeling, needing, or expressing. After Person B has completed verbal empathy, Person A may continue talking, offering the cue, "You know what I mean?" whenever they wish for Person B to reflect back. You'll have 2 minutes. I am going to repeat these instructions. [After the instructions have been given a second time, ask people to raise their hand if they wish to hear them repeated yet once more.]

[Come Home]

INTERACTION 6:

2 minutes. Person B starts. Person A responds after being cued. Use same instructions as Interaction Five, but reverse A and B.

[Come Home]

INTERACTION 7:

3 minutes. Person A starts. Person B decides whether and when to respond.

This time Person A will begin speaking. Person B, practice being fully present with Person A, choosing at each moment to be either silently empathic or to express your empathy verbally. You'll have 3 minutes.

[Come Home]

INTERACTION 8:

3 minutes. Person B starts. Person A decides whether and when to respond. Use same instructions as Interaction 7, but reverse A and B.

[Come Home]

INTERACTION 9:

5 minutes. Parties speak freely.

During this next interaction, you will have 5 minutes to be fully present and to connect with each other in whatever way you choose. If you wish, you can share how this exercise went for you. The title of this exercise is "Practicing Empathy as Connecting Presence."

After 4 minutes, I will give the following signal [demonstrate signal] in case you wish to take the last minute to express appreciation to your partner.

[Come Home]

INTERACTION 10:

1 minute. Both parties are silent.

When I give the signal to begin, once again connect silently with each other, using soft eyes. Allow whatever discomfort to arise without judging it or pushing it away. Then, when you are able, return to offer your full presence to your partner. You will have 1 minute.

After you complete the "Come Home" for this final interaction, suggest that participants stand up, stretch, and rearrange their chairs to join others for the large group debrief.

DEBRIEF QUESTIONS: Use questions below to encourage open sharing:

1. Does anyone wish to share what they learned or noticed?

2. What was the most difficult part? (Why?)

3. What feelings, needs, sensations did you notice during the Come Home segments?

4. Did you learn anything about yourself? About how you listen? About your quality of presence?

SUGGESTIONS FOR PRACTICE IN DAILY LIFE:

1. Every day take a moment to practice offering your full presence to another living being without using language or gestures. Good opportunities include waiting in line or in traffic, watching children or pets at play, greeting or taking leave of someone.

2. Notice whether someone in your environment appears desirous of being heard. Offer your empathic presence.

REFERENCES: Chapters 7, 8

ABBREVIATED VERSION—INSTRUCTIONS TO GROUP:

1. *Pick a partner and sit facing each other. Decide who will be Partner A and who Partner B.*

2. *When I give the signal for the first round to begin, Partner A will talk for 2 minutes while Partner B listens in silence.*

3. *When you hear the bell, Partner B will have 1 minute to empathically reflect back what partner A said.*

4. *In the second round, Partner B will speak for 2 minutes and partner A will then take a minute to empathically reflect back.*

DEBRIEF QUESTIONS FOR ABBREVIATED VERSION:

1. What was it like to talk for 2 minutes without the other person talking?

2. What was it like to listen for 2 minutes without talking?

3. What was it like to empathically reflect back what the other person had said?

ACTIVITY 11.4

Empathy Poker

PURPOSE OF ACTIVITY:

1. To practice empathic listening

2. To explore NVC needs through play

3. To increase our vocabulary of need words

4. To build skill in identifying needs

5. To develop fluency in verbally reflecting back feelings and needs

6. To connect with one's own feelings in the heart/mind and body

BRIEF DESCRIPTION: A group of six to eight participants use a deck of cards to play a game. Players aim at supporting one member of the group to connect with the needs underlying a situation which that person has identified.

MATERIALS NEEDED: For each group of five to seven players:
- ❑ Group Handout: Empathy Poker Dealer Instructions
- ❑ One set of Need Cards (See General Learning Aid G8)
- ❑ A dozen Feeling Cards (See General Learning Aid G6)
- ❑ Optional: 3-minute egg-timer
- ❑ Optional: post-it sticky notes

TIME REQUIRED: 60–90 minutes

GROUP SIZE: A minimum of five players for each small group

SPACE REQUIRED: Each group needs a flat surface for players to lay out their cards. Ideally, the group would be clustered around a table. Sitting in a circle on a comfortable floor would also work. Groups sitting in chairs might improvise by placing a flat surface (e.g., poster board) at least a square yard or meter on their laps. The room needs to be large enough for each group to have its own space.

LITERACY LEVEL REQUIRED: All participants need to be able to recognize single words representing needs and feelings. At least one participant in each small group needs to be able to read the Dealer Instructions.

PROCEDURE:

1. NOTE: Demonstrate the game and make certain everyone is clear on how it is played before dividing the room into small groups. Refer to Instructional Video

demonstration of this activity and to the Handout, "Empathy Poker Dealer Instructions."

2. Ask each group to choose a "dealer" for their first round. Give each dealer

    - a set of Need Cards

    - a dozen Feeling Cards (selected to cover a variety of feelings)

    - an egg-timer

    - a copy of the group handout: Dealer Instructions

REFERENCES: Chapters 7, 8

Empathy Poker Dealer Instructions

INSTRUCTIONS FOR DEALER

1. Pick one of the red feeling cards and hold it so everyone in your group can see it.

2. Say to the group: *"Go inside and see if you can feel what that feeling might feel like."* Give them 30 seconds of silence.

3. Now ask your group, *"What might you look like if you have this feeling? What might other people notice about you?"* Tell them that they are free to move their bodies, make noises, and express their feeling through postures and facial expressions. After a few moments say, *"Keep doing what you are doing but look around and take some peeks at each other!"*

4. When everyone has quieted down ask: *"Can anyone recall a situation in your life that leads you to feel this way?"*

5. Give the group some time to reflect on your question as you deal the deck of blue need cards (face down) to everyone EXCEPT yourself. Do NOT give yourself any cards.

6. Decide who will share a situation in their life that triggers the feeling identified earlier. This person is called the "player." Inform the player: *"As the player for this round, you will not need any cards, so please allow me to use this pile of cards."* Take the player's cards for your own use in this round.

7. Give the following instructions to the player: *"Describe the situation that leads you to feel this feeling. You have up to 3 minutes."*
   [Set 3-minute egg-timer if available.]

8. When the player has finished describing the situation, urge everyone to look at the cards in their hands. Then ask: *"Are you holding any needs in your hand that might be alive for the player in the situation they just described?"*

9. The group will now take turns offering the player one need at a time. Begin with yourself (the dealer). As you place your need card (face up) near the player, address the player in this way: *"[Name of player], are you feeling [selected feeling] because you need [word on the need card you put down]?"*

10. Consider adding a phrase after you name the universal need to help connect to the situation on hand. Example: Instead of "Mary, are you feeling sad because you value connection?" you might say, **"Mary, are you feeling sad because you value connection—an opportunity to connect with an old friend you haven't seen for years?"**

11. Allow people to take turns offering the player one need card at a time, skipping their turn if they have no more to offer. Make sure the player does NOT respond out loud while cards are being placed in front of them.

12. There are two "wild (blank) cards" in each deck. After people have run out of cards to offer the player, those holding wild cards may assign any universal "need" they wish to the wild cards and offer them to the player. (If available, use a post-it sticky note to write the need word on the wild card.)

13. Ask the player to take a moment to look at the needs spread out in front of them. Say to the player: **"Now—one at a time—pick the needs which resonate with you. Whenever you reach for a card please say, 'YES, I FEEL [selected feeling] BECAUSE I NEED [word on card].'"**

    NOTE: Offer the following suggestion if you think it will be useful to the player: "Consider adding a phrase that helps you connect to the universal need." (Example: Instead of "Yes, I feel discouraged because I need support," the player might say: "Yes, I feel discouraged because I need support—support to realize my life's dream of having a home I can call my own.")

14. After the player has completed picking up all the cards they want, ask them: **"Have you connected to all your needs in this situation? Are there other needs that have not been mentioned?"** Encourage the player and others to briefly share what they learned from this round. (If the group desires, use the egg-timer to limit sharing so as to leave plenty of time for additional rounds.)

15. Say to the player: **"For the next round, would you be willing to serve as dealer and do what I did in the last round?"** Hand them these "Empathy Poker Dealer Instructions."

Empathy Mill

PURPOSE OF ACTIVITY:

1. To cultivate awareness of feelings and needs, and to practice hearing and identifying feelings and needs behind other people's words

2. To connect with other participants: this exercise serves well as an "ice-breaker" to support a sense of community in the group

3. To allow participants an opportunity to mutually support one another's learning (each person becomes an "expert" on their own card and can assist others on that piece)

BRIEF DESCRIPTION: Each participant holds a card from which they read off a statement designed to elicit verbal empathy from another person. Participants work in pairs and mill around to find their next partner.

NOTE: Instructions for a more advanced version of this activity are given at the end. In this adaptation, participants write personal trigger statements rather than read them off the cards provided.

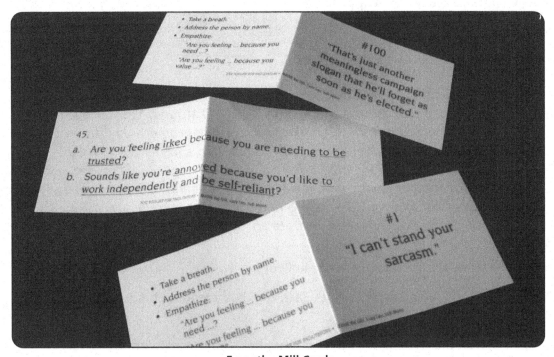

Empathy Mill Cards

MATERIALS NEEDED:

- ❑ A basket of Empathy Mill cards, at least one for each person present (having a few extras is handy in case someone draws a card they don't like). See Specific Learning Aid 11.5: Empathy Mill Cards
- ❑ Feeling and need words posted on walls (or otherwise easily accessible to all participants). See General Learning Aid G5 and G7: Wall Signs, or G1: Learning Guide
- ❑ Name tags and markers to write names (unless everyone knows one another already)

SPACE REQUIRED: A large open space for everyone to stand together and move around comfortably. Remove obstructions to movement such as chairs, stuff on the floor, etc.

TIME REQUIRED: 30 minutes

GROUP SIZE: Minimum ten, maximum based on number of Empathy Mill cards available. Preferable to have even number of participants.

LITERACY LEVEL REQUIRED: Ability to read sentences

PROCEDURE:

1. Name the exercise and explain its purpose: cultivating awareness of feelings and needs by hearing and identifying feelings and needs behind other people's words.

2. Describe activity:

> *For this activity we will be opening up a large circle in the center of the room so that there is space for us all to mill around. You will each be drawing a card from this basket. Each card has something different written on the outside. As you mill around, find another person who is free and share your cards with each other. When you are finished, look for another person who is free. Raise your hand when you need a new partner and you'll be able to find each other more easily. [Name of a volunteer] and I will now demonstrate an interaction.*

3. Demonstrate interaction (with a volunteer):

   a. Each person draws a card. Each card has a front, a back, and an inside.

   b. On the back of each card is a number. The person with the lower number will go first.

   c. Read your card out loud to the volunteer.

d. Before volunteer responds, point to the back of your own card and say:

If our partner is at a loss as to how to respond, all they need to do is look at the back of the card we are holding. On the back of this card it reads: "Take a breath." [Allow time for volunteer to take a breath.] "Address person by name." [Let your volunteer say your name.]

e. The volunteer will now reflect back your feelings and needs by asking "Are you feeling . . . because you need, because you value . . .?"

f. Repeat out loud the feeling and need words which the volunteer used to empathize with you. Explain:

My task is to listen carefully for any feelings and needs being reflected back to me. If I hear a feeling or need word, I will confirm this by simply saying the word out loud as I just did.

g. Now open your card: inside are two examples of what your partner might have said to reflect back to you. The first one is in "classical NVC," and uses the formula given on the back of the card: "Are you feeling . . . because you need/value . . .?" The second one is a bit more "idiomatic." Invite your partner to stand next to you so you can read the contents together.

h. You have finished with your card, so now the two of you will switch roles. This time the volunteer will read their card, and you will offer verbal empathy.

4. Ask if anyone has any questions. Then reiterate the difference between classical and idiomatic NVC. You might, for example, say the following:

Some people are uneasy using the formula "Are you feeling . . . because you are needing . . .?" since it sounds stilted to them; they want to sound real and natural. In real life we each learn to apply NVC in ways that match our personal style of speech. However, for now I am asking you to use the classical NVC empathy formula as a way to practice identifying universal feelings and needs.

5. Point participants to the feeling and need words on the wall (or charts provided): remind them these are not exhaustive lists.

6. Suggest a time frame (e.g., 30 minutes) and encourage participants to engage with as many partners as possible, but without a sense of hurry.

If your respondent is stuck or you are not hearing any feelings and needs, instead of discussing the problem, open your card and read the examples. Have the person try again if they are open to doing so.

NOTE: Get a sense if there are participants who have difficulty reading. Read them their cards and help them learn the lines by heart.

7. Monitor activity—Make sure there is an even number of participants. Encourage pairs not to get stuck in discussion, and help people find new partners.

DEBRIEF QUESTIONS:

1. Does anyone want to share anything they learned from this activity?

2. Was it easier for you to connect with the person's feelings or their needs? Please describe and give examples.

3. Did you notice whether it was easier for you to receive the messages when you focused on the other person's feelings and needs? Please elaborate.

REFERENCES: Chapters 7, 8

INSTRUCTIONS FOR ADVANCED VERSION:

1. Invite participants to reflect on a situation for which they would like some empathy.

2. Ask them to write down what triggered their pain, either:

    a. A direct quote: words they heard someone saying, or

    b. A single sentence describing what happened

3. Have participants work in pairs: one person reads what they had written while the partner reflects back feelings and needs.

DEBRIEF QUESTIONS for ADVANCED VERSION:

1. What was it like being heard by your partner?

2. What was it like to extend yourself empathically to someone who is wanting to be heard?

THE NVC DANCE

12.1 Awareness Exercise:
Visualizing the Three Steps

12.2 Activity: Dancing Fingers

12.3 Activity: Cha-Cha-Cha

KEY CONCEPT 12:
The NVC Dance

Description: The NVC Dance refers to the artful combination and repetition of three steps to engender a flow of compassionate heart-based dialogue:

- Expressing honestly

- Receiving empathically

- Self-empathy

At each moment, the NVC practitioner needs to decide which of these steps to take to create the most connecting dance with his or her partner. Fortunately, it is not necessary for both parties to be familiar with the dance-steps for a dance to take place. [For specific information on each of the three steps, refer to previous sections: #9 Connecting with Self, #10 Honesty, #11 Empathy]

Toolkit exercises in this section give participants opportunity to observe and practice the three steps, to understand how they fit together, and to develop skill in choosing the step to take.

Tips for Facilitators: Be sure that participants have a clear concept of each of the three steps and have worked with each piece separately before practicing the NVC Dance.

Use the Floor Map or copy the Finger Map or a similar chart onto a large surface. Refer to this chart when illustrating the NVC Dance or when a participant is working with their own dance scenario. It is helpful for participants to see which step is being taken, and to know where it fits in the overall picture.

When demonstrating self-empathy as one of the three steps of an NVC Dance, use a visual prop—such as wearing a hat or cupping one's hands over the heart—to indicate that the words being expressed are actually taking place inside the speaker's mind.

AWARENESS EXERCISE 12.1

Visualizing the Three Steps

AIM OF EXERCISE: To practice the NVC dance steps and to visualize dancing through a challenging personal situation.

MATERIALS NEEDED:

- ❑ General Learning Aid G2: Finger Map (a copy for each participant)

INSTRUCTIONS FOR GUIDING AWARENESS EXERCISE:

1. Use the Finger Map to refresh the participants' understanding of the three dance steps: self-empathy, honesty, and empathy.

2. Introduce the exercise:

   > *In this guided awareness exercise, you will have an opportunity to visualize an NVC dance with someone in your life. I would like you to bring to mind someone whose words or behavior you feel unhappy about. Take 5 minutes, either alone or with a partner, to identify a scenario that did or might take place between you and this person.*

3. After all participants have decided on a scenario to work with, provide pen and paper for those who might wish to record the dialogue that comes up in the visualization exercise. Emphasize that some people find writing helpful while others will simply imagine the dialogue in their heads.

4. Read the following slowly, leaving space between each statement for participants to engage in the guided process.

   a. *Sit comfortably. Straighten your spine. Make any necessary adjustments.*

   b. *Focus your attention inward by closing your eyes or gently dropping your gaze to the floor in front of you.*

   c. *Concentrate your attention on your breathing.*

   d. *Simply notice yourself receiving the breath and letting it go. Continue to receive and let go for several breaths. Notice if there is relaxation occurring in your body.*

   e. *Now bring to mind the situation that you chose earlier. Simply imagine it in your mind's eye and observe it. Observe yourself and the other person. What do you see? What do you hear?*

   f. *Make a conscious intention to create a heart connection with the other person. This can be done inside your own heart, without speaking to them.*

g. *Once you have established your intention, focus attention on your own feelings and needs in this situation. This is self-empathy. See if you can open to whatever feelings are present and to touch the needs behind them. Take time to hold your needs with loving attention and to acknowledge how much you value these needs.*

h. *Without hurrying, and when you are ready, turn your attention to the other person and imagine what they might be feeling and needing. This is empathy. When you think you have guessed their needs, hold these needs with equal care and acknowledge how much you value them.*

i. *When you are ready to speak to the other person, choose either honesty or empathy—either honestly express what is going on in you, or verbally empathize by guessing what might be going on in them.*

j. *Imagine how the other person is responding to you. Continue the dialogue with them, switching among the three steps of honesty, empathy, and self-empathy as you see fit. Remember, whenever you get stuck, to return to self-empathy and connect with your own feelings and needs. Those of you who wish may write down the dialogue. We'll take 5 minutes to either imagine or write this dialogue between you and the other person.*

k. *You have just visualized engaging in an NVC dance with a person with whom you are experiencing difficulty. Notice if this has led to any changes in how you perceive either the situation or the other person. You may want to jot down your thoughts to share with us later.*

l. *When you are ready, please open your eyes and slowly return to the circle. Let's take a moment of stillness to look around us with an attitude of curiosity and wonder as to what others experienced during this exercise.*

SHARING CIRCLE:

• My name is _____ .

• A shift in perspective I experienced, or would like to experience, is _____ .

REFERENCES: Chapters 9, 13

ACTIVITY 12.2

Dancing Fingers

PURPOSE OF ACTIVITY:

1. To practice the four NVC components as applied in each of the three parts of the model: honesty, empathy, and self-empathy

2. To practice bringing together the three parts to engage in an "NVC Dance"

BRIEF DESCRIPTION: Participants use color-coded labels on their fingers to guide them through the moves of an "NVC Dance." The exercise includes demonstration and practice for each of the three "dance steps": honesty, empathy, and self-empathy. Participants practice dancing in pairs by bringing together all three parts. This activity serves well as a comprehensive review of the NVC model. The clear delineation of all three parts and four components at each step supports participants in grasping the whole model while applying "classical NVC" in role-play. (Groups who are already fluent in applying the fundamentals of NVC and who wish to engage in "colloquial NVC" may be referred to Activity 12.3 "Cha-Cha-Cha.")

MATERIALS NEEDED:

❑ For labeling fingers: colored stickers (either round dots or small strips) in four colors: yellow, red, blue, green. NOTE: Colored tape, ribbon, or thick yarn may be used instead.
❑ Paper and writing implements

TIME REQUIRED: 2 hours (not including debrief)

GROUP SIZE: Any

SPACE REQUIRED: Enough for participants to work in pairs without mutual interference

LITERACY LEVEL REQUIRED: Ability to write and read sentences

PROCEDURE:

Part 1—Set-up (15 minutes): Go through these steps with participants so that you generate your own scenarios for the demonstration that will follow.

1. Make sure that each participant has a piece of paper about 8" x 11." Ask them to fold it in half and tear along the fold so that they now have two pieces of paper of approximately the same size (about 8" across and 5" long).

2. Ask participants to bring to mind someone who is behaving in a way that they are not enjoying.

3. Ask them to take one of their pieces of paper, and to write down four items of information, numbering the items 1 to 4.

   - *#1, on the top of the page, write your own name.*

   - *Below that, #2, write down a name for the person whose behavior you are not enjoying. (As we will be sharing these scenarios, use a fictitious name if you wish.) Next to the name, specify the person's relationship to you. For example, they may be your boss, roommate, employee, teacher, teenage daughter, a cyclist on the road, etc.*

   - *#3, give this scenario a title which indicates the context. For example, "Recycling at Work," "Replacing Borrowed Tools," "Driving Like a Maniac."*

   - *Finally, #4, write down whatever complaints or judgments you have in this situation regarding the person you identified under #2. For example, "What a selfish coworker, always picking the light tasks and leaving me with the hard ones!"*

4. Ask participants to take what they just wrote and copy it on to their second piece of paper.

5. Instruct participants to secure the two pieces of paper by folding them together:

   Put one piece of paper on top of the other and fold both together. First fold them in half. Then fold again so that the papers are secured to each other and end up a quarter of their original size.

6. Collect everyone's papers (except your own) and place them in a basket or box.

7. Pass out two sets (i.e., eight) colored stickers to each participant to label and stick on their fingers. Use your own fingers to demonstrate what you say below:

   - *The index finger points to what I see and hear. Label this finger "OBSERVATION" or "O," using the color YELLOW to represent light by which to see.*

   - *Holding up the middle finger reflects strong emotions I can't miss. Label this finger "FEELING" or "F," using the color RED to represent heart.*

   - *The ring finger stands for commitment to meeting a need or value. Label this finger "NEED" or "N," using the color BLUE to represent universality as in the vast blue sky.*

- *The little finger completes our hand. Label this finger "REQUEST" or "R," using GREEN to represent "green light" as when we move forward in traffic.*

Part II—Demonstration (15 minutes)

1. Review the three parts of the NVC Dance: "Honesty," "Empathy," and "Self-Empathy." Explain that we will first practice each individual step of the NVC dance and then practice putting them together.

2. Demonstrate the gestures for Honesty, Empathy, and Self-Empathy that we will be using in this activity:

    a. *We will use our right hand to guide us to express honestly. [Place your right hand, palm up, in front of your heart, and wiggle the fingers.]*

    b. *We use our left hand to receive empathically. [Place your left hand, palm up, in front of your heart, and wiggle the fingers.]*

    c. *And for self-empathy, we place our right hand—which represents honesty—on our heart as a gesture of receiving ourselves and listening to our own heart. [Place your right palm on your heart, and wiggle the fingers.]*

3. Establish a scenario for demonstrating the activity.

    a. *I will now take a scenario to role-play. Is there anyone who would like to take the role of the person whose behavior stimulated pain for me? [Wait for someone to volunteer.]*

    b. *Thank you, would you be willing to join me by standing here in front of the room? [Give the volunteer one of the two pieces of paper for your scenario.]*

    c. *I'd like to ask you to address me by the name that is on top of the paper. [Wait for volunteer to address you by name.]*

    d. *Now look at Item #2 and tell me who you are in relationship to me. [Wait for volunteer to respond with, for example. "I am Sue, your coworker."]*

    e. *Tell me what this is about by reading Item #3, the title of the scenario, and saying, "This is about _____ ." [Wait for volunteer to respond with, for example, "This is about 'Recycling at Work.'"]*

    f. *Please read the last item—complaints, judgments, and whatever thoughts I have about you in this particular situation. Start your sentence with, "You are thinking . . ." [Wait for volunteer to respond with, for example, "You are thinking that I am a selfish coworker, always picking the light tasks and leaving you with the hard ones!"]*

Part III—Honesty (20 minutes)

1. Demonstrate the "Honesty" step by making a fist with your right hand, fingers facing up, and thumb tucked inside. Stand next to the volunteer and turn to them whenever you are expressing a component in Steps d, e, f, g, below.

   a. *My right hand will now guide me to express myself honestly to my _____ (e.g., coworker), using the four components of NVC.*

   b. *But first I ask myself: do I hold a genuine intention to connect with this person on a heart-to-heart level? My thumb, the strongest finger, represents consciousness of intention. If I realize I have no intention to connect human to human, then there is no point in going through the charade of applying the four NVC components. I can choose to blame, guilt-trip, shame, bribe, threaten, or coerce others to change their behavior.* [Take a moment to demonstrate how you might go inside to check out your intention.]

   c. *Once aware of my intention to connect, I can release my thumb and focus on the four components.* [Release thumb from your right fist.]

   d. *The first component is yellow, for observation. This is the observation I express to my _____ (e.g., coworker):* [Uncurl your index finger as you state the observation.]

       "_____." (e.g., *"Each time we do recycling, I notice you take the aluminum cans and leave the newspapers and cardboard boxes."*)

   e. *The second component is red, for feeling. This is the feeling I express to my (e.g., coworker):* [Uncurl middle finger while you express the feeling.]

       "_____." (e.g., *"I feel disappointed."*)

   f. *The third component is blue, for need. This is the universal need I express to my _____ (e.g., coworker):* [Uncurl ring finger as you express the need.]

       "_____." (e.g., *"I value equal sharing."*)

   g. *The fourth component is green, for request. This is the present request I make to my _____ (e.g., coworker):* [Uncurl little finger as you make the request.]

       "_____." (e.g., *"Would you agree to carry at least four boxes of the paper stuff when we do recycling together?"*)

   h. *I have now offered the gift of honesty out of an intention to connect.* [Extend your right hand, palm up, fingers uncurled.]

2. Invite participants to practice what was just demonstrated. Give the following instructions:

> • *Please take one set of papers from the basket. If you pick your own, simply put it back and get another.*
>
> • *Find a partner and role-play the scenario as was just demonstrated.*
>
> • *Remember to uncurl your fingers as you move through the five pieces: intention, observation, feeling, need, request.*
>
> • *You will have 10 minutes to practice expressing honestly. I'll signal as we approach 5 minutes so you can switch roles.*

Part IV—Self-Empathy (20 minutes)

1. Demonstrate the "Self-Empathy" step by inviting back the volunteer who had assisted you earlier. Remind them of their relationship to you in the role-play and restate your expression of honesty.

> *(e.g., You are my coworker and I just expressed my honesty by saying to you "Each time we do recycling, I notice you take the aluminum cans and leave the newspapers and cardboard boxes. I feel disappointed because I value equal sharing. Would you agree to carry at least four boxes of the paper stuff when we do recycling together?")*
>
> a. *Ask the volunteer role-playing the other party to respond to you by rejecting your request in a way that is likely to be difficult for you to hear. [Example: "You are always complaining. Can't you just pitch in and stop worrying about doing a bit more than your share once in a while?"]*
>
> b. *My right hand over my heart will now guide me to extend self-empathy using the four components of NVC. [Place your right fist against your own heart, thumb tucked in.]*
>
> c. *But first I ask myself: do I hold a genuine intention to connect with myself? Am I willing to open up to whatever feelings come up? Am I feeling patient and courageous enough to be present to myself for this? My thumb, the strongest finger, represents consciousness of intention. [Take some silence to demonstrate how you might sit with your intention to connect with yourself.]*
>
> d. *Once aware of my intention to connect, I can release my thumb and focus on the four components. [Release thumb from fist.]*
>
> e. *Demonstrate each of the four components, specifying the color, and giving a concrete example of how you would express that component to yourself. Uncurl the finger that corresponds to the component before moving on to the next component.*

- Example of observation: *"When I hear my coworker say, 'You are always complaining. Can't you just pitch in and stop worrying about doing a bit more than your share once in a while?'..."*

- Example of feeling: *"I feel discouraged..."*

- Example of need: *"...because I want to be able to express myself so as to be understood without judgment."*

- Example of request: *"Am I willing to take a few moments and open up to how much I value this need for understanding? To simply hold and be with this need for a while?"*

Take a few moments with your right hand over your heart to demonstrate silent self-empathy.

2. Invite participants to practice what was just demonstrated. Give the following instructions:

- *Find another partner and role-play your scenario as was just demonstrated.*

- *Remember to uncurl your fingers as you move through the five pieces: intention, observation, feeling, need, request.*

- *Please take 10 minutes to practice self-empathy. I'll give a signal as we approach 5 minutes so you can switch roles.*

Part V—Empathy

1. Demonstrate the "Empathy" step with the same volunteer. Replay the scenario by offering your original honesty statement and having the other party respond with their difficult-to-hear message.

Example: **You:** "Each time we do recycling, I notice you take the aluminum cans and leave the newspapers and cardboard boxes. I feel disappointed because I value equal sharing. Would you agree to carry at least four boxes of the paper stuff when we do recycling together?"

Coworker: "You are always complaining. Can't you just pitch in and stop worrying about doing a bit more than your share once in a while?"

2. *In the last part, when I heard their response to my honesty, I demonstrated how I might engage in self-empathy. In this part, I will demonstrate how I might receive this person empathically. If I have fully empathized with myself, I am now open and able to hear the pain in their response. I recognize that until they are heard, it is unlikely that they will be able to hear what's going on for me. The step I now choose is to receive them empathically.*

3. Make a fist with your left hand, fingers facing up, thumb tucked inside, and place it in front of yourself. Say:

   a. *My left hand will now guide me in receiving empathically, especially to hear the other party's feelings and needs.*

   b. *But first I ask myself: "Do I hold a genuine intention to connect with this coworker on a heart-to-heart level?" My thumb, the strongest finger, represents consciousness of intention. If I realize I have no intention to connect human to human, then there is no point in going through the charade of applying the four NVC components. [Take a moment to demonstrate how you might go inside to check out your intention.]*

   c. *Once aware of my intention to connect, I can release my thumb and focus on the four components. [Release thumb from your left fist.]*

   d. *The first component is yellow, for observation. I focus on what the other party might be observing, what they are seeing or hearing. [Uncurl your left index finger as you guess their observation.] Example: "When you hear my request that you take out four boxes of the paper stuff. . . ."*

   e. *The second component is red, for feeling. [Uncurl your left middle finger as you guess their feeling.] Example: ". . . do you feel a little miffed. . .?"*

   f. *The third component is blue, for need: [Uncurl your left ring finger as you guess and reflect back their need.] Example: ". . . because you would like some flexibility and ease around how we work together?"*

   g. *The fourth component is green, for request. [Uncurl your left little finger as you guess and reflect back their request.] Example: "Do you wish that I had simply hollered when I needed you to give me a hand?"*

   I would like to offer a note regarding this component. In the process of receiving empathically, we often postpone guessing and reflecting back the other party's request. In omitting the request, our intention is to provide space for the other party to touch additional layers of feelings and needs.

An example of empathic receiving without the request component:

   - *"When you hear my request that you take out four boxes of the paper stuff, do you feel a bit miffed because you would like some flexibility and ease around how we work together?"*

   - *The other party might respond by saying: "Yeah, you always try to get people to do what you want by coming up with more rules: recycling, four boxes, 4:00 p.m., glass here, cardboard there, cans flattened. . . ."*

- *Their response gives us opportunity to hear another layer of feeling and need that may not have surfaced if we had reflected back the request piece earlier. Our empathic reflection of what they just shared may sound like this: "Do you feel frustrated because you'd like more input in how things are done?"*

   h. *I have now offered empathy to the other with the intention of hearing what is in their heart. [Extend your left hand, palm up, fingers uncurled.]*

4. Invite participants to practice what was just demonstrated. Give the following instructions:

   - *Find another partner to work with your scenario and practice receiving empathically as was just demonstrated.*

   - *Remember to uncurl your fingers as you move through each piece: intention, observation, feeling, need. You may omit the request piece if you wish.*

   - * *Please take 10 minutes, with each of you using 5 minutes to practice empathy with the scenario you picked.*

Part VI—Putting the steps together (30 minutes)

1. *We have now practiced each of the three steps and are ready to put them together to engage in an NVC Dance. At each moment, I can check inside myself to decide which step to take:*

   - *I can express myself honestly [Hold out right hand, palm up.]*

   - *I can empathize with myself [Hold right palm to heart.]*

   - *I can empathically receive the other person [Hold out left hand, palm up.]*

2. Demonstrate an NVC Dance by extending the role-play based on your original scenario. (Or you may prefer using a different volunteer or a different scenario.)

   a. Each time before speaking, pause and specify which of the three steps you are intending to take.

   b. Accompany your words with hand and finger motions.

   c. Remind participants that self-empathy takes place internally and that our words are not being heard by the other party.

   d. Continue the dance until you sense a shift in energy indicating that both parties hear and value each other's needs. Mention to the group that it is not necessary in this exercise to extend role-plays beyond this point nor to explore practical solutions.

e. At the end, check in with the other party in the role-play. Ask whether they are able to sense a heart connection, or what they would need in order to feel connected.

3. Invite questions from participants to make sure everyone is clear on how to practice the NVC Dance. Mention the following points:

- *Find a new partner with whom to practice the NVC Dance as was just demonstrated.*

- *You may either stick to the same scenario or trade your set of papers with someone else.*

- *Remember to use hand and finger motions to indicate which of the three steps or four components you are engaged in at a particular moment.*

- *Go slowly and take time to check in with yourself before deciding which of the three steps to take.*

- *Choose self-empathy whenever you feel stuck.*

- *You have 20 minutes. Take 10 minutes for each of you to practice the NVC Dance using the scenario you picked.*

DEBRIEF QUESTIONS:

1. What did you learn from this activity?

2. What was the most difficult part for you?

3. What did you notice about using your thumb and connecting with your intention before each statement?

SUGGESTIONS FOR PRACTICE IN DAILY LIFE:

1. Take a few minutes on a regular basis to practice with your hands and fingers until the motions feel natural.

2. Either during or after a challenging encounter, imagine yourself expressing with honesty, receiving empathically, and offering yourself self-empathy. Let your dancing fingers guide you through each step of the dance.

REFERENCES: Chapters 1, 13

Cha-Cha-Cha

PURPOSE OF ACTIVITY:

- To develop clarity as to which step to take while sustaining an NVC dance

- To practice flowing among the three dance steps

BRIEF DESCRIPTION: Participants practice the three steps of the NVC Dance through role-playing a personal situation. Working in groups of three, individuals track the three steps either by standing on labeled papers on the floor or by flipping a three-sided "tent card." NOTE: This activity is for those who have already learned and are able to apply each of the four components of the NVC model.

MATERIALS NEEDED:

- ❑ A "tent card" for each small group. See Specific Learning Aid 12.3A: Tent Cards. Tent cards have three sides and allow speakers as well as listeners to track which of the three dance steps speakers are currently engaged in.
- ❑ For each small group, a set of three 8 ½" x 11" papers labeled respectively: HONESTY, EMPATHY, SELF-EMPATHY. See Specific Learning Aid 12.3B: Step-Trackers.

Tent Cards

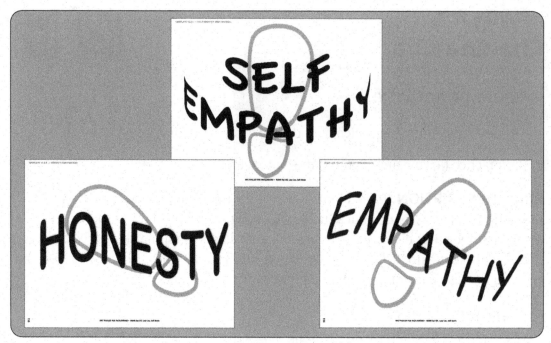

Step-Trackers

TIME REQUIRED: 1 hour

GROUP SIZE: At least three

SPACE REQUIRED: Enough for groups of three to work without mutual interference

LITERACY LEVEL REQUIRED: No reading required except for labels on tent cards indicating the three dance steps.

PROCEDURE: NOTE: Item #4 below calls for a role-play that can efficiently demonstrate the steps of the NVC Dance. You might prepare it ahead of time with a volunteer or you might use a puppet to represent the party with whom you are dialoguing.

1. Introduce the activity

   > *In this activity we will be practicing the NVC Cha-Cha-Cha. When engaging in NVC, we have the opportunity at each moment to choose one of three dance steps: honesty, empathy, or self-empathy. We will be role-playing personal situations, practicing choosing the step to take and then carrying it out.*

2. Define the three dance steps

a. Solicit responses from participants or offer your own or the following definitions of the three steps:

i. **Honesty:** I express what I am observing, feeling, needing, requesting.

ii. **Empathy:** Whether silently or verbally, I place my attention on what the other might be observing, feeling, needing, requesting.

iii. **Self-Empathy:** I tune in silently to this moment's inner experience—sensations in my body, emotions, needs that are met or not met. I am aware I am thinking without being caught up in the content of the thoughts themselves.

As you refer to each of the three steps, hold the corresponding labeled paper over your head to show participants. Then place it on the floor in front of you. Arrange the three pieces of paper on the floor with the letters facing you in the form of an upside down triangle: SELF-EMPATHY in the back row, EMPATHY and HONESTY in the front row next to each other.

If participants are unable to easily see the papers on the floor in front of you, take another set and attach the papers to the wall behind you, placing SELF-EMPATHY on top, and EMPATHY and HONESTY below it such that they correspond to their positions on the floor.

b. Ask participants how they determine which step to choose at a particular moment.

3. Demonstrate the Cha-Cha-Cha

Skip back and forth quickly among the three labeled pieces of paper on the floor as you demonstrate the structure of the three-step Cha-Cha-Cha. Use the following or a similar script. [The letters H, SE, E indicate the paper you are stepping on: Honesty, Self-Empathy, Empathy.]:

> *I might start with Honesty (H) to express myself. When I hear pain in their response, I might move to Empathy (E), as I know they need to be heard before they would be able to hear me as I express myself again (H). I hear they are still in pain, and this time, I know I need to attend to myself (SE) before I can engage effectively and hear (E) what's going on with them. Once they are heard, I might express myself again (H), and be more easily able to hear what's going on for them (E). But if it's difficult, I always have the choice of (SE) coming home to myself, before engaging the other person by either receiving them (E) or expressing what's going on for me (H).*
>
> *I dance the Cha-Cha-Cha by combining and repeating these three steps over and over again to sustain the flow of compassionate connection*

> *between us—which is the intention of NVC. One marvelous aspect of this dance is that my partner does not need to know the dance steps to be drawn into dancing with me.*

4. Illustrate role-play

   Inform participants that you will now role-play a concrete situation to demonstrate the Cha-Cha-Cha.

   a. Make sure your role-play touches each of the three steps at least a couple of times.

   b. Take the role of the NVC dancer. As you speak, step on the piece of paper that corresponds to the dance-step you are illustrating.

   c. If you use a puppet to represent the other party, hold it out so that it faces you when "she or he" speaks. Drop your hand when you are speaking your own role.

   d. If you use another person to role-play the other party, you may need to turn sideways toward the participants. Be sure to adjust the positions of the labeled papers on the floor and on the wall accordingly.

   Mention that dances come in various speeds. The Cha-Cha-Cha is a quick dance in that we are moving relatively fast from one step to the next. Quick dances offer more opportunity for participants to experience the flow between the dance steps. Slow dances offer more opportunity to practice executing each individual step with thoroughness.

Sample Cha-Cha-Cha role-play:

Specify the role you are taking and the situation in one sentence:

> *I am talking to my boss about driving back and forth from the office to make a delivery that is located 2 minutes from my home.*

Speaker: (H) I'm frustrated to be driving 3 hours every Friday afternoon to make this delivery when I could be doing it on my way home and saving a lot of time. Would you be okay if I did that?

Boss: You are always just thinking about what's convenient for YOU.

Speaker: (SE) [Silent self-empathy: Feeling sad. Heaviness in chest area. Needing to be understood. . . .]

Speaker: (E) Are you wanting to trust that the interests of the company are being taken into consideration?

Boss: Yep, that's it. This company treats you workers well, but only if you're there for the company too.

Speaker: (H) I feel encouraged hearing you say that because I'd like to propose something that would also benefit the company. Are you willing to hear it?

Boss: If you keep it down to fifty words or less. There are more words and ideas coming out of you than three people put together.

Speaker: (SE) [Silent self-empathy: Whew, I feel annoyed hearing him bring that up. I'd appreciate some acceptance, just being okay with who I am. Hmmm. I guess I can extend some acceptance to myself in this moment by simply opening to this experience of annoyance. Feeling warm, shoulders tight, a bit heaviness of heart. . . .]

Speaker: (H) Okay, in short I'm spending from 2:00 to 5:00 p.m. driving out and back to make that delivery. If I did it on my way home, I could put in an extra hour and a half here at work, leave at 3:30, and still be home early. Wouldn't that be a win-win?

Boss: Are you kidding? How about the van?

Speaker: (E) Sounds like you're worried that it will be safe over the weekend?

Boss: Ummm, it's not that; I know you're careful. But what if some work order comes up over the weekend. . . .

Speaker: (E once again) So is it that you want to rely on a vehicle being available here at all times?

Boss: Yeah, we need that.

Speaker: (H) How would it be if I left the keys to my car here?

After demonstrating the role-play, ask for questions. Make sure that participants understand what each of the three dance steps consists of, and the circumstances that would prompt us to choose a particular step over another.

5. Small-group practice

    a. Divide participants into groups of three.

    b. Suggest that each participant take 5–8 minutes to dance the Cha-Cha-Cha using a personal situation.

c. Ask that a second person play the other party in the situation. Remind this person to vary their responses so that the speaker gets a chance to practice all three steps of the dance (e.g., if the other party is stuck in pain, the speaker may not have opportunity to practice the Honesty-step within the time allotted).

d. Remind speakers to state the role and the situation in just one brief sentence so that time is available for dancing, rather than discussing, the situation.

e. Ask the third person in the triad to observe the Cha-Cha-Cha and to offer feedback to the speaker regarding the steps they choose. Speakers may request ongoing feedback or wait until the end of the role-play.

f. Inform participants that they may practice by either standing (using the papers on the floor) or sitting (using tent cards). Show how a speaker would flip a tent card toward themselves to indicate the step they have chosen. Mention that the tent card is constructed so that the speaker's choice is also visible to others in the group.

g. Suggest that groups engage in a 2-minute debrief after each role-play.

h. Pass out a set of step-trackers and a tent card to each triad.

i. Inform groups that they have 30 minutes, and that you will be signaling them at 10-minute intervals.

DEBRIEF QUESTIONS:

1. Describe any experience you had of either gravitating toward or avoiding any of the three steps.

2. Did you notice any hesitation or confusion in determining which dance step to take next? If so, how did you resolve it?

3. What part of the role-play was most challenging for you when you were the speaker?

4. What did you learn in the role of observer?

SUGGESTION FOR PRACTICE IN DAILY LIFE: Experiment for a period of time with clearly distinguishing the three dance steps when you interact with another person. Notice if steps unconsciously transmute and meld into one another. For example, we may think we are offering attention to another person (empathizing) by following up on a subject they raised, when in fact we may be drawing attention away from them and unaware that we are in fact expressing ourselves and asking to be heard.

REFERENCES: Chapters 1, 13

MAKING LIFE CHOICEFUL

13.1 Awareness Exercise: Beyond Rebellion and Submission

13.2 Activity: Power Against vs. Power With

13.3 Activity: Practicing Freedom and Choice

KEY CONCEPT 13:

Making Life Choiceful

Description: The essence of NVC lies in the consciousness of needs. With the awareness of what we are needing from moment to moment, we realize that everything we do or say is motivated by an attempt—whether skillful or unskillful—to meet a need that is stirring in us. Freedom comes in the recognition that there is choice in everything we do or say—that nothing and no one can coerce us into doing something we do not choose to do. We may not take pleasure in all our options, but by applying NVC to connect to the underlying need, we come to appreciate every choice we make for the way it serves our life.

We replace the oppressive world of "have to," "must," "should," "ought to," "supposed to," "can't" and "got to" with the empowering awareness of choice. We no longer stop at red lights because we "have to." We recognize that we have a choice to stop or not stop, and to decide based on our own needs and values. The need might be for safety, the preservation of life and health; it might be for order, or we might value cooperation or community; or it might be for security and protection from potentially damaging consequences. When we make conscious choices based on our own needs, we are no longer imprisoned in the world of submission and rebellion: we neither give in to the authority of others nor do we resist their authority. Instead, we step into the freedom of our own choices.

Toolkit exercises in this section provide practice in recognizing the availability of choice, especially in difficult moments, and in connecting to our needs.

Tips for Facilitators: We strongly recommend the use of the activities presented in Chapter 9 of Marshall Rosenberg's *Nonviolent Communication: A Language of Life*, 3rd edition, "Translating 'Have to' to 'Choose to,'" (page 136) and "Cultivating Awareness of the Energy Behind Our Actions" (page 138).

AWARENESS EXERCISE 13.1

Beyond Rebellion and Submission

AIM OF EXERCISE:

1. To experience the freedom of not having to either submit or rebel

2. To practice replacing rebellion and submission with an awareness of needs and values

INSTRUCTIONS FOR GUIDING AWARENESS EXERCISE: Read the following instructions slowly, allowing time between statements for the participant to engage with each step.

1. *Adjust your body so that you are sitting comfortably with your back straight.*

2. *You may close your eyes if you choose or softly focus your gaze about 6 feet in front of you.*

3. *Breathe out—letting go—and then breathe in—receiving.*

4. *Take a few breaths—letting go and receiving . . . letting go and receiving . . .*

5. *Now think of something someone wants you to do but which you do not want to do. [Verify that everyone has completed this step before moving on.]*

6. *Imagine yourself submitting to their wishes. As you see yourself submitting, what body sensations do you experience? Take time to scan and rescan your body, noticing tension, pulsing, heat, cold, etc. [10 seconds]*

7. *Now imagine yourself rebelling against what they want. As you see yourself rebelling, what body sensations do you experience? Again take time to become aware of the body sensations that result from your imagining yourself rebelling. Really experience them.*

8. *Take a moment to release yourself from the space of rebellion by focusing on your breathing—simply notice your breath coming in and going out.*

9. *Now return to your thoughts about the other person. Try to hear what they are wanting in this situation. Ask yourself what needs of yours would be thwarted if you do what they want? Imagine yourself holding that need in your right hand. Take a few moments to cherish that need as you hold it in your hand.*

10. *Now ask yourself what need would be thwarted for them if you do not do what they want? Imagine yourself holding this need in your other hand. Spend a few moments cherishing this need.*

11. *See if you can let go of the request they made of you. Simply focus on the two needs—yours and theirs. Hold both needs tenderly as you breathe and relax . . . in and out . . . relaxing . . . in and out . . . holding both needs precious. . . .*

12. *Now envision yourself stretching out both hands toward the other person as you continue to hold a need in each hand, and imagine exploring strategies together that would meet both needs.*

SHARING CIRCLE:

- My name is _____ .

- I am holding my need for _____ in one hand and the other person's need for _____ in the other hand.

SUGGESTION FOR PRACTICE IN DAILY LIFE: When asked to do something you don't want to do—or when you think you are expected to do something you don't want to do—try holding out both hands. Place your need gently in your dominant hand and the other person's need in the other hand.

REFERENCES: Chapters 5, 9, 13

ACTIVITY 13.2

Power Against vs. Power With

PURPOSE OF ACTIVITY:

1. To recognize when we are exercising "power against" someone—either overtly (through "power and control") or covertly (through "victim stance")

2. To explore the difference between "power against" and "power with"

3. To practice the application of "power with"

BRIEF DESCRIPTION: After an introduction and demonstration on how to move from "power against" to "power with," participants practice in groups of three to transform a "stuck" personal situation into choices that serve life.

MATERIALS NEEDED:

❑ Individual Handout: Power Against vs. Power With for each participant

TIME REQUIRED: 60 minutes

GROUP SIZE: Any size

SPACE REQUIRED: Enough space (or good acoustics) for groups to work without being distracted by one another

LITERACY LEVEL REQUIRED: Able to read and write

PROCEDURE:

1. Introduce the concept of "power against":

    Many of us have been educated to believe that if things aren't going the way we want, we have to get other people to change their behavior. This attitude belies a conscious or unconscious belief that in order for me to feel good, whole, successful, "enough," etc., I need you to be or behave a certain way. In this state of mind, we easily blame or judge others, make demands of them, and deny responsibility for our own situation. This often leads to our pitting our power against the other by taking one of two stances:

    a. *"Power and Control"—applying overt power to coerce someone to behave as we would like. We may, for example, display force, impose punishment, act out our anger, withdraw love and support, or threaten to do any of the above.*

  b. *"Victim Stance"—applying covert power to manipulate someone to behave as we would like. We may, for example, try to guilt-trip, shame, flatter, or "be nice" to someone.*

  When we speak or act out of these two stances, our behaviors increase separation and decrease well-being.

2. Demonstrate the relationship between two forms of "power against": overt and covert power. Give each participant a copy of Individual Handout 13.2.

Sometimes we shift from one stance to another, exerting both overt force and covert manipulation to produce the effect we want in the other party. Although these two stances employ different strategies, they are basically similar. In both instances we experience ourselves lacking internal power to meet our own needs and dependent upon the behavior of others. In both instances, whether we express it or not, we may judge or blame the other party, deny responsibility for our own situation, and believe it necessary for the other person to change in order for us to be happy.

 a. Go over the following diagram on the Handout:

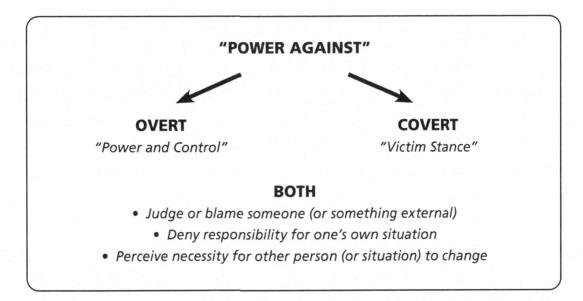

"POWER AGAINST"

OVERT
"Power and Control"

COVERT
"Victim Stance"

BOTH
- *Judge or blame someone (or something external)*
- *Deny responsibility for one's own situation*
- *Perceive necessity for other person (or situation) to change*

 b. Use a concrete example (your own or the one below) to illustrate the two ways in which "power against" might be applied.

Example:

I hear the bus driver mutter an ethnic slur at a couple as they are stepping off the bus. If I am angry and operate out of "power against," I might either:

a. *Apply overt force to pit my power against that of the bus driver. To act out my anger I might call him a name, report him to his company, threaten to report him, etc. This will most likely create an experience of deeper separation for myself as well as for the driver.*

b. *Apply covert force to manipulate the other into changing as I want them to. For example, I might remark loudly to the passenger next to me, "Don't you think public servants should be trained to respect people of all races?" While we may take the high moral ground and try to shame or guilt-trip the other party, it is unlikely that they will change their behavior out of a genuine concern for what we want.*

Emphasize that when we succeed in "getting what we want" through either overt or covert power (i.e., through "power against"), we pay a heavy price in the form of alienation—in ourselves and in the other—thus contributing to more separation in the world.

3. Introduce the concept of "power with" and explain the relationship between power and vulnerability.

> *In this exercise we explore how we can let go of both overt and covert force by recognizing our own internal power and our capacity to address our needs. To shift from an external to an internal source of power requires vulnerability—a willingness to vulnerably recognize and name our needs. Out of the vulnerability of being fully connected to our needs—naming them as well as valuing them—we come to discover ways to meet those needs.*
>
> *When tempted to apply "power against" to force change on someone, I can remember my other source of power: "power with." Let me illustrate the steps I use to engage this power:*

NOTE: Copy the "Power With" diagram (top of next page) on the board or simply sketch a large infinity symbol, adding the arrows and the letters a, b, c, d as indicated on the diagram.

Sweep your hand along the arrows and point to the places on the diagram that correspond to the following four points to describe the process:

> a. *First I recognize the vulnerability of that moment when I experience being "hit in the face" by the driver's remark. This moment—experienced variously as "losing control," "groundlessness," "at a loss," "stopped in one's tracks," "sudden overwhelm," "having the rug pulled," "not knowing"—is precious because it is this moment of vulnerability—when all of a sudden the world is not what our thoughts say it should be—that holds the potential for new, fresh possibilities. So the first step is simply to pause and recognize that I have just arrived at a moment of vulnerability.*

"POWER WITH"

POWER AND VULNERABILITY

(a) An unexpected feeling (of surprise, anger, fear, shame, confusion, etc.) tells me I've moved to the vulnerability side.

(d) I step into my power when, grounded in my own values, I can see the other as fully human with needs as precious as my own. With this power I trust myself to take effective action to address my needs.

(b) I embrace my vulnerability by pausing and opening fully to this moment's feelings and needs. Through this connection, I rediscover my internal power to value myself, out of which arises my power to value others.

(c) This returns me to the power side.

b. *Next, I allow myself to experience this vulnerability by connecting to my feeling and needs. In the example with the bus driver, I may recognize feelings of anger, sorrow, or fear, and my needs for respect and understanding toward all people.*

c. *I consciously hold these needs (for respect and understanding) in my heart until I can fully experience their value for me. When grounded in needs, I am able to embody my own inner power and core strength.*

d. *When I am coming out of my inner power and core strength, I have much greater capacity to see the bus driver with empathy and to guess his needs (e.g., safety or respect).*

- *I make an effort to cherish both sets of needs—my own and what I guess to be his—by consciously holding both sets of needs in my heart.*

- *When I no longer view the other party with eyes of judgment, but with empathy, I have stepped into a different kind of power in relationship to them. "Power with" is the power to inspire connection, such that both parties care about each other's needs and work together out of that place of caring.*

- *Once I am in this place of power in relationship to the other party, I am ready to approach them to express and hear mutual needs. For instance, I might say to the bus driver, "Hearing your remark to the couple getting off the bus, I feel sad because I so care about everyone being respected. Then I thought what might have been going on for you, and wondered if you've had some scary or unpleasant situations on the job . . . and perhaps what you're also wanting is respect and to be safe with the people you are serving . . .?" This is the beginning of a conversation where you are supporting both your own power and the power of the bus driver. When the bus driver trusts that their needs and concerns are being heard and valued, they are much more likely to want to hear and address yours. Being together "in cahoots" with each other generates considerable power to meet both your needs.*

4. Summarize.

    Instead of viewing "vulnerability" as the opposite of "power," we come to value power and vulnerability as two aspects of a single process. We learn to move between the two, from one to the other and back again, following the flow of this infinity symbol. [Illustrate this movement by tracing your finger along the symbol as if drawing a figure "8" on its side.]

    Let's return to our earlier example. When I feel vulnerable, instead of exerting force (either overtly or covertly) to change the bus driver, I pause and acknowledge my vulnerability by getting in touch with feelings and needs. With awareness grounded in what I value in this moment, I experience the internal power that allows me to recognize the other party's humanity and their needs. By holding both my own and the bus driver's needs at heart, I can exercise "power with" to effectively engage in dialogue that addresses my needs.

    In the course of our conversation, I might once again find myself feeling vulnerable. If so, I return and reground myself in an awareness of my needs and thereby regain internal power. And in this way I continue to flow, stepping between power and vulnerability as I move toward meeting my needs.

5. Ask participants to recall and write down the following:

    a. A situation where they chose to use overt force, pushing their point of view to diminish the power of others.

    b. A situation where they perceived themselves as "victim" and tried to manipulate someone into doing what they wanted.

    Mention that they are to write down only the situation, not how they reacted to it.

6. Instruct participants to work in groups of three.

    a. *Participant A, read one of the situations you wrote down.*

    b. *Participant B, give an example of how Participant A might have applied overt force in that situation.*

c. *Participant C, give an example of how Participant A might have applied covert force in the situation.*

d. *Participant A, with the help of B and C, identify your need in that situation.*

e. *All three of you together, spend a minute to consciously hold and value this need. Can you actually connect with the preciousness of this need in your heart? You may or may not come across a strategy to address the need. The key lies in experiencing the power of knowing and valuing your need.*

f. *If you are able to consciously hold and value Participant A's need, then take a moment to guess the other party's need. Hold one need in each hand and value them both. [NOTE: Do this step only if you have completed step e to your satisfaction.]*

g. *Exchange roles so that Participant B now reads a personal situation. Continue rotating roles until you have completed all six situations (a through f) or until time is up. You have half an hour for this activity.*

DEBRIEF QUESTIONS:

1. What do you recognize about your habitual behavior when you encounter a situation that triggers vulnerability in you?

2. Were you able to experience the power of knowing and accepting your needs? If so, describe that experience.

SUGGESTIONS FOR PRACTICE IN DAILY LIFE:

1. In the course of the day, notice when you engage in using "Power Against" someone. Reflect on whether you applied overt or covert power. Then connect with your underlying need in the situation and experiment with moving between power and vulnerability.

2. If you perceive someone using "Power Against," either overtly or covertly, imagine what their needs might be. Support them in gaining power from within by helping them recognize and accept their own need.

REFERENCE: Chapter 10

Power Against vs. Power With

"POWER AGAINST"

OVERT

"Power and Control"

COVERT

"Victim Stance"

BOTH

- *Judge or blame someone (or something external)*
- *Deny responsibility for one's own situation*
- *Perceive necessity for other person (or situation) to change*

"POWER WITH"

POWER AND VULNERABILITY

(a) An unexpected feeling (of surprise, anger, fear, shame, confusion, etc.) tells me I've moved to the vulnerability side.

(d) I step into my power when, grounded in my own values, I can see the other as fully human with needs as precious as my own. With this power I trust myself to take effective action to address my needs.

(b) I embrace my vulnerability by pausing and opening fully to this moment's feelings and needs. Through this connection, I rediscover my internal power to value myself, out of which arises my power to value others.

(c) This returns me to the power side.

ACTIVITY 13.3

Practicing Freedom and Choice

PURPOSE OF ACTIVITY:

1. To understand and practice power of choice in what we do and say

2. To discover an abundance of personal resources from which we can choose to meet needs

3. To practice accepting the reality of a situation before exercising our power to respond

BRIEF DESCRIPTION: Participants are presented with three concepts in the form of reminders that support the power to choose:

1. "I have a wealth of resources."

2. "I always have choice in what I do or say."

3. "I can accept reality or I can resist it."

In groups of three or four, participants focus on a given scenario and role-play to apply the three concepts by:

- Exploring ways to accept a difficult reality,
- Brainstorming available personal resources,
- Responding to the situation at hand by making conscious choices based on awareness of needs.

MATERIALS NEEDED:

- ☐ For each participant: Individual Handout 13.3A: Cultivating Our Power to Choose
- ☐ For each small group of three or four participants: Group Handout 13.3B: Playing the Card We've Been Dealt (prison) or 13.3C (general community). NOTE: This handout may be offered to the group either in the form of a single sheet of paper or cut into six separate individual "cards."

TIME REQUIRED: 1 hour

GROUP SIZE: Any

SPACE REQUIRED: Enough for small groups to work without mutual interference

LITERACY LEVEL REQUIRED: At least one person in each small group with ability to read and write

PROCEDURE:

1. Introduce the "three reminders that support our power to choose." (See boxed text below.) Accompany the outlined material with your own understanding and personal examples.

2. Address Items 1 and 2 on Individual Handout 13.3A: Cultivating Our Power to Choose in one of two ways:
   - Facilitate a discussion with the whole group or
   - Include these items as part of the small group work (below).

3. Divide participants into groups of three or four.
   - Give each group a copy of the Group Handout "Playing the Card We've Been Dealt" (13.3B for prison community or 13.3C for general community).
   - Give each participant a copy of the Individual Handout (13.3A: Cultivating Our Power to Choose).

4. Allow 45 minutes for group work (or 30 minutes if Items 1 and 2 of the Individual Handout have already been addressed in the large group.)

5. Debrief by inviting each group to share what they learned that might be of benefit to other participants.

THREE REMINDERS THAT SUPPORT OUR POWER TO CHOOSE

Reminder #1: "I have a wealth of resources."

1. "Resource" refers to a thing or a quality—tangible or intangible—that I can make use of to meet a need. Our personal resources constitute a large treasure chest upon which we draw to make life more wonderful for ourselves and for others.

2. We each have a wealth of personal resources.

   a. For example: life energy, time, skills, intelligence, creativity, patience, relationships, physical strength, material possessions, money, health, community, courage, love, sense of humor, various "knacks," reputation, experience, fortitude, integrity, wisdom, will power, etc.

   b. We often don't recognize a resource until we notice its shortage, e.g., "I didn't realize my eyesight was a resource until a blind woman asked me to lead her across the street, [or] . . . when my eyes started to strain from the data-entry work."

Reminder #2: "I always have choice in what I do or say."

1. We often associate "choice" and "freedom" with the availability of pleasant experiences or preferred circumstances.

    Example:
    *   "I went with my friend for ice cream. They had run out of chocolate so I had no choice but to eat a lousy vanilla cone. What a waste of calories and two bucks!"

    *   "I have no freedom to do anything inside prison."

2. NVC encourages us to reframe "choice" as something we make rather than something we are given.

    Example:
    *   Instead of thinking "I have no choice but to eat a lousy vanilla cone," I can remind myself, "I always have choice in what I eat or do." If I choose to eat a vanilla cone even though I consider vanilla a "lousy" flavor:
        a. I may be making this choice to meet my needs for play, connection, and ease.
        b. It may not meet my need for yumminess (beauty of taste).
        c. If meeting the need for yumminess is more important for me in this moment than fun and connection, I might make a different choice. For example, instead of eating the vanilla ice cream, I might chew on the delectable squid jerky I keep in my handbag, or go to another ice cream shop, or look for something scrumptious at the supermarket.

3. In a similar vein, we regard "freedom" as something we consciously create rather than something provided to us by others.

    Example:
    *   Instead of thinking, "I have no freedom in prison," I can remind myself: "I can practice freedom anywhere." As a prisoner, are they making me serve time or am I making time serve me (i.e., I make time serve my needs)?

    *   I am free when I invest my personal resources consciously in service of what I value (needs).

    *   I am not free when my actions are unconsciously motivated, reactive, or impulsive (coming out of habit energy, conditioning, or ingrained patterns).

    *   I am free when I determine my thoughts and emotions.

    *   I am not free when I unconsciously believe my thoughts, especially those that engender separation (fear and anger), e.g., thoughts of wrongness, shame, and blame.

Reminder #3: "I can accept reality or I can resist it."

"We are all here for a single purpose: to grow in wisdom and to learn to love better. We can do this through losing as well as through winning, by having and by not having, by succeeding or by failing. All we need to do is to show up openhearted for class. Fulfilling life's purpose may depend more on how we play than on what we are dealt."
—Rachel Naomi Remen (physician, author, storyteller)

1. Reality is the hand we have been dealt: what is true in this moment.

   - The bucket holding my favorite ice cream is empty: that's reality.

   - A farmer's field is flooded: that's reality.

   - I got a diagnosis of cancer: that's reality.

   - You are in a state prison: that's reality.

2. We have as much choice in each of these situations as in a situation where we have won the lottery if "choice" refers to how we respond to a situation rather than to the availability of desirable options. Our freedom and assertion of choice do not depend on us "winning, having, or succeeding."

3. When we recognize and accept reality for what it is, we avoid investing our resources resisting, denying, cursing, or condemning the hand we've been dealt.

4. When we judge someone or a situation, it is difficult to see the person or the situation clearly. Accepting reality gives us clarity to engage in choice and freedom—to expend our resources consciously and to play our cards creatively to meet this moment's need.

5. The choice I make in this moment affects the future. Accepting reality implies neither resignation nor fatalism. It is accepting what is true in this moment and making more effective choices based on seeing clearly.

DEBRIEF QUESTION: Small groups: What have you learned that might be of benefit to share with participants in the whole group?

SUGGESTIONS FOR PRACTICE IN DAILY LIFE:

1. Reflect on the gifts you have to offer. Take an hour to create an inventory of your personal resources. (If you do this with a friend, they may be able to help you see your own wealth even more clearly.)

2. Be aware of moments where you have difficulty accepting reality as it is. Notice when you think in terms of what "should," "shouldn't," "is supposed to," or "ought to" happen. Allow yourself to pause and appreciate your ability to recognize these moments.

3. Identify an area in your life where you experience powerlessness or see yourself as having little or no choice. What is the "card life has dealt you"? Experiment with applying Item 3 in the Handout (13.3 "Cultivating Our Power to Choose").

REFERENCES: Chapters 9, 12

Cultivating Our Power to Choose

This is a small group activity. Please read out loud and respond together as a group to the items below:

1. Go over the three reminders that support us in living a life grounded in freedom and choice. Take turns summarizing each concept and see whether everyone in the group shares the same understanding.

   a. "I have a wealth of personal resources."

   b. "I always have choice in what I do or say."

   c. "I can accept reality or I can resist it."

2. Give a real example (taken from your own lives) to illustrate each concept.

3. Pick one of the six scenarios (Group Handout 13.3B or C: Cards Life Has Dealt Us). As a group, assume the role of the primary character in the scenario and apply the three reminders in the following sequence:

   a. Recognize resources:

      Brainstorm, naming all the resources—personal qualities and material resources—that you possess as individuals in this group. Ask one member to record the list.

   b. Accept: How might you fully accept this moment's reality?

      • State the reality in the form of an NVC observation.

      • Devise one or several strategies that would support you in fully accepting what is already true. You might, for example, take turns expressing what you are feeling in relationship to this reality. Or you might create a ritual that helps you move through disbelief, denial, resistance, resentment, etc.

      • Name the unmet needs in this situation. Pick one need that seems most prominent and take time to connect with it fully. Hold this need silently: be aware of how (and how much) you value it or yearn for its fulfillment.

   c. Choose freely:

      • Review the list of resources you brainstormed and highlight the items most likely to serve you in responding to this particular "card which life has dealt."

- While being grounded in a clear awareness of your current need(s), name ways you might choose to respond to the situation at hand.
- Ask whether these choices take into account the needs of all those who are touched by the situation (and what need of yours might be served by considering this question).

4. When you have completed the process, decide what you have learned that would be valuable to share with participants in the large group during debrief.

Cards Life Has Dealt Us:

PRISON

1. You are ready to apply for parole. However, you are told that, due to your recent argument with an officer, you now need to complete a six-month anger-management program before your application will be reviewed. You have tried several times to explain that the so-called argument was due to misunderstanding on the part of the officer, but no one in authority has accepted this.	2. You were just informed that your mother died of a heart attack. Over the last two years, you have been longing to see her in order to let her know how sorry you are for what you have done.
3. You are being released next week from prison to a halfway house in the community. You have been told that drugs are rampant in that building. You want to stay clean and are terrified of being assigned to live there.	4. Yesterday, your friend was turned down by the parole board for the third time. This morning, when you went to meet him for a walk, you found him hanging from a rope, dead.
5. You are determined to make good use of your time in prison in order to be a successfully contributing member of society when released. You work hard at your job and are pursuing college courses. Now the government is cutting education funds to prison and also eliminating jobs contracted through private businesses. You estimate that you will lose both your job and college program within three months.	6. You are eighteen years old and have been arrested and sentenced for the first time. You are being sent to an adult prison that has a reputation for brutality and racial violence.

Cards Life Has Dealt Us:

GENERAL COMMUNITY

1. You have been steadily promoted and building a career at the same company for ten years. You just learned from the CEO that the company has quietly completed a transaction to outsource your entire department.	2. Your baby girl was found in her crib dead. The doctor diagnosed it as SIDS (Sudden Infant Death Syndrome).
3. Due to a volatile stock market, you learn you have lost nearly your entire savings of thirty-five years.	4. You are a twenty-year-old who does not believe in war. You have stated your position as a CO (Conscientious Objector) to the government. You now receive a letter informing you that you have been drafted and are to report for duty in one month.
5. You are a parent of three young children. A known sex offender has just moved onto your street.	6. You have just returned to the community after serving ten years in state prison for a sex offense. You filled out nearly fifty applications for housing before finding your current home. Your criminal history has now come to the attention of a handful of neighbors. Even though you have a legal right to live here, they have asked you to leave, hinting that they will "make life miserable" if you don't.

EXPRESSING AND RECEIVING A NO

14:1   Awareness Exercise:
       Expressing No

14:2   Activity: Three Ways to Hear
       a No

14.3   Activity: Expressing No
       in NVC

KEY CONCEPT 14:

Expressing and Receiving a No

Description: Whether expressing or receiving a no, we perceive no not as a rejection but as an expression of a need which is seeking to be met. We express an NVC no by communicating the current need that prevents us from complying with someone's request. Likewise, when we hear someone say no to our request, we focus on hearing what need they are saying yes to in this moment which is preventing them from saying yes to our request. Our intention is to stay heart-connected, understanding and valuing each other's needs, even if we choose not to participate in each other's strategies to meet a particular need.

Toolkit exercises: In this section draw our awareness to the habitual reactions that prevent us from hearing the yes behind someone's no. Practice is provided for translating no into mutual needs as well as staying in touch with ourselves and our bodily reactions when asked to do something we don't want to do.

Tips for Facilitators: Many of us find it difficult to say no. In *Speak Peace in a World of Conflict*, Marshall Rosenberg writes, "Many women . . . have been educated from childhood to believe that loving women have no needs. [As for men. . .] courageous men have no needs." (p. 44) Before facilitating the exercises in this section, reflect on any resistance you commonly experience to turning down someone's requests to you. Are there certain needs that are challenging for you to own or to actively fulfill for yourself?

By understanding our resistance to saying no, we can become more aware of our relationship to our needs. We may have difficulty owning a certain need because it does not fit the image we hold of ourselves, or we may feel anxious about a need because we don't believe we have what it takes to meet this need on our own. For example, we might tell ourselves that we should not need (or do not deserve) to relax. In this case it may be difficult to say no to someone's request for our time if we happen to be "just sitting around reading a novel." Or we may have difficulty saying no because we don't trust that our needs for acceptance and inclusion can be met when we don't do what others want of us.

As we practice NVC, we become aware of the value of "giving from the heart" and come to understand why "everyone pays" when giving is done out of obligation, fear, shame, guilt, or the hope for love or reward. However, many of us are conditioned such that saying no brings up enormous anxiety. Due to our inability to say no, we may end up "giving in" or "giving up" rather than "giving from the heart." By examining our resistance to saying no and by listening carefully to what we are telling ourselves in such situations, we are deepening our capacity to live and give authentically from the heart. When we have an urge to comply with someone's request, we might pause and check for any hints of irritation, resentment, or anxiety and notice thoughts such as:

- They'll get angry at me if I don't.
- They won't like me.
- It's not polite not to.
- They have so much more on their plate than I do, and there is nobody else to do it.
- It's not nice to refuse.
- I don't have to do this, but I'll do it as a favor for them.
- They should appreciate me.
- I'm being nice to them; they should be nice to me too.
- I shouldn't be stuck with this.
- I am trying to accommodate them and they should know that.
- I'll do it to be caring (compassionate, kind, generous, a good person).

It is often helpful to check with the physical sensations in our body. When we say yes to someone's request because it truly meets our own need or value for e.g., kindness or compassion, our bodies move with conviction even if the task at hand is not a pleasant one.

AWARENESS EXERCISE 14.1

Expressing No

AIM OF EXERCISE:

1. To increase the ability to connect with our own needs when asked to do something we don't want to do

2. To practice listening to our bodies when we experience resistance to what someone is asking of us

3. To develop skill in translating no into mutual needs and then exploring strategies for meeting those needs

INSTRUCTIONS FOR GUIDING AWARENESS EXERCISE: Read the following out loud slowly, allowing time between each sentence for participants to follow the instructions at an unhurried pace:

1. *Sit comfortably, with back straight. Make any adjustments in posture that would help you feel both relaxed and alert.*

2. *Either close your eyes or softly drop your gaze to a spot on the floor close in front of you.*

3. *Begin by focusing attention on the breath, noticing breathing in and breathing out.*

4. *As you breathe in, allow yourself to receive. Then let go as you breathe out. With each out-breath, allow your body to let go and relax a little bit more.*

5. *Now imagine a situation where someone is asking you to do something that you don't want to do.*

   - *Picture the person.*

   - *Hear the person's voice making the request of you.*

   - *Notice any sensations in your body—perhaps tightening of muscles, change in breathing or heart rate, heat, pressure, constriction, . . .*

   - *Allow yourself to simply be present with these sensations. No need to judge, analyze, explain, or think about what is going on. Just feel what the body is feeling.*

   - *Keep breathing, receiving and letting go, receiving and letting go, . . .*

6. *Now imagine yourself saying no to this person's request.*

   - *See your own posture and hear the sound of your words.*

- *Notice what is happening in your body now. [Pause]*

- *Again, breathe in and receive; breathe out and let go. Take a few more breaths.*

7. *Now imagine yourself being in a space where you are able to look directly at this person. See if you can sense the need they are trying to meet when they make their request of you. What might be the universal need or value behind their request?*

8. *Bring your attention back inside again. This time connect with your own need: what need of yours are you wanting to protect when you resist their request?*

9. *As you become aware of both your own need and the other person's need, imagine yourself approaching the other person with this understanding. See and hear yourself saying the following words to them, "When you make that request of me, I am guessing you are needing _____ . And I would like you to know that I need _____ . Would you be willing to explore with me ways to get both our needs met?"*

10. *Bring your attention inside again. Scan your body from head to toe. Notice any physical sensations. What is happening with your muscles, breath, heart rate, . . .?*

11. *Take a few more conscious breaths in and out, receiving and letting go. Receiving and letting go, . . .*

12. *As we complete this visualization process, take a moment to reflect on what you have experienced or learned in this exercise.*

SHARING CIRCLE:

1. My name is _____ .

2. In doing this exercise, I discovered or rediscovered _____ about myself.

SUGGESTIONS FOR PRACTICE IN DAILY LIFE:

- When asked to do something that triggers resistance in you, ask yourself: If I were to comply with their request, what need of mine and what need of theirs might be met or unmet?

- Practice responding in a way that acknowledges the importance of both their need and yours.

REFERENCES: Chapters 5, 6, 7, 9, 13

ACTIVITY 14.2

Three Ways to Hear a No

PURPOSE OF ACTIVITY:

1. To hear the need the other person is saying yes to when they say no to our request

2. To be aware of our habitual reactions when we hear a no

BRIEF DESCRIPTION: In groups of four, participants take turns role-playing:
- Someone who issues a "no" statement
- Someone who hears the no and focuses on what's wrong with the speaker
- Someone who hears the no and focuses on what wrong with themselves
- Someone who hears the no and focuses on need(s) the speaker might be saying yes to

MATERIALS NEEDED:
- ☐ Group Handout: List of "No" Messages. Choose Handout 14.2A for prison or Handout 14.2B for general community.

TIME REQUIRED: 1 hour

GROUP SIZE: Four or more

SPACE REQUIRED: Adequate for groups to work without mutual interference

LITERACY LEVEL REQUIRED: Ability to read and write sentences

PROCEDURE:

1. Ask participants to either recall or imagine a situation where someone says no to them.

2. Request two or three participants to volunteer a "no" message they have heard or can imagine hearing.

3. Give participants a minute to write down one or several "no" messages from their own lives.

4. Review the three choices that are available when we hear a no.

   a. We can place our attention on what's wrong with the person who is delivering the no. In our mind, we criticize them and their refusal to comply with what we want.

b. We can place our attention on what's wrong with ourselves. We hear rejection as an indication of our own inadequacy and in our mind we criticize ourselves or the request we put out.

c. We can place our attention on hearing the need the other person is trying to meet when they say no to us. We try to understand the need to which they are saying yes that prevents them from saying yes to what we are asking.

Emphasize that in this activity we are practicing hearing and interpreting a no rather than responding orally to another person.

5. Demonstrate the exercise.

   a. Invite four volunteers to stand in front of the group.

   b. Say to the first volunteer:

      i. *Bring to mind a scenario where you say no to someone.*

      ii. *Tell us the relationship between yourself and the person to whom you are saying no. (For example: "I am a contractor. The person I am saying no to is a member of my construction crew.")*

      iii. *Face the other three people and deliver your "no" message to them as if they were the other party. (For example: "No, you can't take tomorrow off. Don't you realize we are way behind schedule and how much money that's costing?")*

   c. Say to the second volunteer:

      i. *Focus attention on what's wrong with this person for saying no.*

      ii. *Express your judgments out loud. (For example: "All he can think of is money and his own butt.")*

   d. Say to the third volunteer:

      i. *Focus attention on what's wrong with yourself or the request you made which elicited the no.*

      ii. *Express your self-judgments out loud. (For example: "I knew it was selfish to ask for something like that.")*

   e. Say to the fourth volunteer:

      i. *Focus attention on the speaker's need. Guess the need they were saying yes to when they said no to what you wanted.*

      ii. *Say your guess out loud. (For example, "I wonder if the boss is needing support and is concerned about resources being well-spent.")*

6. If desired, have volunteers rotate positions and engage in a second demonstration.

7. Invite participants to form groups of four. Give each group a list of "no" messages (Group Handout 14.2A or B) and the following instructions:

   a. *Take turns playing the four roles as demonstrated earlier by the volunteers.*

   b. *First person: offer a "no" message. Please use either a "no" message from the group handout or one you wrote yourself. Remember to specify your relationship to the other party.*

   c. *Second person: Judge the speaker for saying "no" to you and then express your thoughts out loud.*

   d. *Third person: Judge yourself for having been rejected and then express your thoughts out loud.*

   e. *Fourth person: Guess the speaker's need(s) to which they are saying yes when they say no to you. Use phrases such as, "I guess they value . . ." "I wonder if they need . . ."*

DEBRIEF QUESTIONS:

1. Describe anything you learned from this activity that may affect how you hear the next no that comes your way.

2. What might you do to nourish your capacity to hear the yes behind someone's no to you?

SUGGESTIONS FOR PRACTICE IN DAILY LIFE:

1. When you hear no, stop and breathe. Reflect on your three choices as to where to place attention.

2. Develop an ear for hearing the yes behind a person's no. You can practice when watching TV or overhearing others' conversations as well as through personal interactions.

REFERENCE: Chapter 10

List of "No" Messages: PRISON

Imagine a situation where an inmate, having approached the person indicated below, receives the following "no" messages from them:

1. **Counselor:** "That correctional plan you came up with won't work. You need to follow the one we laid out for you."

2. **Partner:** "I'll decide when to come visit. I don't need you to tell me how to live my life."

3. **Parole board:** "We are not ready to grant you parole at this time. Come back in two years."

4. **Parole officer:** "Your request is too general. I haven't a clue what you are trying to get at. The answer is no."

5. **Cellmate:** "No way. Why should I turn my music down for you?"

6. **Classmate:** "I don't feel like doing you another favor. You didn't even acknowledge what I did for you last week."

7. **Coparent:** "I don't bring the kids because it's sad for them to see you here."

8. **Halfway house:** "We regret that your request for residency has been turned down. We are unable to accommodate individuals with your crime history."

9. **Father:** "Get real. You're not a kid anymore and I'm not Sugar Daddy who forks over whatever you want."

10. **Baseball captain:** "What makes you think you are qualified to play today when you haven't attended practice all month?"

11. **Instructor:** "The class is full. You registered way too late."

12. **Workout partner:** "Not today. I feel like jogging by myself."

13. **Cellmate:** "Stop asking me stupid questions. You have been bugging me all day."

14. **Officer:** "Health care is closed. You will have to wait till tomorrow."

15. **Supervisor:** "No, you can't take time off just because you feel like it. You don't even look sick."

16. **Your son or daughter (or another family member):** "I don't really need you to call every week 'cause I don't have that much to say anyway."

17. **Scrabble partner:** "I can't play with you tonight because I am working on the open house."

18. **Friend:** "The reason I'm not showing you the letter is because you'll blab about me all over the place."

19. **Nurse:** "Sorry, we don't give inmates prescription painkillers."

20. **Classmate:** "Thanks for the offer but I want to do the homework myself."

List of "No" Messages: GENERAL COMMUNITY

In the following situations, the person receiving the "no" message is the second individual indicated, e.g., "child" in Item #1 below.

1. **Parent to child:** "You know the rules. No movies on school nights."

2. **Teenager to parent:** "I got a date so I can't help you with the chores tomorrow."

3. **Passerby to panhandler:** "Do you think money is easy for me to come by?"

4. **Newspaper editor to letter writer:** "We don't publish letters that contain profanity."

5. **Community member to director of nonprofit organization:** "I have decided not to accept your request to serve on the board. As it is, I hardly ever see my family."

6. **Partner to partner:** "I don't feel like going for coffee. How about a walk?"

7. **Park administrator to artist:** "You can't leave your sculpture here. It's a public garden; not everyone appreciates modern art."

8. **Guest to host:** "Thanks for your offer, but I am boycotting bottled water. I think free water is a human right."

9. **Friend to friend:** "I can't lend you any more money. You promised last time and you never paid back."

10. **Neighbor to neighbor:** "I was told you just got out of prison. If you need to talk to me, here is my number at work, but don't be coming over to the house."

11. **Committee member to colleague:** "No, I am not coming for wine and cheese. We spent the whole day sitting and talking. I've had enough group-time!"

12. **Mother to adult child:** "No, don't touch the cake in the frig! I made it for my bridge club."

13. **Student to teacher:** "I didn't do the homework because it's a stupid assignment."

14. **Star-player to teammates:** "Sorry I won't be at the game this weekend. We go to church as a family on Sunday mornings."

15. **NVC community members to local trainer:** "This is a major event so we've decided to invite out-of-town trainers to handle the presentation."

16. **Landlord to tenant:** "Please don't give my name as a reference. I don't like to be called unless I have glowing things to say about someone."

17. **Church member to minister:** "I'm not donating more money until our church deals with the discrimination against women and gay people."

18. **Housemate to housemate:** "I don't care if it is your great-aunt's Chinese antique; can't you see that the living room is already one huge clutter?"

19. **Supervisor to employee:** "You can't come to work unless you are wearing a uniform."

20. **Parent to teenager:** "I don't care if all your friends have their driver's license. You are not getting yours until you graduate."

ACTIVITY 14.3

Expressing No

PURPOSE OF ACTIVITY:

1. To understand and practice expressing the three elements of an NVC "no"

2. To cultivate awareness of the underlying needs which lead us to feel reluctant to say no in certain situations

BRIEF DESCRIPTION: We begin with a review of the three elements of an NVC "no" and an exploration of common needs behind difficulties in saying no. Participants practice in small groups, expressing no in role-play situations outlined in a handout. They then work in pairs on personal situations, connecting with the needs underlying their reluctance to say no and experimenting with the three elements to articulate an NVC "no" for a difficult situation.

MATERIALS NEEDED:
- ❑ Board or flipchart, with two markers of different colors
- ❑ Pencil and paper
- ❑ For each small group, a copy of Group Handout 14.3A (prison) or 14.3B (general community): Situations for Expressing No
- ❑ For each pair, a copy of Group Handout 14.3C: Instructions for Pair Practice

TIME REQUIRED: 1 hour

GROUP SIZE: Four to six or more

SPACE REQUIRED: Adequate for small groups or pairs to work without mutual interference

LITERACY LEVEL REQUIRED: Sentence-level reading and writing

PROCEDURE:

1. Illustrate the three elements of an NVC expression of no, using your own example or the one given below. Example: Your program administrator requests, "Would you upgrade and manage the PA system for the upcoming event?"

   Three elements of an **NVC "No":**

   a. One: Let the other party know that you heard their request as a gift. Listen for their underlying need and see the request as an opportunity being extended for you to use your power to meet a precious human need they have.

Example: "I appreciate your trust that I can contribute to this important event by running the sound system."

b. Two: Express the need that is preventing you from saying yes to their request. Example: "I feel overwhelmed when I think about my schedule, and want to follow through on current commitments before I accept new responsibilities."

c. Three: Recognize the other party's need and express your concern for how it may be met. Example: "I do hear your need for support. Would you like me to ask my nephew if he is free?"

2. Raise the topic of why it is often difficult for some of us to say no.

a. Invite participants' input and list their responses on the board. Leave some space at the end of each item. Example: "I sometimes find it hard to say no because . . .
   - Then people won't like me."
   - I feel I'm being selfish."
   - People would be disappointed in me."
   - I might not get asked or included in the future."

b. Ask participants to name the needs behind the reasons that are listed on the board. Explore whether there may be layers of needs for a single item. Use a different color to write the need words next to the corresponding item on the list. Example:
   - *Reason*: "I feel I'm being selfish."
   - *Possible needs*: Compassion, contribution ("I don't want to be selfish. I want to contribute to other people's well being.")
   - *Possible deeper needs*: Self-acceptance, relief from pain ("I don't like the feeling of being selfish, i.e., I don't like the pain I feel when I judge myself to be selfish.")

c. Emphasize that whether it be yes or no, an NVC response is always grounded in an awareness of the need we are trying to meet.

3. Small group practice
   a. Divide participants into even-sized groups of four to six members each.

   b. Give each group a handout. Use either Handout 14.3A (Prison) or 14.3B (General Community): Situations for Expressing No.

   c. Instruct group members to take turns practicing saying no, using the situations in the handout.

   d. Review again the three elements of an NVC "no."

   e. Inform participants that they have 20 minutes for this part of the activity.

4. Pair practice

   a. Provide 2–3 minutes for individuals to silently recall and write down one or several situations where they have (or had) difficulty saying no.

   b. Request groups to break into pairs and give each pair a copy of Handout 14.3C: Instructions for Pair Practice.

   c. Go over the instructions and make sure everyone is clear on how to proceed.

   d. Inform participants that they have 10 minutes to practice in pairs on their own situations.

DEBRIEF QUESTIONS:

1. What aspect of expressing no in NVC is most challenging for you?

2. How do you see yourself integrating what we just practiced in your day-to-day living?

SUGGESTIONS FOR PRACTICE IN DAILY LIFE:

1. Train yourself to pause before saying no in order to become fully aware of the need to which you are saying yes.

2. Notice any situation in your life where you are repeatedly saying no (i.e., telephone solicitors, cocktail invitations). Imagine how you might express no in a way that acknowledges the other person and fully embodies the three elements you practiced today.

REFERENCE: Chapter 10

Situations for Expressing No: PRISON

1. Your cell mate has procured some heroin and invites you to join him in getting high.

2. You are going out on a pass and your buddy asks you to make a phone call to his ex-girlfriend to tell her how much he has changed and that she should come to visit him to see for herself.

3. Your job as a peer counselor is to offer a listening ear to fellow inmates who need a place to talk. Today you spent nearly the whole day empathizing with person after person, and now it's recreation period and you are eager to play ball. However, another prisoner approaches you to say they just had a big fight and asks you to help them work through it during recreation period.

4. You are being asked by a prison official to work as an institutional driver. This is a job of trust in the prison but your goal right now is to get your high school diploma and prepare yourself for future employment.

5. You are being asked by your NVC teammates to facilitate one of the exercises at the NVC workshop coming up this weekend. You don't want to do this because you are nervous about participants at the workshop who might disrespect you for your crime history.

6. You are a volunteer who goes inside prison to offer NVC. You are being asked by an inmate in your workshop to deliver a small heart they had carved for their mother, who attends your NVC practice groups on the outside.

Situations for Expressing No:

GENERAL COMMUNITY

1. Your colleague who sits at the next desk says to you: "I'm planning on calling in sick tomorrow. If the supervisor asks about me, will you tell her that I was coughing and sneezing and had a headache today?"

2. Your teenager says to you: "Everyone I know has an iPhone except me. If you could only see how much I'm missing out on life, you'd be getting me one."

3. Your longtime next-door neighbor is running for mayor. You do not agree with her political views. She says to you: "We're coming to the home stretch, but it's a close race, and I need all the help I can get. I know you've been laid off so I wonder if I can ask you a big favor. Would you be willing to leaflet our neighborhood tomorrow? It'll take no more than an hour."

4. Your in-laws are on the phone saying: "We just heard about this great airline deal: terrific prices, but you have to stay at least a month at your destination. Since we haven't seen you and the kids for so long, we thought this would be a wonderful opportunity to spend some time together rather than another one of those hurried hello-and-goodbye visits. We'd like to go ahead with it, if it's okay with you."

5. Your supervisor says, "In the future, I'd like for you to just send out a standard form letter to candidates we reject rather than calling them individually and spending time on people whom this firm will never see again."

6. Your partner says: "Of course it's not a scam. I went to school with a guy who's doing this and he's already made a mint. If we pull out our savings and do this tomorrow, we'll be twice as rich in three months. Come on, it's the chance of a lifetime!"

Expressing No: Instructions for Pair Practice

Make sure you have each written down one or several situations where you have (or had) difficulty saying no to someone. Take turns, giving each partner an opportunity to work through the following process:

1. Tell your partner two things, using one brief sentence:

    a. What is being asked of you in this situation (to which you wish to say no)

    b. What your relationship is to the person who is asking

2. Tell your partner the reason(s) why you have difficulty saying no in this situation. Again, be brief and state your reasons with just a few words.

3. Together with your partner, explore the needs underlying your reasons for why you have difficulty saying no in this situation. Remember that there may be several needs or layers of needs.

4. Finally, express no in NVC to your partner as if they were the other party in the situation.

    i. Let them know that you hear their request as a gift. If you hear the need underlying someone's request, we can see that they are extending an opportunity for us to use our power to meet a precious human need.

    ii Express the need that is preventing you from saying yes to their request.

    iii. Recognize the other party's need and express your concern for how it may be met.

5. Ask your partner to orally reflect back all three elements of your no. Partners may use the formula, "I heard you say, (i) . . ., (ii) . . ., and (iii) . . ."

APPRECIATION AND CELEBRATION

15.1 Awareness Exercise: Celebrating Our Joy

15.2 Awareness Exercise: Self-Appreciation

15.3 Activity: Giving Someone an Appreciation

15.4 Activity: What Keeps Us From Expressing Our Appreciation?

15.5 Activity: A Secret Eye for Appreciation

15.6 Activity: Receiving Appreciation

Appreciation and Celebration

Description: NVC encourages the expression of appreciation as a way to celebrate life when our needs are met. When we are grounded moment to moment in the consciousness of needs, we recognize how often our needs are in fact being met, and this awareness of fulfillment brings joy and gratitude to our lives.

In NVC we celebrate by connecting to needs that are being gratified. When this comes about through someone's action or words, we express appreciation to that person by letting them know (a) specifically what they did or said, (b) how we feel, and (c) what need of ours is met. Appreciation is a way of inviting the other party into our celebration, and letting them know how their choices have contributed to our life.

NVC appreciation is not to be confused with conventional compliments such as "You did a great job," or "You are an excellent cook." The latter are positive judgments which place the speaker in the role of judge determining who or what is good or bad. Positive judgments, like negative judgments, reinforce a world where we make choices dependent on external sources of approval or disapproval rather than on an awareness of our own needs.

Toolkit Exercises: The exercises in this section offer practice in expressing and receiving NVC appreciation, in cultivating awareness of how we are affected by something we enjoy, and in celebrating our capacity to contribute to each other.

Tips for Facilitators: Many people turn to NVC when they encounter pain, tension, or conflict. This may lead facilitators to spend most of the group's time on situations where needs are not being met and forget how powerfully NVC can enhance joy and well-being in all situations. We suggest that expressions of celebration and appreciation be naturally woven into each session, and that participants have regular opportunities to practice giving and receiving NVC appreciation.

Celebrating Our Joy

AIM OF EXERCISE:

1. To practice being aware of how we are affected by something we enjoy

2. To practice appreciation by focusing on three NVC components

INSTRUCTIONS FOR GUIDING AWARENESS EXERCISE: Before beginning the guided awareness exercise, remind participants of the three elements of NVC appreciation—(1) observation, (2) need, (3) feeling—as expressed in the following ditty:

> I appreciate you
> When I tell you true
> How your act impacted on me:
> - What you did or said,
> - How I was fed,
> - And the feelings I feel inside me.

Read the following slowly, allowing time between each statement for participants to reflect:

1. *Adjust your posture so you are sitting comfortably with your back straight.*

2. *Either close your eyes or drop your gaze to the floor.*

3. *Be aware of your breathing. Simply feel the rising and falling of your belly or chest as the breath enters and leaves your body.*

4. *Now remember something you enjoyed and bring it to the present.*

   - *What was happening?*

   - *How were you fed by what happened? (What need of yours was fulfilled?)*

   - *How do you feel now as you remember what happened?*

   - *Sit with that feeling and simply enjoy the body sensations you experience as you celebrate this feeling.*

5. *Now bring to mind someone whom you are appreciating.*

   - *Bring their presence to your consciousness.*

   - *What did they do or say that you are celebrating?*

- *How were you fed by what they did? (What need was met in you?)*

- *How do you feel now as you recall what they did and how you were fed?*

- *Now imagine going up to this person. Imagine telling them what they did, how you were fed and the feelings that come up for you as you recall this.*

- *Notice what happens in your body as you celebrate this person and what they did that affected you.*

SUGGESTIONS FOR PRACTICE IN DAILY LIFE: Every day notice something you enjoy for which you feel grateful. Articulate to yourself:

- What you are observing that is contributing to joy or gratitude,

- The needs that are fed,

- The feelings you feel.

You can practice this while waiting for a bus, doing housework, going to sleep, taking a walk, etc.

REFERENCE: Chapter 14

AWARENESS EXERCISE 15.2

Self-Appreciation

AIM OF EXERCISE:

1. To practice appreciating ourselves

2. To become aware of the feelings and thoughts that prevent us from fully appreciating ourselves

INSTRUCTIONS FOR GUIDING AWARENESS EXERCISE: Read slowly, allowing approximately 15 seconds between statements for the participant to follow instructions for each step:

1. *Adjust your posture so that you are sitting comfortably with your back straight. Either close your eyes or drop your gaze softly to the floor in front of you.*

2. *Focus your attention on your breathing. Inhale and receive. Exhale and let go. Breathe easily and freely, receiving and letting go of each breath without hurry.*

3. *Are you enjoying your breathing in this moment? If so, appreciate your body and its ability to receive and let go. Do this by feeling your feelings and enjoying the need you are meeting. If you are not happy with your breathing, mourn this by naming the unmet need, recognizing its value, and holding it with care.*

4. *Turn your attention to your body. Is there one thing that you appreciate about your body? Pause and take joy in this by making an observation about an aspect of your physical being that you appreciate.*

5. *Is there one thing you said today that you are happy with? What was it? What needs did you meet? As you recall this now, how do you feel?*

6. *Is there one action you took today that you are happy with? What did you do? What needs did the action serve? How do you feel about it in this moment?*

7. *Is there something you have accomplished in your life that you are happy with? What did you do? Which of your needs were fulfilled through this accomplishment? Was there a deeper need beneath the need you just named? How are you feeling right now? Take a moment to feel this feeling.*

8. *Is there something in your life that you did that you have never acknowledged? What keeps you from appreciating it? Take this opportunity to acknowledge it. Are you experiencing any resistance*

to appreciating it? If so, what need are you trying to meet by resisting appreciating your action?

9. *Think of a moment in the past when you appreciated yourself or appreciated something you did. Do you recall how you felt?*

10. *In going through this exercise of appreciating yourself*

    — *your breathing, your body, your words, your actions*

    — *what comes up for you? Are you comfortable appreciating yourself or do you tell yourself that you shouldn't appreciate yourself? Take a moment to explore any thoughts of "I shouldn't" associated with self-appreciation.*

11. *As we end this exercise, consider one statement you would like to share with the group about your experience here.*

12. *When you are ready, open your eyes slowly, and look around the room. See if you can extend an attitude of appreciation toward each participant for having devoted this time to appreciating themselves.*

SHARING CIRCLE:

1. My name is _____ .

2. One statement about this exercise I would like to share is _____ .

SUGGESTIONS FOR PRACTICE IN DAILY LIFE:

1. Upon completion of a task, however minor, appreciate your accomplishment by naming the need you met and pausing to feel your feeling in your body.

2. If you notice reluctance to appreciate yourself, try expressing the appreciation as if you were addressing another person: "When I notice you doing _____ , I feel _____ because I value _____ ."

REFERENCE: Chapter 14

ACTIVITY 15.3

Giving Someone an Appreciation

PURPOSE OF ACTIVITY:

1. To practice the three components of an NVC appreciation

2. To practice receiving appreciation with an awareness of feelings and needs

BRIEF DESCRIPTION: Facilitator reminds participants of the three components used for expressing NVC appreciation. Participants apply these three components by writing an appreciation they would like to offer someone. They then work in pairs and express this appreciation orally to a partner who plays the role of the person whom they wish to appreciate. The latter practices fully receiving the appreciation by staying heart-connected through awareness of both parties' feelings and needs.

MATERIALS NEEDED:

- ❏ Paper and pen for each participant
- ❏ (Optional) Floor Map (See General Learning Aid G3)

TIME REQUIRED: 30–40 minutes

GROUP SIZE: Any

SPACE REQUIRED: Adequate for working in pairs

LITERACY LEVEL REQUIRED: Writing is included in the exercise, but those who wish may compose an appreciation in their heads without writing anything down.

PROCEDURE:

1. Remind participants of the three components of an NVC appreciation. You may use the following ditty:

    > I appreciate you
    > When I tell you true
    > How your act impacted on me.
    > - What you did or said,
    > - How I was fed,
    > - And the feeling I feel inside me.

    NOTE: Consider using the Floor Map to accompany this ditty:

    a. Stand on the piece labeled Observation on the Honesty part of the Floor Map while saying, "What you did or said."

b. Stand on Need and say, "How I was fed."

c. Stand on Feeling and say, "And the feeling I feel inside me."

2. Offer an appreciation to someone in the group using these three components.

Example: "Ali, when Josef came in after we had started, you moved over and invited him to sit next to you. I noticed that my eyes began to tear up, my mouth went into a smile and my shoulders relaxed. I had the sense of shared responsibility for the circle and I feel so grateful."

3. Invite participants to think of something someone did or said that they appreciate, and to write down (or compose in their heads) an appreciation which includes the following three components:

a. What the person did or said,

b. What you feel when you recall what they did or said (both your emotions and any physical sensations in the body), and

c. What need or value was met in you.

4. Tell participants that they will be choosing a partner to stand in for the person whom they wish to appreciate. Demonstrate this activity, using an appreciation that is personally meaningful to you. Example:

a. Choose a person and say: "Will you stand in for my Uncle Joe? I would like you to listen by offering me your full attention. See if you can hear what I am feeling and what need of mine is being gratified. You do not need to respond out loud."

b. Offer the appreciation: "Uncle Joe, remember the summer I turned ten and you took me to the big circus in the city? I still feel the joy of that because I really get how much you cared about my dream to see a real circus."

5. Ask the volunteer ("Uncle Joe" above) whether they are willing to assist you in demonstrating how to receive appreciation in a way that further deepens the joyful connection being made. If not, then demonstrate the NVC process of receiving appreciation, below, by playing both roles.

> *As a recipient of appreciation, instead of responding with "Oh, shucks, it was nothing," we can open to a joyful moment of gratitude by staying in heart connection. When receiving appreciation, we listen with our full attention, and may respond in the following manner:*
>
> • *We may reflect back the person's feelings and needs so they know their appreciation has been fully received.*

Example: "Wow, are you saying that 20 years later, when you think of our adventure in the big city, you're still feeling grateful . . . remembering that I cared about you and your big dream to see the circus?"

- *Express the feelings and needs that come up for you as you listen to their appreciation.*

Example: "I am just so awed and moved to hear how something I did—which was pure fun for me—has contributed to your happiness over so many years!"

As you may have noticed, these two responses correspond to the two parts of the NVC Model: (1) empathically receiving the other person's feelings and needs, and (2) honestly expressing our own feelings and needs. Please remember that when we receive someone, it is the quality of attention to their feelings and needs that makes for empathy—not the specific words we use.

6. Invite participants to choose a partner with whom they will be practicing offering and receiving appreciation. Give the following instructions:

   a. *Take turns role-playing, one person giving appreciation and the other receiving. When you role-play the recipient, please remember to:*

      (1) *listen with your full attention,*

      (2) *connect with the feelings and needs being expressed by the speaker,*

      (3) *choose whether or not to reflect back orally,*

      (4) *and then express the feelings and needs that come up for you as recipient of the appreciation.*

   b. *Take 5 minutes for each exchange.*

   c. *After you have completed both exchanges, come out of your roles and share your experiences and learning from this activity. How was it for you to offer appreciation in this way? How was it to be the recipient? You'll have 5 minutes to debrief with each other.*

7. After 15 minutes, reconvene the whole group and debrief.

DEBRIEF QUESTIONS:

1. What did you and your partner learn during your debrief that might benefit the rest of us?

2. What would support you to give and receive appreciation in real life in the manner we just practiced? What would hinder you?

3. Would it be easier for you to offer a written or an oral appreciation? Why?

SUGGESTION FOR PRACTICE IN DAILY LIFE: Write, phone, or see one person whom you would like to appreciate. Express your appreciation using the three NVC components we practiced. Be aware of your feelings before, during, and after you do this. What needs were met or not met at each stage?

REFERENCE: Chapter 14

ACTIVITY 15.4

What Keeps Us From Expressing Our Appreciation?

PURPOSE OF ACTIVITY: To explore what keeps us from expressing our appreciation

BRIEF DESCRIPTION: Participants bring to mind someone who did or said something they appreciate(d), but to whom they have yet to communicate this appreciation. Working individually and in small groups, participants explore if they are meeting a need by not expressing appreciation. They are encouraged to give voice to their appreciation and to practice verbalizing it while feeling the accompanying sensations in the body.

MATERIALS NEEDED:

- ☐ Individual Handout 15.4: What Keeps Me From Expressing My Appreciation?
- ☐ Writing implements and paper for all participants
- ☐ Flip chart or board would be helpful

TIME REQUIRED: 30 minutes

GROUP SIZE: Any size

SPACE REQUIRED: Adequate seating for all participants

LITERACY LEVEL REQUIRED: Basic reading and writing

PROCEDURE:

1. Review the three components of NVC appreciation:

    a. (Observation) What someone did or said

    b. (Feeling) How I feel about what they did or said

    c. (Need) The need in me that was met through their words or actions

2. Lead the whole group through the following process:

    a. *Bring to mind someone whose words or action you appreciate but to whom you have yet to express any appreciation.*

    b. *Imagine approaching this person and telling them (a) what they did or said that you appreciate, (b) how you feel about it, and (c) what need was met for you. Experiment with expressing these three components using language that is natural and authentic for you.*

c. As you imagine offering this appreciation, get in touch with your body sensations and any feelings that come up. Allow yourself to pause and feel this experience fully.

a. Write down the appreciation you just imagined offering.

b. Now ask yourself what keeps you from expressing appreciation to them? There may be several answers—jot them down.

a. Now I would like to ask three or four of you to briefly share your reasons for not voicing your appreciation. Your sharing may help the rest of us become more aware of what holds us back. [Write the reasons in abbreviated form on the board.]

b. Having jotted down your reason(s), go back and translate each one into need language. What need of yours are you trying to meet by not giving the appreciation?

a. Say the need words out loud so that I may record them on the board. [Write the need words on the board.]

3. Distribute the handout, "What Keeps Me From Expressing My Appreciation?" and ask participants to form groups of three or four.

4. Give the following instructions:

a. Read the handout and ask which item(s), if any, resonate with your own experience.

b. Explore and share with each other your thoughts as to why you may not express appreciation.

c. Name the need(s) that you may be trying to meet by not expressing appreciation. Notice any shift in energy (or release, such as laughter) as you name these needs for each other.

d. Finally, take turns reading the appreciation you had written earlier, choosing someone in the group as a surrogate for the person to whom you would like to express it.

DEBRIEF QUESTIONS:

1. What did you learn about what keeps you from expressing appreciation?

2. How would you like to apply what you have learned?

SUGGESTIONS FOR PRACTICE IN DAILY LIFE:

1. Offer someone appreciation. If you feel uncertain, consider writing down your appreciation before expressing it to the other person. Notice your own energy as you offer appreciation as well as the other person's energy as they receive it.

2. Use email as an opportunity to practice expressing written appreciation. Take time to pause and connect with yourself as you compose and send off an appreciation.

REFERENCE: Chapter 14

What Keeps Me From Expressing My Appreciation?

1. I fear the pain of not being able to express my appreciation clearly.

2. I fear the pain of not seeing my intention or words being received or understood.

3. I fear the pain of being viewed by others in ways I consider negative. For example, being viewed as:

   a. "manipulative," "fake," "insincere"

   b. "sentimental," "uncool"

   c. _____

4. I fear the pain of "falling apart" or "getting too emotional" when I try to express my appreciation.

5. I believe the other person already knows that I appreciate them.

6. I believe the other person is simply doing their job.

7. I believe that the other person either does not need or does not want my appreciation.

8. I believe that the other person expects or is eager for me to give appreciation (thus inclining me toward resistance).

9. I believe that the other person does not deserve appreciation due to some other behaviors I have seen in them.

10. I believe that appreciation might "spoil" or alter our relationship, making it less manageable (e.g., such that it requires more personal attention or calls on me to connect beyond roles and hierarchy).

11. I believe that talk is cheap and action is what counts.

12. I believe that verbalizing appreciation introduces formality and distance in close, familial relationships (by implying that words are needed to express what intimately-connected hearts naturally already share).

13. _____

ACTIVITY 15.5

A Secret Eye for Appreciation

PURPOSE OF ACTIVITY:

- To celebrate our capacity to contribute to each other's well-being

- To practice expressing appreciation in NVC

BRIEF DESCRIPTION: Each participant anonymously tracks another participant over the duration of the training. At the end of the period, the former expresses appreciation for something that the latter did or said. NOTE: Use this activity for groups that have opportunities to interact over an extended period, e.g. multi-day workshops, on-going courses, weekly practice groups, etc.

MATERIALS NEEDED:

- ❑ Name tags and markers for each day of the training
- ❑ A small piece of paper for each participant
- ❑ A basket or box
- ❑ Paper and writing instrument for each participant (optional for groups under twenty-five)

TIME REQUIRED:

- Several minutes to offer instructions at the beginning of a training and to offer reminders as needed.

- The amount of time required to share appreciation depends on the size of the group. Allot approximately 2 minutes for each person present. NOTE: for groups beyond twenty-five, give participants 10 minutes to write down their appreciation and another 20 for several volunteers in the large group to share the appreciation they received.

GROUP SIZE: Any

SPACE REQUIRED: No special space needed

LITERACY LEVEL REQUIRED: For groups numbering beyond twenty-five, reading and writing required

PROCEDURE:

1. Explain the purpose and process of this activity.

Often we tend to notice when our needs have not been met. We miss out on the appreciation and celebration we could be enjoying if we were also able to pay attention to how our needs are being met. For this activity, we will each anonymously track another person in the group, and our goal is to notice something this person says or does which addresses a need or value we hold dear. It could be something very small . . . something we usually may not notice, such as holding the door open for someone. . . . When we pay attention, we recognize that this small gesture can meet our need for consideration, respect, or caring. . . . We might realize that this little gesture and others like it indeed make our world a more beautiful place. At the end of our time together, there will be an opportunity to express what we noticed, what needs of ours are met, and how we feel about it.

2. Draw lots to determine who each person will be observing: ask each person to print their name on a piece of paper and fold it in four. Collect all the papers in a basket and pass the basket around for each person to draw one name. Encourage everyone to keep it a secret as to whom they would be observing.

   NOTE: For groups of people who don't know each other, ask each person to say their name before they draw from the basket. At the end, go around once more so that each person has an opportunity to silently identify the person whose name they have drawn. Make sure each person is wearing a name tag throughout the training.

3. Over the course of the training, remind participants to continue their secret observation, jotting down what they see or hear, and getting in touch with the needs that are met.

4. Toward the end of the training,

   - if it is a large group,
     i.   ask participants to write down their appreciation in the form of observations, feelings, and needs and give this to the person they have been observing.
     ii. Invite several people to read out loud to the group the appreciation they just received.
     iii. Then ask them, "How do you feel hearing this appreciation? What needs of yours are met or unmet?"

   - if the group is smaller than twenty-five,
     i.   ask participants to orally express their appreciation directly to the person they were tracking. Remind them to include their observation, need, and feeling.
     ii. Allow the listener to receive the appreciation fully and then ask them to reflect back the observation, feeling and need they heard in the speaker, e.g., "I hear you appreciate my saying to the group on the

second day that I was bored with this workshop. I hear that you felt relieved because it met your needs for honesty and openness."

iii. Now ask the same person to express what they feel and need as they hear the appreciation, e.g., "I'm feeling amused and also touched because I value being seen and accepted for who I am."

DEBRIEF QUESTIONS:

1. What was your experience in anonymously "tracking" another person in the group?

2. What was it like to offer appreciation?

3. What was it like to receive appreciation?

4. What did you learn?

SUGGESTIONS FOR PRACTICE IN DAILY LIFE:

1. Think of someone in your life with whom you are currently experiencing tension. Anonymously track this person for a predetermined length of time (e.g., a month), and see if you can find something over the course of each day (or each major interaction) to appreciate. Identify your observation, feeling, and need.

2. Identify one thing you appreciate on the first day of a month. On each successive day, challenge yourself to notice something or someone else to appreciate, matching the number of items to the day of the month (i.e., twenty items on the twentieth of the month). If you enjoy journaling, you can write your appreciation at the closing of each day. Remember to include observation, feeling, and need.

REFERENCE: Chapter 14

ACTIVITY 15.6

Receiving Appreciation

PURPOSE OF ACTIVITY: To practice receiving and acknowledging appreciation

BRIEF DESCRIPTION: Participants practice four elements in receiving and acknowledging appreciation. In Part I, they role-play in pairs using specific appreciation they would like to receive from someone in their lives. In Part II, volunteers from the group offer and receive real-time appreciation from each other.

MATERIALS NEEDED: None

TIME REQUIRED: 30–40 min

GROUP SIZE: Two or more

SPACE REQUIRED: Enough for individuals to move around and to seek partners with whom to pair off

LITERACY LEVEL REQUIRED: None

PROCEDURE:

Part I

1. Introduce the subject by asking participants: When someone offers you an appreciation what is your habitual response?

2. Introduce how NVC encourages us to receive appreciation.

When someone voices appreciation toward me:

    a. *I first pause and "breathe in" the appreciation, especially if I am feeling awkward, uncertain or resistant.*

    b. *I focus my attention to listen for three things:*

        i. *What I did or said,*

        ii. *What need of theirs was met as a result, and*

        i. *How they feel about their need being met in this way*

    c. *I acknowledge their appreciation by empathically reflecting back what I hear to be their:*

    (i) observation, (ii) need, and (iii) feeling.

    d. Finally, I may choose to express my own feeling and need in this moment.

3. Offer the following example followed by a second example of your own:

    Suppose someone says to me, "You did a great job listening when I was sharing." I might receive this appreciation in the following manner:

    a. I pause and take a breath.

    b. I listen for what they are observing, needing, and feeling.

    a. I acknowledge the appreciation out loud, expressing myself in either "classical" or "colloquial" NVC:

- *(Classical) "It sounds like just by my being present, listening and reflecting back, you felt more at ease to freely express what you had in mind? And are you feeling some relief right now?"*

- *(Colloquial) "Happy you got to speak your truth and be heard?"*

    b. After they receive this acknowledgment, I might share NVC honesty:

- *"I feel moved when I hear you say that because I really want to show up in a way that lets people express themselves freely. I am grateful you took time to give me that feedback."*

1. Give instructions for the activity:

    a. Take some time to think of two appreciations you would enjoy hearing from two different people. Using a piece of paper for each appreciation, write down:

- *From whom you would like to receive this appreciation. State their relationship to you, e.g., "father," "neighbor," "supervisor," etc.*

- *What you would like them to say to you. Write the words exactly as you would like to hear them.*

    Please write legibly so that others can read your writing.

    b. Find a partner, hand them one piece of paper, and ask them to address you in the following way:

- *"I am your [e.g., father, neighbor, supervisor, etc.]. There have been some words I've been wanting to say to you. [Partner reads the appreciation you wrote on paper.]."*

    c. Receive the appreciation using the steps demonstrated.

      i. Breathe in the appreciation.

    ii.   *Listen for the speaker's observation, need, and feeling.*

    i.   *Acknowledge the appreciation by reflecting back. (For this activity, please use "classical NVC.")*

    ii.   *(If desired:) Express your own feeling and need.*

a.   *After you and your partner have exchanged roles, and both of you have had a chance to practice, take a few moments to share your experience of receiving and acknowledging appreciation.*

b.   *Raise your hand to indicate that you are looking for a new partner to practice your second appreciation.*

c.   *Let's take a couple of minutes to quietly write down our two appreciations. We'll then work with partners for about 15 minutes.*

Part 2

1.   Ask participants if anyone has an appreciation they would like to offer to someone in the room. If someone volunteers, have them ask the person they have in mind whether they are willing to receive the appreciation.

2.   If both are willing, invite them to give and receive appreciation in the presence of the group.

3.   Offer this opportunity to additional pairs of volunteers as long as the group seems to be learning and valuing the witnessing of this giving and receiving of appreciation.

DEBRIEF QUESTIONS:

1.   What do you consider to be the key elements to receiving an appreciation?

2.   Which of these elements are you most comfortable or uncomfortable with?

3.   Have you gained anything from this activity that you would apply in life?

4.   What would impede you from receiving appreciation in the way we practiced today?

SUGGESTION FOR PRACTICE IN DAILY LIFE: When hearing an appreciation, focus on the other person and guess what is alive for them in that moment.

REFERENCE: Chapter 14

ANGER

16.1 Awareness Exercise:
     Cherishing the Need Behind
     Our Anger

16.2 Activity: Stimulus or Cause

16.3 Activity: SSSTOP

16.4 Activity: Powergrounding

16.5 Activity: Anger Poker

Anger

Description: NVC stresses that anger is caused by a certain type of thinking. We get angry when we think that someone (or something) should or should not be or behave the way they are being or behaving. This kind of thinking alienates us from our own needs. Furthermore, anger prompts a desire to punish, often propelling us to make choices that are not likely to contribute to our needs being met. NVC suggests a series of steps to transform anger and to reconnect to our own needs:

- Stop, breathe, and feel the experience of anger in the body

- Identify the stimulus of the anger—what was actually observed, free of evaluation

- Identify the "should-thinking" that is the cause of the anger

- Translate the "should-thinking" into needs

- Open to the feelings that come up when we connect to the unmet needs

- Present a clear request to address any unmet needs

Toolkit exercises in this section, in addition to focusing on each of the above steps, also provide practice in approaching the other "expensive emotions" of guilt, shame, and depression.

Tips for Facilitators: Let participants know the value of anger. Anger reminds us that we have a precious unmet need. Its job, like that of an alarm clock, is to wake us up. When we wake up to the need that is being thwarted, anger has done its job and is no longer needed. Once we connect with our need, anger usually diminishes on its own unless our minds return to focusing on thoughts about the situation, in which case anger is regenerated and can grow and grow to gobble up our energy and peace of mind. Emphasize that we have a choice as to where we choose to focus our energy and attention: on our needs or on thoughts of what should (or should not) be.

AWARENESS EXERCISE 16.1

Cherishing the Need Behind Our Anger

[NOTE: For this Awareness Exercise, provide paper and pen for participants who wish to jot down fleeting thoughts.]

INSTRUCTIONS FOR GUIDING AWARENESS EXERCISE: Read the following slowly, leaving space between each statement for the participant to engage in the guided process.

1. *Sit comfortably. Straighten your spine. Make any necessary adjustments.*

2. *Focus your attention inward by closing your eyes or gently dropping your gaze to the floor in front of you.*

3. *Bring your attention to your breathing.*

4. *Try letting go when you breathe out. When you breathe in, see if you can receive with ease, without straining.*

    a. *On each exhalation, experiment with letting go. Without pushing the breath out, simply release until your lungs feel comfortably empty.*

    b. *On each inhalation, experiment with receiving. Without reaching and grasping, simply accept the breath of life until your lungs are comfortably full.*

    c. *Notice the sensation of breathing as you effortlessly receive on the in-breath and effortlessly let go on the out-breath.*

    d. *How do you feel now as you breathe, receiving and releasing, receiving and releasing . . .?*

5. *Now bring to mind a situation around which you feel angry.* (20 seconds)

6. *Feel your body sensations.*

    a. *Notice if anything is happening to your muscles as you think of this situation; notice the muscles in your jaw, neck, chest, gut, shoulders . . .*

    b. *Notice any changes in your breathing.*

    c. *Notice these changes with curiosity, without judging. And if you do judge yourself or the changes in your body, can you simply notice that? Simply notice that you are judging?*

7. Now go back and think about the situation that brings up anger for you. What are you saying to yourself about the situation, about yourself, or about the other party? (If you wish, jot down the thoughts as they arise.) [30 seconds]

8. Say this sentence to yourself: "These thoughts are the cause of my anger." [Facilitator, read this sentence twice.]

9. Now ask yourself: "What need in me is being thwarted here? What do I need or value in this situation? What is my unmet need?"

   When you become aware of the need and when you experience a sense of clarity that this indeed is what you yearn for, open yourself to receiving it—the same way you received life breath a few minutes ago. Receive it, hold it, value it, and see its beauty.

10. Once again, go inside your body and notice any changes in your muscles or in your breathing. Simply notice without judging, either favorably or unfavorably, whatever changes or physical sensations there are.

11. In the next 2 minutes, take time to enjoy your breath—breathing in and receiving, breathing out and letting go—all the while holding in your heart the need you so deeply value.

SHARING CIRCLE: Give the following instructions:

1. For this Sharing Circle, you will each have a turn to say your name and the need you are holding. When you have spoken these two words, please pause and look around the circle.

2. While you do this, the rest of us will receive you with our full presence. As we listen and receive your words, we will silently repeat them to ourselves: your name and the need you are holding.

3. Open yourself to the experience of being fully received in the circle.

4. When you are ready, nod to the person on your left to signal that you are complete and to invite their turn.

5. Let's each take 5 to 10 seconds.

6. I'll start. [Model the procedure by taking the first turn.]

   NOTE: As facilitator, you probably did not do the exercise yourself, so simply say your name and a need that is being met or unmet for you in the moment.

REFERENCE: Chapter 10

ACTIVITY 16.2

Stimulus or Cause?

PURPOSE OF ACTIVITY:

1. To recognize that the cause of anger lies in our thinking

2. To learn to distinguish stimulus from cause of anger

BRIEF DESCRIPTION: Groups of five to ten participants sit in a circle around a table or on the floor. Each participant holds a "slap card" with the word "Stimulus" on one side and "Cause" on the other. One person reads or makes up a statement and challenges the group with the question, "Stimulus or Cause?" The rest of the group responds in unison by slapping their card down to reveal their choice of either "Stimulus" or "Cause." If all cards are in agreement, the group goes on to the next statement. Otherwise, each person has an opportunity to explain their reasoning, starting with those whose choice is in the minority. Anyone may flip their card over at any time if they change their mind upon hearing other people's reasoning. When all cards are in agreement, a new round begins.

MATERIALS NEEDED:

☐ For each participant: "Slap Card" (See Specific Learning Aid 16.2: Slap Cards)

☐ For each group: Group Handout 16.2 Stimulus or Cause? (Use 16.2A for prison and 16.2B for general community.)

TIME REQUIRED: 20–30 minutes

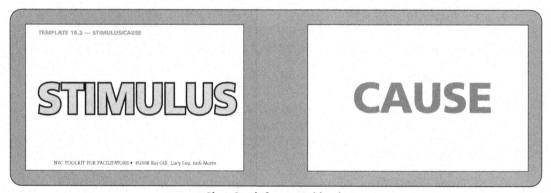

Slap Card, front and back

GROUP SIZE: Minimum five

SPACE REQUIRED:

*   Large flat surface: groups need either to be sitting at a table or on the floor

*   Size of room needs to be large enough for groups to engage without mutual interference

LITERACY LEVEL REQUIRED: Sentence-level reading

PROCEDURE:

1. Ask the question, "What makes us angry?" using a story from your own life or the following example. Review the NVC distinction between "cause" and "stimulus" of anger.

   Example:

   > *I was wearing my new white shoes. As I stepped off the bus, two teenage boys, laughing and slapping each other, dashed past me. One of them tripped over my foot and left a dirty scuff mark on my left shoe. When I looked at it, I felt angry. I thought: "These guys shouldn't be running and fooling around on the sidewalk. They should be more respectful in public space." Later on the same day, I was helping an elderly patient get into a wheelchair when he lost balance, stepped on me, and left a dirty scuff mark on my other shoe. When I looked down, I felt disappointed. I would like to have been able to enjoy the beauty of my new shoes today.*

   > *Even though the stimulus in both instances was a dirty scuff mark on my shoe, I was angry in the first instance but not in the second. Why? In the first instance I had thoughts about what "should" or "should not" happen. The cause of my anger is the thought: "These guys shouldn't be running and fooling around on the sidewalk. They should be more respectful in public space."*

   > *I was not angry in the second instance because I had no "should-thinking" going on in my head.*

2. Group Practice

   When you are satisfied that participants have grasped the concept of "stimulus vs. cause," offer the following instructions for the activity:

   a. *For this activity, you will form groups of about half a dozen people.*

   b. *You will each get a "slap card." One side reads "Stimulus" and the other "Cause."*

   c. *Each group will receive a handout with a list of statements. Take turns reading a statement from the handout. Then ask the question, "Stimulus or Cause?"*

   d. *The rest of you in the group, as you listen to the statement, determine whether this statement is expressing the "stimulus" or the "cause" of the speaker's anger.*

e. When you hear the question "Stimulus or Cause?" everybody, slap your card down on the table or floor so that the word you chose is facing up.

f. Take a look at all the cards on the surface.

g. Are they all in agreement? If so, go on to the next statement.

h. If not all cards agree, listen to one another's reasons for the choices that were made. Start with those who chose in the minority.

i. At any moment, while listening to one another's reasoning, anyone may flip their card over to the other side.

j. When all cards are in agreement, move on to the next statement.

k. There may be occasions when you cannot come to agreement. What's important is that you understand one another's reasoning before moving on.

l. You are welcome to make up your own statement instead of reading one from the handout. When delivering a statement, remember to use an angry tone.

m. Once you get the hang of it, try doing this activity at a clipped pace.

n. You'll have 15–20 minutes.

3. Demonstrate by making one or two statements and slapping down your card after the question, "Stimulus or Cause?" Form groups of five to ten members, and make sure there is adequate floor or table space for each group. Pass out Slap Cards and Handout.

DEBRIEF QUESTIONS:

1. What is the advantage of differentiating stimulus from cause of anger?

2. How do you know whether you are identifying a stimulus or the thoughts which are causing your anger?

3. Describe any disagreements your group encountered in determining whether a statement was "stimulus" or "cause."

SUGGESTION FOR PRACTICE IN DAILY LIFE: When you feel angry, write down all your angry thoughts on the left side of a piece of paper. Then on the right side, articulate the stimulus (or stimuli) for your anger, using observations free of evaluation.

REFERENCE: Chapter 10

Anger—Stimulus or Cause? PRISON

Take turns reading the statements given below or make up your own statement when your turn comes up. Imagine that the speaker of the statement is angry. After you make the statement, challenge your group by asking, "Stimulus or Cause?"

Others in the group now slap down their card, choosing to show either:

- **STIMULUS** of anger (an NVC *observation*—what we see or hear without any evaluation), or

- **CAUSE** of anger (thinking that implies that someone—or something—*should or should not* have behaved a certain way, i.e., was wrong in some way or another.)

1. He was looking at me and said, "Fatso."

2. He is trying to put me down.

3. You blame other people for your own problems.

4. The officer spoke to me loudly—at a volume I am not used to hearing.

5. The officer was yelling at me like I was deaf or something.

6. My cell mate is stealing cigarettes from me and thinks he can get away with it.

7. My cigarettes are not at my house where I had left them.

8. Good mothers don't hit children.

9. Your last visit here was over a month ago.

10. You just spilled coffee on the floor.

11. I sent a kite three weeks ago and they ignored me.

12. You are being careless with your coffee.

13. You haven't bothered to visit me for over a month.

14. I saw her hit the child on the head more than five times.

15. The parole board should have asked what I am currently doing to improve myself.

16. The parole board did not ask what I am currently doing to improve myself.

17. She didn't even say hello to me when she arrived.

18. I heard him say, "I'm better off than the rest of you."

19. He thinks he is better off than the rest of us.

20. My boss just went off and gave my job away to someone else.

21. My boss said he would like someone else to take over the job I had been doing.

22. My request for a trailer visit was denied.

23. They're making me look bad.

24. I sent a kite three weeks ago and have not received a reply.

25. They asked so many questions that they made me miss dinner.

Anger—Stimulus or Cause? GENERAL COMMUNITY

Take turns reading the statements given below or make up your own statement when your turn comes up. Imagine that the speaker of the statement is angry. After you make the statement, challenge your group by asking, "Stimulus or Cause?"

Others in the group now slap down their card so that it shows either:

- **STIMULUS** (an NVC *observation*—what we see or hear without any evaluation), or

- **CAUSE** (thinking that implies that someone—or something—*should or should not* have behaved a certain way, i.e., was wrong in some way or another.)

1. She was looking at me and said, "Some people just don't know how to look after themselves."

2. She was judging me for not taking care of myself.

3. My friend Mia spoke to me loudly—at a volume I am not used to hearing.

4. Today I heard you say: "The doctor was rude to me. He is always putting me down." Yesterday I heard you say, "People in helping professions are so abusive."

5. You tend to blame others for your own problems.

6. My son thinks he can get away with stealing cookies from the cookie jar.

7. I put two dozen cookies in the jar this morning and now there are twenty.

8. People who hit their children are not worthy of being parents.

9. She pulled the crying child off the floor and hit him on the head at least five times.

10. You just spilled coffee on the carpet.

11. My friend, whose brain was damaged at birth, came home last week with a cell phone plan she now says she can't pay for.

12. You are careless with your coffee.

13. My brother hardly bothers to visit our mother since she moved to a care home.

14. My brother has visited my mother twice since she moved to a care home a year ago.

15. You take so much air time other people don't have a chance to express themselves.

16. I heard him say, "I'm better off than the rest of you."

17. My boss just went off and gave my job away to someone else.

18. My boss said he would like someone else to take over the job I had been doing.

19. I heard you use this phrase several times while talking with me today: "Do you feel _____ because you need _____?"

20. We're being cheated of our rights.

21. You're getting all worked up again!

22. The muscles over your lips are tight, your brow is furrowed and you are sweeping the floor faster and with more energy than I would expect.

23. You keep repeating, "Do you feel _____ because you need _____?"

24. You people just don't understand me.

25. I gave you a $20 bill for this postcard and you're giving me 43 cents in change.

ACTIVITY 16.3
SSSTOP

PURPOSE OF ACTIVITY:

1. To understand the cause of anger

2. To practice a process for diminishing anger without suppressing it

3. To learn to connect with the feelings and unmet needs that lie beneath anger

BRIEF DESCRIPTION: The facilitator introduces the use of a flowchart on the floor to guide participants through the steps of "expressing anger fully" in NVC. After they have learned the steps, participants each receive a handout of the flowchart to work through a personal situation in a small group and then on their own.

MATERIALS NEEDED:

☐ Specific Learning Aid 16.3: SSSTOP Flowchart (two sets) NOTE: Refer to photo on how to arrange one set on the wall and the other on the floor.

☐ Individual Handout 16.3: SSSTOP

☐ General Learning Aid G1: Learning Guide (one per person)

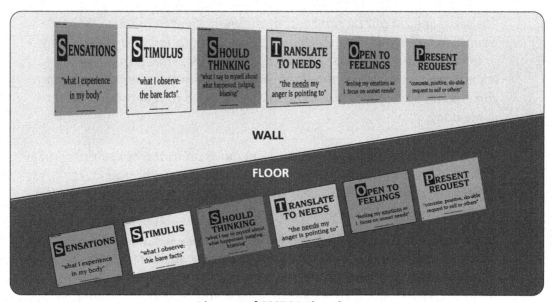

Diagram of SSSTOP Flowchart

TIME REQUIRED: 80 minutes

GROUP SIZE: Any

SPACE REQUIRED: Adequate for groups of four to work without mutual interference

LITERACY LEVEL REQUIRED: Minimal

PROCEDURE:

Part 1—Explanation of the SSSTOP Flowchart Steps

1. Place one SSSTOP Flowchart horizontally across the wall in front of which you will be standing, about a foot above your head. (See photo on previous page.) Arrange the pieces from left to right (S-S-S-T-O-P), leaving a foot of space between pieces. Place another flowchart on the floor directly in front of you such that the pieces are aligned with the ones on the wall.

2. Point to the flowchart on the wall and the word it spells "S-S-STOP"

   > *As soon as I become aware of anger, I remember to STOP. I stop and breathe.* [Demonstrate]

3. Stand on the first piece of the chart: SENSATIONS

   > *The first and very important step to prevent myself from being hijacked or swept away by the force of anger is to come home. I do this by simply bringing my consciousness into my body and feeling my physical sensations.* [Close your eyes to demonstrate how you might bring your attention inward.] *The sensations might be tightness in the chest, heat in the face, a pounding heartbeat, constriction in throat, a sensation of urgency in my arm to strike out, shortness of breath, palpitation, vibration, tingling . . . It's not important to find the right words to name these sensations; I can come home by simply allowing myself some space to feel the sensations in my body.*

   > 4. *When I am back home in the body, I can move on to the next step: STIMULUS.* [Take a step sideways to stand on the next piece of the flowchart.] *STIMULUS refers to what actually or factually occurred that triggered the anger. We state the stimulus in the form of an NVC observation.*

   > 5. *The third S refers to SHOULD-THINKING.* [Step on the next piece of the chart.] *This is the cause of our anger. Anger is caused by our thinking that someone (or something) should (or should not) be or behave the way they are. We identify our should-thinking and articulate our thoughts of judgment, blame, and criticism in order to clearly see the cause of our anger.*

   > 6. *The next step is T for Translate.* [Step on the next piece of the chart.] *We translate our should-thinking by listening closely to each blaming thought and hearing the need it is pointing to. There may be many layers of needs, but each time we touch a need, we pause to own it, experience it, and acknowledge its value.*

7. *The next step is O: Open to feelings.* [Step on next piece of flowchart.] *As we touch our unmet needs, we will encounter feelings that have been hidden under our anger. We encourage ourselves to open up to whatever emotions might come up in this process of transforming anger. You may want to use your Learning Guide to identify the feeling you are experiencing.*

8. *"Expressing anger fully" in NVC requires courage and strength of heart and mind. It is not a linear process. For example,* [Continue standing on O: Open to Feelings]

   - *As I open to certain feelings, other thoughts might come up* [Step back to "S:Should-Thinking" on the flowchart]

   - *which I may then want to translate* [Step to "T:Translate to Need"],

   - *or I might recall another incident* [Step to S:Stimulus]

   - *and be overwhelmed by a rush of feelings that remind me to ground myself once again in my body* [Step to S:Sensation].

   - *Sometimes I may have one foot here* [Keep one foot on S:Sensation]

   - *and one foot here* [Stretch to place other foot on O:Open to Feelings], *but as long as I stay within SSSTOP,*

   - *I trust that I will eventually get clarity to move forward in meeting my needs.* [Step onto P:Present Request on the flowchart.]

9. *P stands for PRESENT REQUEST—a request presented in concrete, positive language which invites an immediate response. The request may be to yourself or to another person, and may be a request for connection to dialogue about the situation at hand.*

Part II—Demonstration and Practice

1. Ask a participant to volunteer a situation they would like to use to demonstrate the steps of the flowchart.

2. Guide the volunteer through the process, inviting them to stand on the piece of the flowchart that corresponds to each step. (If no one volunteers, use a personal or hypothetical example to illustrate the process.)

3. Ask if there are any questions regarding the steps of the flowchart. When there are no more questions, give participants a couple of minutes of silence to recall times in their lives when they have felt angry.

4. Distribute the handout and divide participants into groups of four.

5. Instruct participants to take turns using the flowchart to work through a personal experience of anger. Suggest that they take about 10 minutes per person, asking for support and feedback from the group if desired.

6. Reconvene the whole group for participants to share questions and insights generated during the small-group practice.

7. Provide another 10 minutes for participants to practice individually, using the flowchart to work through a different angry situation they have experienced.

DEBRIEF QUESTIONS:

1. Did you learn anything about your own anger through this exercise?

2. What feelings were you able to touch beneath your anger?

3. Name some circumstances in your life where you can easily imagine yourself applying the SSSTOP process. What are some circumstances where you might experience reluctance or resistance in using SSSTOP?

4. What would support you in using SSSTOP the next time you find yourself angry? Be as specific as possible.

SUGGESTIONS FOR PRACTICE IN DAILY LIFE:

1. Next time you find yourself angry, stop, breathe, and name your unmet need. Take back your power by making one move toward meeting that need.

2. Keep an Anger Journal. For each instance of anger, write out the six pieces you have learned through SSSTOP: S (Sensation), S (Stimulus), S (Should-Thinking), T (Translate to Needs), O (Open to Feelings), and P (Present Request). After many entries, see if you detect any patterns in your anger history. For example, are there repetitions of certain stimuli, needs or feelings?

REFERENCE: Chapter 10

SSSTOP

S SENSATIONS

Physical **sensations** in the body, e.g. heat, tightness, tingling, heaviness . . .

S STIMULUS

What actually or **factually** happened? Observation without evaluation

S SHOULD THINKING

Cause of anger: Thinking that someone or something **should** or **should not** be or behave in a certain way. This can take the form of judgment, blame, criticism ...

CUT ALONG DOTTED LINE TO LAY THE 6 PIECES OF "SSSTOP" IN ONE STRAIGHT LINE

T TRANSLATE TO NEEDS

Translate "should-thinking" by hearing the unfulfilled **need(s)** beneath it.

O OPEN TO FEELINGS

Open to **emotions** that come up when we touch our unmet needs, e.g. feelings of fear, hurt, shame, sorrow, despair ...

P PRESENT REQUEST

Making a present **request** in concrete, positive language moves us towards meeting the need beneath our anger

ACTIVITY 16.4

Powergrounding

PURPOSE OF ACTIVITY: To learn a way to protect ourselves from being hijacked by anger

BRIEF DESCRIPTION: Powergrounding is a 30-second technique consisting of six conscious breaths. During the last three breaths, participants focus attention on physical sensations—first in the face, then neck and shoulders, and finally chest and belly. In this activity participants are invited to practice powergrounding in a variety of situations, ranging from stimulus-free silence to confrontational "in-your-face" provocation.

NOTE: As much as possible, introduce this activity early in the course of a workshop or training so there is opportunity for repeated practice throughout the remainder of the group's time together.

MATERIALS NEEDED:
- ❑ Board or flipchart
- ❑ Timer (or watch with second hand)
- ❑ Optional: bell

TIME REQUIRED:

- Initial session: 30 minutes, including debrief

- Practice (to be interspersed throughout the training): 30 seconds each time

- Review at the end of the training: 5 minutes

GROUP SIZE: Any

SPACE REQUIRED: Space to sit, stand, and mill around

LITERACY LEVEL REQUIRED: None

PROCEDURE:

1. Explain the purpose and process of powergrounding:

   a. *NVC offers a series of steps allowing us to translate anger into an awareness of underlying needs. Once aware of our own needs, we have choice as to how to meet them.*

   b. *The nature of anger is such, however, that often it sweeps us off our feet. Before we are able to focus on the NVC steps to translate anger,*

we may already have acted out in ways we would later regret.
[Give example, preferably from your own life.]

    c.   *How do we ground ourselves so we are not swept away, but can effectively engage the NVC process that empowers us to meet our needs beneath the anger? [Optional: solicit responses from participants.]*

    d.   *Powergrounding is a simple 30-second technique that we can use anytime anywhere to protect us from being hijacked by anger. It consists of taking six conscious breaths, focusing on bodily sensations in the fourth, fifth, and sixth breaths. [Let's try it together now.]*

2.   Guide participants through the process of powergrounding. Use your own breathing to measure the pause between steps.

    a.   *Let's take a moment and find a comfortable seated posture. Bring your attention inward. You may want to close your eyes.*

    b.   *Take three breaths, being aware that you are breathing. [Pause.]*

    c.   *On the fourth breath, imagine breathing into your face. Feel the face.*

    d.   *On the fifth breath, breathe into your neck and shoulders. Feel the sensations in the neck and shoulders.*

    e.   *On the final breath, breathe into your chest and belly. Feel the sensations in your chest and belly.*

3.   Repeat the instructions with different wording:

    a.   *We'll do this once again, so you can remember the steps on your own.*

    b.   *Get comfortable, close your eyes, and take three conscious breaths. [Pause.]*

    c.   *On the fourth inhalation, bring the breath into your face. As you exhale, feel the face.*

    d.   *On the fifth breath, inhale into the neck and shoulders. As you breathe out, feel the sensations in the neck and shoulder area.*

    e.   *Now breathe into your chest and belly. As you exhale, feel what it feels like in the chest and belly.*

4.   Check for questions regarding the six breaths. Write the sequence on the board or flipchart:

    a. First
    b. Second
    c. Third

d. Fourth—face

e. Fifth—neck and shoulders

f. Sixth—chest and belly

5. Ask participants to memorize the sequence, and if desired, guide them through it one more time. Then allow a minute of silence for participants to practice the six breaths at their own speed without cues from you. (Leave the information on the board.)

6. Explain that you'll now be offering a series of different situations for them to practice using the same six breaths. Inform participants that they will have one minute to practice powergrounding for each situation, and to keep repeating the sequence of six breaths until the minute is up. (If a bell is available, use it at the end of each situation to signal the transition to the next situation.)

a. *Situation #1. Get your body into a cramped, uncomfortable position. Now powerground.*

b. *Situation #2. This time sit up straight, open your eyes wide, and powerground.*

c. *Situation #3. Stand up with eyes open and powerground.*

d. *Situation #4. Still standing, powerground while moving your neck and head slowly.*

e. *Situation #5. Powerground while moving your body—arms, legs, torso . . .*

f. *Situation #6. Now walk around the room without looking at other people while you powerground.*

g. *Situation #7. This time, powerground while walking and looking at other people.*

h. *Situation #8. Now find a partner and stand in front of each other. (If numbers are not even, have one group of three facing one another in a triangle.) Powerground without looking at each other.*

i. *Situation #9. Close your eyes for a moment. . . . Now open your eyes and look intently at your partner while you practice powergrounding.*

j. *Assign roles to partners (in preparation for Situation #11): Before we move on, I'd like for you and your partner to decide who will be A and who will be B for a situation that will come later. Would all A's please raise their hand? Thank you.*

k. *Situation #10. Now, close your eyes again. Bring to mind someone toward whom you feel angry. [15-second pause] Does everyone have someone in mind? Good. Now imagine that this person is standing in front of you in this moment as you open your eyes and powerground in their presence.*

l. Situation #11A.

  i. *Close your eyes. This time, as you recall the person toward whom you feel angry, take a few moments to imagine the words and gestures they might use that would most trigger you. [20 seconds]*

  ii. *Open your eyes. Partner A, using just a few words, tell B how they can role-play the person in a way that would be most effective in triggering you. What words or gestures might they use? It can be short because what your partner will be doing is to repeat the same trigger over and over again to provoke you. [Allow 20 seconds for A to tell B what to say or do.] Partner B, if A is unable to come up with any words or gesture, simply use your creativity to work on unsettling them. For example, try insulting, sneering, getting up close, blowing smoke in their face, etc. Let's close our eyes and pause for just a second before beginning.*

  iii. *Now begin. Partner B, behave in a way that is likely to trigger your partner. Partner A, imagine this to be the person you're angry with and powerground for 1 minute.*

m. Situation #11B

  i. *Stop, close your eyes and take a moment here to simply breathe.*

  ii. *Now we'll reverse the situation. Partner B, take a few moments to instruct A on what they might say or do to effectively trigger you. [20 seconds]*

  iii. *Close your eyes for a moment. . . . Okay, now begin. Partner A, try to unsettle your partner. Partner B, imagine this to be the person you're angry with and powerground for 1 minute.*

n. Situation #12

  Now take a moment to thank your partner and return to your seats.

  i. *Close your eyes and recall someone or something you're angry about. [It can be the same situation you role-played earlier or a different one.]*

  ii. *Keep thinking about this situation and how angry you feel about it. [45 seconds]*

  iii. *Stop! Stop thinking and powerground. [1 minute]*

  iv. *Check in to see where you are right now in relationship to the angry thoughts and feelings you had conjured up earlier.*

7. Debrief, inviting participants to share experiences or use the questions given below ("Debrief Questions").

8. Emphasize that powergrounding:

   a. May be used anywhere and anytime (as long as 30 seconds are available): waking up in the morning, driving, waiting in line, before we start an important conversation, walking, showering, when we notice something pleasurable, when we notice something painful, when we go to bed . . .

   b. Becomes increasingly "fail-proof" in "emergencies" the more often it is practiced on a daily basis.

9. Offer as many opportunities as possible to practice powergrounding during the remainder of the training period. Simply say "Powerground!" and take a 30-second pause.

10. Reserve 5 minutes toward the end of the training period to powerground once again. Encourage participants to come up with creative ways and places to introduce this practice into their daily lives. Review "Suggestions for Practice in Daily Life" (below).

DEBRIEF QUESTIONS:

1. Which of the situations in the series we practiced was easy or difficult for you? Describe how and when you felt comfortable or uncomfortable powergrounding.

2. What did you discover in the experience of consciously stopping, breathing, and connecting with your body?

3. Would you like to apply this practice in your daily life? If so, what would support you in or prevent you from incorporating it successfully?

SUGGESTIONS FOR PRACTICE IN DAILY LIFE:

1. Review a routine day in your mind and identify several spots where you would like to practice powergrounding. To develop powergrounding into a daily habit, articulate your intention every morning for two weeks and check in with yourself at the end of each day.

2. Identify stressful situations that you encounter frequently in a week (day, or month). Powerground as you mentally focus on one of these situations. Resolve to powerground each time you approach this situation.

3. Practice powergrounding in a beautiful setting or when you are feeling peaceful. Take time to feel pleasure, comfort, or delight in the experience of connecting with your breath and body sensations.

4. In the midst of a difficult interaction with someone, pause to powerground. You might tell the other party, "I'm taking 30 seconds to ground (collect, or center) myself." Do this as often as necessary. You may find that simply slowing down the dialogue allows both of you to feel more spacious.

REFERENCE: Chapter 10

ACTIVITY 16.5
Anger Poker

PURPOSE OF ACTIVITY:

1. To practice distinguishing cause of anger from its stimulus

2. To practice identifying needs underlying anger

3. To practice empathy

BRIEF DESCRIPTION: This activity is similar to Empathy Poker (Activity#11.4) and is played in small groups. Instead of a stack of feeling words to choose from, the central player uses three cue cards to state:

(a) their anger,

(b) the stimulus they observed, and

(c) the cause of their anger (i.e., their "should-thinking").

Others in the group take turns offering need cards to identify possible unmet needs beneath the central player's anger.

MATERIALS NEEDED—For each group of five to seven players:
- ❑ Group Handout 16.5: Anger Poker Dealer Instructions
- ❑ General Learning Aid G8: Set of Need Cards
- ❑ Specific Learning Aid 16.5: Set of Anger Poker Cue Cards
- ❑ Optional: post-it sticky notes

TIME REQUIRED: 45–60 minutes

GROUP SIZE: Ideally six participants to each small group (seven is acceptable, or possibly five)

SPACE REQUIRED: Each group needs a flat surface for players to lay out their cards. Ideally, the group would be clustered around a table. Sitting in a circle on a comfortable floor would also work. Groups sitting in chairs might improvise by placing a flat surface (e.g. poster board) of at least a square yard or meter on their laps. The room needs to be large enough for each group to have its own space.

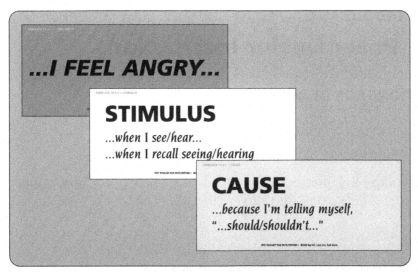

Set of Anger Poker Cue Cards

LITERACY LEVEL REQUIRED: All participants need to be able to recognize single words representing needs. At least one participant in each small group needs to be able to read the Dealer Instructions.

PROCEDURE:

1. Familiarize yourself with this activity using the following resources:
   - Group Handout 16.5: Anger Poker Dealer Instructions (see next page)
   - Instructional Video Clip of Activity 11.4: Empathy Poker
   - Instructional Video Clip "Facilitating an NVC Circle," which includes a presentation of Anger Poker

2. Demonstrate the game and make certain everyone is clear on how it is played before dividing the room into small groups of five to seven participants each.

3. Ask each group to choose a "dealer" for their first round. Give each dealer:
   - A set of Need Cards
   - A set of Cue Cards
   - A copy of Group Handout 16.5: Anger Poker Dealer Instructions
   - Post-it sticky notes (if available)

4. Allow a minimum of 45 minutes or up to 2 hours for groups to engage in this activity.

5. Reconvene participants for debrief, asking them to share what they learned, enjoyed, or found difficult.

REFERENCE: Chapter 10

Anger Poker Dealer Instructions

INSTRUCTIONS FOR DEALER

1. Encourage the group to select a "player" for this round. The player will be sharing an angry experience.

2. Give the player the three cue cards. Deal the deck of need cards evenly to everyone else (including yourself, the dealer).

3. Instruct the player:

    -   *Recall a situation where you feel or felt anger.*

    -   *Pick a cue card, read it out loud and fill in the phrase that would complete the card. Then place the card down in front of you. You may read cue cards in any order you wish.*

4. Instruct the group:

    -   *Let's take a look at our hands. Are we holding any needs that we sense the player might want to connect to in this situation?*

    -   *We'll take turns, each offering a need card to the player. I'll go first.*

5. Offer a need card to the player, using the phrase, "player, when you are angry because you tell yourself that . . . abc . . . should/shouldn't . . . xyz . . . are you needing [need word on card]?"

    NOTE: Consider adding a phrase after you name the universal need to help connect to the situation at hand. For example, look at the italicized phrase below after the speaker offered "trust" as the need: "John, when you are angry because you tell yourself that your room-mate is a liar, are you needing trust—*to be able to count on the people around you*?"

6. When you have completed your statement, place the card down near the player. Request that the player NOT respond out loud while group members are offering their need cards.

7. Group members continue offering need words that might support the player in connecting to their heart. They skip their turn when they've run out of cards to offer.

8. There are two "wild (blank) cards" in each deck. After people have run out of cards to offer, those holding wild cards may assign any universal "need" they wish to the wild cards and offer them to the player. (If available, use a post-it sticky note to write the need word on the wild card.)

9. Give the player a moment to look at all the needs spread out in front of them. Instruct the player: "Now—one at a time—pick the needs which resonate with you. Whenever you reach for a card please say, "Yes, I need... [followed by word on the card]."Encourage the player to add a phrase if it helps them connect to the universal need. (Example: Instead of "Yes, I need community," the player might add, "Yes, I need community—people who share my ideals and care about me.")

10. After the player has completed picking up all the cards they want, ask them: "Have you connected to all your needs in this situation? Are there other needs that have not been mentioned?" Encourage the player and others to briefly share what they learned from this round.

11. To begin the next round, ask the person who was the player to assume the role of dealer. The group will now select a new player.

MOURNING AND FORGIVENESS

17.1   Awareness Exercise: Mourning and Forgiveness

17.2   Activity: Healing a Childhood Memory

17.3   Activity: Oops

KEY CONCEPT 17:

Mourning and Forgiveness

Description: When we make mistakes, do or say things we wish we hadn't, we often judge ourselves and feel shame, guilt, or anger toward ourselves. NVC offers a compassionate and productive process to relate to our mistakes—one that fosters our ability to learn and grow from past mistakes and allows us to experience regret without blaming or hating ourselves. We explore the following questions during the NVC process of mourning and self-forgiveness:

- What did I do or say which I now wish I hadn't?

- What thoughts do I have of myself for having done or said that?

- What do these thoughts indicate about my present needs, i.e., what needs of mine are not met from having done or said that?

- What feelings come up for me when I sit with these needs?

- What need was I trying to meet when I did or said what I did?

- Given my current awareness of both sets of needs—my present needs as well as the needs I was trying to meet at that time—how might I have chosen differently, or how would I choose differently in a future situation?

Toolkit exercises in this section offer participants practice in applying the NVC mourning and self-forgiveness process to heal past events in their own lives.

Tips for Facilitators: Some people think that, because of the magnitude of the injury that their actions have caused, they have no right to forgive themselves and thus continue to hold themselves in judgment. In such an instance, encourage the person to focus on the need that they are trying to meet by holding themselves in judgment, or the need that prevents them from forgiving themselves. Once they connect with that need, they may be ready to explore strategies to meet that need and to let go of the prison of self-judgment.

Mourning and Forgiveness

AIM OF EXERCISE: To free up the energy we use to protect ourselves from painful past events so that it becomes available to meet present needs

PREPARATION FOR AWARENESS EXERCISE:

1. Before beginning the guided awareness exercise, ask participants to recall a painful past event.

   I'd like to ask you to bring to mind a past event that continues to trigger anxiety, shame, or an urge to protect or defend yourself. The incident may consist of something you did or something that happened to you. Please take 5 minutes for this. You may find it helpful to write it down.

2. Explain that the object of this exercise is not to cultivate forgiveness toward others, but to reclaim our power to serve our own needs.

3. Offer participants some centering strategies.

   During the course of this guided awareness exercise, if you experience an overwhelm of memories and emotions, try one of the following strategies to re-center:

   a. *You can return and connect with your breath, noticing breathing in and breathing out, receiving and letting go of each breath.*

   b. *You can focus on some details of your memory that carry no emotional significance.*

   c. *As we move through the exercise, you will be summoning the presence of a being who, for you, is nonjudgmental and capable of keeping you safe today. If you become overwhelmed, you can simply pause, notice what you are experiencing, and in your mind's eye, speak to this being, telling them what you are feeling in this moment—either emotionally or physically in your body.*

Confirm that participants are clear on how to use these centering strategies.

INSTRUCTIONS FOR GUIDING AWARENESS EXERCISE:

Read the following slowly, leaving space between each statement for the participant to engage in the guided process.

1. Sit comfortably. Straighten your spine. Make any necessary adjustments.

2. Focus your attention inward by closing your eyes or gently dropping your gaze to the floor in front of you.

3. Focus your attention on your breathing. Simply experience yourself receiving breath and letting go of breath.

4. Now imagine yourself in a place where you feel safe and free.

5. Take time to make yourself comfortable there and to notice your surroundings.

6. Return to your breath, noticing yourself breathing in and breathing out, receiving breath and letting go of breath.

7. If at any time during this exercise you notice any resistance to the process, try to give space to that. Honor your experience as it is with a gentle awareness.

8. Now bring to mind a being in whose presence you feel completely safe. This being is powerful and will protect you. They welcome you with unconditional love, fully accepting you just as you are. Invite this being to join you in the safe place you chose earlier.

9. When you are ready, tell the loving being about the event you recalled and jotted down. Describe what happened.

10. Remember, if you begin to feel overwhelmed, you can pause and use one of the following centering strategies:

    a. Go back to your breathing, receiving breath and letting go of breath.

    b. Or focus on a detail that has no emotional significance.

    c. Or you can center your attention on the here and now, on what you are feeling and on the sensations in your body. Tell the protective being what is happening for you right now, right here.

    You may either continue with these centering strategies or, if you feel ready, you may return to the story you were describing to the compassionate being.

11. When you have completed your sharing, take a moment to notice what it feels like to be empathically received by the compassionate being.

12. Now, as you recall the incident, tell the compassionate being what you were needing during that time. What universal needs and values were prominent for you in the situation you described? Notice the deep appreciation with which the compassionate being is receiving the needs you just named. Imagine them embracing the needs with tenderness and respect. Stay here together, recognizing the preciousness of the needs. (Allow 15 seconds of silence.)

13. *Now you are being asked whether you would like to receive this need into your heart where it will be treasured. If you say yes, notice yourself receiving this valuable quality—allowing either yourself or the compassionate being to place it carefully into your heart. If you are not ready to receive it, watch the compassionate being bring it into their own heart where it will be kept safe for you.*

14. *Now check in with yourself. What do you feel and need right now in this moment, having had this experience with the loving being? If you wish, share your feelings and needs with this friendly presence who has accompanied you in this exercise. Notice how gently this being receives each of your needs, regarding each with great care. If you are able, join them by taking a moment to cherish the needs you just identified. Otherwise, simply notice how they are being valued. (15 seconds)*

15. *Now the being is asking you whether you wish to place the needs you just named in your own heart. If you say yes, place them in your heart with care. Otherwise, watch the compassionate being put your needs lovingly into their heart where they will be carried for you.*

16. *As you prepare to take leave, tell the loving being how you have experienced your time together. Let them know if you wish to connect again.*

17. *Now bid goodbye to the being whom you have invited for this journey.*

18. *Recall the two sets of needs you identified during this exercise: the needs you had during the incident and the needs you have now. Can you imagine yourself holding both sets of needs with equal care?*

19. *When you are ready, come back to the circle and open your eyes. Look around. Welcome those in the circle with you, knowing that we each are holding cherished needs and values.*

SHARING CIRCLE:

- My name is _____ .

- One thing I would like to share is _____ . (Encourage participants to use only one sentence or phrase. If deeper sharing is desired, either limit the number of speakers or divide group into twos and threes.)

REFERENCE: Chapter 9

ACTIVITY 17.2

Healing a Childhood Memory

PURPOSE OF ACTIVITY:

1. To experience being fully heard and understood over a painful childhood experience

2. To understand how our interpretation of a past event affects our current reactions in life

3. To connect with the present unmet need(s) behind our interpretation of a past event

BRIEF DESCRIPTION: Participants recall a specific situation from childhood that triggers pain for them. Working in pairs, one person offers a description and interpretation of their childhood story. Their partner listens empathically until they sense that the speaker has been fully heard and received. The speaker then shares how their interpretation of this event continues to influence the ways they react to current situations. Together, the partners explore possible unmet need(s) behind the interpretation.

MATERIALS NEEDED:

☐ Group Handout 17.2: Healing the Inner Child—Guidelines for Role-Play.

TIME REQUIRED: 60–90 minutes

GROUP SIZE: Any size

SPACE REQUIRED: This exercise requires that there be adequate distance between participant pairs so that partners can speak and hear each other without straining.

LITERACY LEVEL REQUIRED: None

PROCEDURE:

1. *Many of us have had experiences in childhood that left us with pain. We may have been punished, for example, for being "stupid," ridiculed for being "fat," or labeled "clumsy" or "irresponsible." Some of the labels could even have been positive: we were held up as "the responsible one" or "the best in the class." Children can easily hear positive labels as demands or expectations on the part of grown-ups. We may end up taking such labels to heart or believing that our interpretation of a particular childhood experience constitutes "reality." As adults, we may continue to operate out of our reaction to these labels and*

interpretations, preventing us from responding to current situations in ways that best meet our needs. For example, someone in your family may have told you repeatedly that you were stupid so that, even today, you have difficulty trusting your own inner wisdom.

2. Inform participants that this activity will provide an opportunity
    a. to recount a painful childhood incident
    b. to role-play ourselves as the child right after the incident by telling an empathic listener partner what's going on for us
    c. to understand how this incident continues to affect us today and to connect with our current unmet needs

3. Ask participants to recall a situation from their childhood that is still affecting their lives in a way that leaves them unable to respond freely in the present. Use the following questions:
    a. How old were you?
    b. What was the setting?
    c. Who was involved?
    d. What happened? Please express what "factually" happened by making observations free of evaluation.

4. Use a situation in your own life to illustrate how you would respond to the four questions you just gave.

    Example: I was ten years old. I was looking after my little brother when he ran out into the street. I ran after him, trying to catch him and protect him from getting run over. A car driving up came to a sudden halt, tires squealing and horn blowing. The driver opened his window and said: "You stupid idiot! Do you want to get killed?" in a voice that carried inside our house. My mother ran to the scene, and said to me in an equally loud voice,

    "Why did you leave your little brother alone when you were supposed to be looking after him! Do you know what a poor example you are for him?" Then she began to cry and added: "You have no common sense. You never did. I really wonder if you ever will." Taking my brother in her arms, she held him and rocked him and told me to go to my room.

5. Now recall how it felt to be the child whose experience you just described. Demonstrate how you would role-play the child that you were. Step into the child's shoes and describe what was going on for them right after the incident. Invite someone with skills in empathic listening to take the role of the listener. If no such person is available, role-play both the child and the empathic listener through the use of puppets or by switching voices and body positions.

Example (based on earlier story)

> **Child**: "My little brother could have been killed. I am so stupid."

> **Listener**: "Are you feeling pretty scared because you want your brother to be safe?"

> **Child**: "Yes, but he is so fast. I let my eyes off him for 1 minute and there he is out on the road."

> **Listener**: "Are you wanting to trust that you know how to look after him safely?"

> **Child**: "Yes, he wants to make things hard for me, sneaking out of my sight and then doing something he's not supposed to. He knows how to get me into trouble."

> **Listener**: "It sounds like you could use some co-operation when you are looking after him."

> **Child**: "Yea, I'm always the one to get punished. They think he is a goody-goody and I'm the one who is irresponsible."

> **Listener**: "Are you wishing that your side of the story could be heard and respected?"

> **Child**: "Mom never listens to me. She just tells me I'm wrong and that I am stupid and have no common sense. Maybe I am stupid. I just can't figure out a way to get her to understand."

> **Listener**: "Would you like it if your mom saw your viewpoint and really understood the situation—maybe even show how you might handle situations you find pretty challenging?"

> **Child**: "Gee, that would sure be nice. Just the thought of that makes me feel better."

> **Listener**: "I am noticing a shift in your energy. Is there anything else you would like to share at this time?"

6. In the next step, share your interpretation of the incident and explain how this interpretation affects your current life. Invite someone to receive you empathically and to reflect back the need underlying each statement you make.

Example (based on earlier story):

> **Speaker**: "I continued throughout my life thinking that I have no common sense, and that my way of doing things will probably be wrong or just not good enough. When I think this way, I don't take initiative. I don't volunteer to do things unless I have someone telling me exactly what to do."

Listener: "It sounds as if you would like to be able to trust your intuition and your ability to figure out how to do things rather than rely on the explicit directions of someone outside yourself?"

Speaker: "Yes, occasionally I do something on my own and I am amazed when it turns out well. But mostly I don't even try."

Listener: "So are you wanting more confidence to trust your own intuition and ability?"

Speaker: "But not on things that would end up in a catastrophe if I did them wrong!"

Listener: "So you'd like to try ways of paying attention to your intuition and practice common sense in areas where it's unlikely there will be dire consequences?"

Speaker: "Right, I really want to do that. I imagine I would begin to trust my own judgment more and turn this around."

7. Ask if anyone is willing to role-play their childhood regarding an event which still exerts on effect on them.

   a. Invite the volunteer to answer the four questions listed under #3.

   b. Ask them to role-play the child by telling you what's going on for them.

      • Demonstrate being fully present as you listen with empathy. Focus on the feelings and needs behind their story and reflect these back to the speaker.
      • Continue until you sense that their need to be heard has been satisfied. You may notice a sigh, a silence, or their muscles relaxing. Ask them, "Are you complete or is there something else you would like me to hear?"

   c. Now ask the volunteer to switch to their adult self and tell you how they interpret the event and how this interpretation affects their current life.

      • Once again, listen with empathy until the speaker appears to be complete.

8. Take time with the volunteer to debrief by asking them to respond to the following questions:

   a. In what way, if any, was it helpful to be heard and to hear yourself and your needs as a child?

   b. In what way, if any, was it helpful to have another person hear how your childhood experience continues to exert an effect on you today?

c. What need(s) would you like to meet as the adult you are today?

d. How are you feeling right now?

9. After completing the demonstration with the volunteer, ask participants for questions or reflections. Decide whether the group requires another role-play to demonstrate this activity.

10. When you are satisfied that everyone understands the procedures, distribute the handouts and divide the group into pairs.

11. Tell participants that they have 40 minutes to work with their partners, and that you will remind them to switch roles after 20 minutes.

DEBRIEF QUESTIONS:

1. What was most helpful to you in this exercise of sharing a memory from your past?

2. Is there some other work you might like to do to reinforce what you learned from this exercise? For example, you may want to draw or write about the experience in your journal. You may want to explore how in future situations you would respond differently rather than fall into the habitual reactions you have just identified.

SUGGESTION FOR PRACTICE IN DAILY LIFE: When you find yourself reacting to a situation, ask yourself the following:

1. What am I telling myself?

2. Where is this reaction coming from?

3. What need am I wanting to meet right now?

REFERENCES: Chapters 9, 13

Healing the Inner Child: Guidelines for Role-Play

Decide who will be the first speaker to describe their childhood experience. The other person will serve as Listener.

ONE: ROLE-PLAY CHILD

Speaker: Imagine yourself at the age when you experienced this event. Use the child's voice to tell your listener:

1. How old you are,
2. What the setting was,
3. Who was involved,
4. What actually (factually) happened, as well as
5. Your interpretation of the event
   In other words, as a child, what would you be telling yourself about the event, about what you did or about what happened to you during the event?

Listener: Receive the speaker empathically, focusing on and reflecting back the needs underlying each of their statements. Continue until the speaker is satisfied that they have been fully heard.

TWO: ROLE-PLAY ADULT

Speaker: Tell the listener how your interpretation of this childhood event affects your current life.

Listener: Listen to the speaker with full attention, guessing and reflecting back the needs behind each statement. Continue until the speaker is satisfied that they are fully understood.

THREE: DEBRIEF TOGETHER

Listener: Encourage the speaker to share their experience of this activity by asking questions such as:

a. In what way, if any, was it helpful to be heard and to hear yourself and your needs as a child?
b. In what way, if any, was it helpful to have another person hear how your childhood experience continues to exert an effect on you today?
c. What need(s) would you like to meet as the adult you are today?
d. How are you feeling right now?

ACTIVITY 17.3

Oops

PURPOSE OF ACTIVITY: To practice a healing process to address something we did or said that we now regret

BRIEF DESCRIPTION: This exercise consists of a demonstration of the NVC process of mourning and self-forgiveness followed by individual practice and group sharing. Participants apply the process to a personal situation with the guide of a worksheet and then share learning and insights.

MATERIALS NEEDED:

❑ Individual Handout 17.3: Mourning—Healing the Past

TIME REQUIRED: 60 minutes

GROUP SIZE: Any

SPACE REQUIRED: Minimal

LITERACY LEVEL REQUIRED: Some writing required

PROCEDURE:

1. Review the process of mourning and self-forgiveness

   a. **Mourning** consists of acknowledging and accepting where I am now:

      i.   recognizing the thoughts and self-judgments about what I did or said,

      ii. connecting to the underlying unmet needs behind these thoughts, and

      iii. opening up to whatever feelings of sorrow, remorse, anguish, etc., that are generated by these unmet needs

   b. **Self-forgiveness** is the ability and willingness to acknowledge and understand the needs I was *trying* to meet when I did or said what I did. It consists of empathically receiving the self (or that part of me) that did what I now regret.

   c. **Learning from past mistakes.** It is only after we have healed—fully mourned and embraced ourselves in forgiveness—that we move forward to grow, exploring new strategies which honor both sets of needs that were uncovered in our mourning and self-forgiveness process.

2. Invite a volunteer to help demonstrate the process by recalling something they did or said in the past that they now regret.

a. Ask the volunteer: "What is present right now for you?" Use the following questions to guide them through the process of mourning (Refer to handout):

  i. *"What did you do or say that you now wish you hadn't? (Just the observable facts.)"* Write the answer on the board.

  ii. *"How do you think about what you did or said? Are there stories or self-judgments that run through your head when you think about the choice(s) you made?"* Write the answer in abbreviated form on the board.

  iii. *"What do you feel and need right now as you think those thoughts?"* Write the feeling and need words on the board.

  iv. *"In this moment, which of the needs listed is (are) most important for you; which would you identify right now to be the key need(s)?"* (When a person is able to touch their most important need(s) in the moment, they often experience a shift in energy.) On the board circle the key need(s).

b. Now ask the volunteer to focus on the past event:

  "What need(s) were you trying to meet when you did or said whatever it was that you now regret?" Write their answer on the board. If more than one need is named, ask the volunteer to identify and circle the key need(s).

c. After the volunteer has fully connected with the experience of mourning and self-forgiveness and can acknowledge the preciousness of the need(s) behind the regrettable choice, invite them to take a few minutes to brainstorm strategies that would allow them to address both sets of needs that were uncovered.

3. Decide whether or not to engage in a second demonstration with a different volunteer.

4. Distribute Individual Handout 17.3: Mourning—Healing the Past, and ask participants to use the process that was just demonstrated to address one thing they did or said that they currently regret. Encourage participants to take about 15 minutes to write their reflections on the handout.

5. After everyone has had a chance to work through the process on paper, ask for a volunteer to share their work. Use the board to record their words just as you had done with the volunteer in the demonstration (Item 2, above).

DEBRIEF QUESTIONS:

1. What do you habitually do when you recognize regret?

2. What needs are met by your doing this exercise today?

3. In doing this exercise, what other needs have come up for you?

4. Describe any "aha's" you may have gotten from this exercise.

5. What step in the worksheet, if any, was particularly difficult for you?

SUGGESTION FOR PRACTICE IN DAILY LIFE: When you find yourself regretting something you did or said, even something very minor, go through the process you learned in this exercise. Notice how you feel before and after, and articulate to yourself specific pieces of learning or growth you received from having made the "mistake."

REFERENCE: Chapter 9

Mourning—Healing the Past

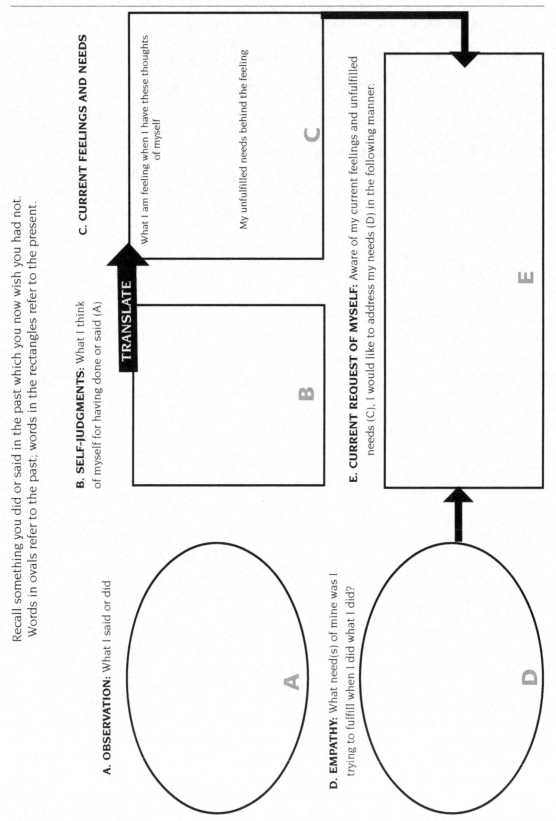

Recall something you did or said in the past which you now wish you had not. Words in ovals refer to the past; words in the rectangles refer to the present.

A. OBSERVATION: What I said or did

A

B. SELF-JUDGMENTS: What I think of myself for having done or said (A)

B

TRANSLATE

C. CURRENT FEELINGS AND NEEDS

What I am feeling when I have these thoughts of myself

My unfulfilled needs behind the feeling

C

D. EMPATHY: What need(s) of mine was I trying to fulfill when I did what I did?

D

E. CURRENT REQUEST OF MYSELF: Aware of my current feelings and unfulfilled needs (C), I would like to address my needs (D) in the following manner:

E

RESOLVING CONFLICTS

18.1 Awareness Exercise: Resolving Conflict

18.2 Activity: Destroying Enemies by Breathing "EH?"

18.3 Activity: Conflict Lineup

18.4 Activity: Disarming Epithets

18.5 Activity: Stepping Into Another's Shoes

KEY CONCEPT 18:

Resolving Conflicts

Description: NVC offers us tools to translate anger and negative judgments toward people into an awareness of unmet needs. By dissolving the enemy images that we project onto people, we replace reactivity with the power that comes from trusting that all needs can be met once we are connected at a heart level. When we use NVC to mediate a conflict, we first support the parties in hearing one another's feelings and needs. When both parties are satisfied that their needs have been heard and valued, we assist them in formulating concrete requests of one another to address the unmet needs in this situation. As mediator, our role is not to generate solutions but to facilitate an open heart space where the parties hear and acknowledge one another's needs. We do not take responsibility for the outcome, but trust that the parties themselves are their own best resource for arriving at a successful solution once they are able to hear one another's needs.

Toolkit exercises in this section provide practice in mediating conflict, dissolving "enemy images," and transforming anger, resentment, and violent urges.

Tips for Facilitators: Conflicts are often caused or exacerbated by one party criticizing, blaming, or judging the other. In NVC, we direct attention toward what is in each person's heart and support contestants to hear the need behind whatever strategies they are using. When mediating between two parties, it is helpful to check in with ourselves and to notice whether we are taking sides and judging any party for being right, wrong, worthy, or unworthy. If we are aware of such thinking, we can stop and explore the needs behind our judgments. This might be done by taking a few conscious breaths, focusing our attention inward, and asking ourselves, "What am I needing or valuing when I have these thoughts?" If the judgments continue to hang on in our minds, consider taking time out. We can acknowledge to the group that we are practicing for ourselves what we hope to support in them—which is to connect fully with the needs beneath any judgmental thinking. While we may not always be able to transform judgments into needs, we can continue to model NVC with integrity if we reconfirm our intention to connect and take time out for the internal work required to realize our intention.

AWARENESS EXERCISE 18.1

Resolving Conflict

AIM OF EXERCISE—To create internal spaciousness for resolving conflict by:

1. Grounding in a place of love and respect,

2. Opening our eyes to see both sides of an issue,

3. Valuing the needs of both parties while waiting for strategies to emerge

INSTRUCTIONS FOR GUIDING AWARENESS EXERCISE:

In this awareness exercise we will be creating the internal spaciousness that supports us in resolving conflict. Choose a situation where you are either in conflict with someone else or with yourself. If there are two parts of yourself which are in conflict, you may want to give each part a name, such as "Babbling Bruce," "Good Daughter," or "Mr. Can-Do." Before we begin the guided awareness exercise, take 3 minutes, either alone or with a partner, to clarify the conflict you would like to focus on.

After 3 minutes, read the following slowly, leaving space between each statement for the participant to engage in the guided process.

1. *Sit comfortably. Straighten your spine. Make any necessary adjustments.*

2. *Focus your attention inward by closing your eyes or gently dropping your gaze to the floor in front of you.*

3. *Focus your attention on your breathing.*

4. *Feel yourself receiving air and then letting it go, receiving and letting go. . . . Take several conscious breaths, bringing your attention to the present moment, to the here and now.*

5. *Now imagine a safe place with enough space for three people to sit in a triangle while seeing and hearing one another clearly. Let the vision of such a place present itself to you, or create one in your mind. Take 1 minute to observe your safe place. . . . What does it look like? Are there any sounds? Smells? Is it warm, cool, breezy?*

6. *Now invite into this place someone or some being whom you deeply trust—a being who is a great source of compassion and understanding for you. For the rest of this exercise, I'll be referring to this being as the "Compassionate One."*

7. Allow the Compassionate One to take a seat. Then take a seat yourself. After you are both settled, invite the person or the part or yourself with whom you are having a conflict to take the third seat. If the conflict is between two parts of yourself, choose the part you'd like to play and then invite the other part to take the third seat.

8. Imagine that you are seated in the triangle, closing your eyes and coming home, being present to yourself.

9. Now imagine yourself, when you are ready, opening your eyes. You see the other two in the triangle: they are still sitting in stillness, eyes closed, being present to themselves and to this moment. Take a look at each of them.

10. Now the Compassionate One opens their eyes and looks at you with deep appreciation and love. These eyes see you without judgment. They see your true feelings and needs, beholding you and your needs with great respect.

11. Allow yourself to fully receive this caring look from the Compassionate One. Then watch the Compassionate One turn toward the other party and offer the same tender respect, holding the feelings and needs of the other party with care.

12. When you are ready—and at the invitation of the Compassionate One—turn your gaze toward the other party. Open to their feelings and needs in this conflict. What might their heart be feeling or needing?

13. If you find yourself blaming or judging, go back to the Compassionate One. You may or may not be able today to receive the other with their needs. If not, then simply watch the Compassionate One alternating attention between you and the other party, between your needs and theirs.

14. The Compassionate One is now taking your needs and placing them very gently in one hand. They lay that hand, the one that is close to you, palm-up on their lap. After a while they take the other party's needs and place them in the other hand. You are looking at the Compassionate One sitting in stillness, both hands resting, palms up, on their lap. If you feel ready, do the same: hold your own needs in one hand and the other party's needs in the other hand just as the Compassionate One is doing.

15. Perhaps the other party is wanting to join you now by doing the same, holding your needs in one hand and their own needs in the other. If the other party seems unable to do so at this time, simply stay with the Compassionate One who is continuing to hold the two sets of needs. If the other party is ready to join you, then perhaps all three of you will share this moment by simply and lovingly holding the two sets of

needs, one in each hand. Don't rush to strategize for solutions. Stay focused on the needs. If you are holding both parties' needs, a strategy is likely to present itself in time. [1 minute]

16. *We are now drawing to a close. If you would like more time to complete the process, consider making an appointment to return to the space you have created, asking the Compassionate One and the other party to join you at that time.*

17. *In your mind's eye, take leave first of the other party and then of the Compassionate One.*

18. *When ready, return your focus to this room.*

SHARING CIRCLE:

- My name is _____ .

- One need I am holding is _____ . One need I believe the other party is holding is _____ .

- Consider using the following questions to debrief this awareness exercise, either all together or in small groups of 3:

  a. What was your experience?

  b. What helped or prevented you from holding both sets of needs in your hands?

  c. What is left unfinished in your process?

  d. Would you like to make an agreement with yourself to continue the process?

REFERENCE: Chapter 10

Destroying Enemies by Breathing "EH?"

PURPOSE OF ACTIVITY:

1. To reduce animosity, violence, and anger

2. To practice holding both parties' needs in a moment of tension

BRIEF DESCRIPTION: Participants work with personal situations that stimulate anger and "enemy images." With the assistance of a partner who role-plays the undesired stimulus, participants practice grounding themselves through conscious breathing and a verbal reminder ("EH?"—Empathy Honesty) to connect with their own and the other party's need.

MATERIALS NEEDED:
- ❑ Paper and writing instruments

TIME REQUIRED: 30 minutes

GROUP SIZE: Two or more

SPACE REQUIRED: Enough to work in pairs

LITERACY LEVEL REQUIRED: Writing is helpful, although not absolutely necessary if participants are able to hold situations in their head.

PROCEDURE:

1. Introduce the subject:

    Abraham Lincoln once said, "Am I not destroying my enemies when I make friends with them?" NVC gives us power to destroy our enemies by turning them into friends. When someone speaks or behaves in ways that stimulate anger, resentment, or violent thoughts in us, how do we turn our minds around in that very moment? This is what we will be practicing.

2. Instruct participants to work individually to produce materials for the activity:

    a. *Write down what someone might do or say that leads you to see them as "enemy"—an opponent or someone who stands against you. Enemy images, alienation, or a sense of separation can occur with*

> *strangers as well as with those closest to us, in situations involving major issues as well as incidents we label as "minor" or even "petty."*

Examples:

> i. I was feeling vulnerable and sharing something personal at our morning meeting when the new office-clerk got up and asked for coffee.
>
> ii. My partner walks in the door and says: "Why isn't supper ready? You're home all day with the kids and can't even get food on the table by the time I return?"

b. Take about 5 minutes to come up with one or several examples of what someone did or said (or what someone might do or say) to stimulate anger, resentment, or violent thoughts in you.

c. While participants are working, write one of the above examples on a piece of paper or generate a personal example and write it down. You will be using this example to demonstrate the activity below.

3. Demonstrate the activity.
Let's now practice how we might create friends out of enemies. [Ask for a volunteer to help demonstrate.]

a. *We'll work in pairs, taking turns to practice while our partner role-plays the words or behavior that triggered us.*

b. *First I choose one of the situations I wrote, and read it to my partner. [Example: I was feeling vulnerable and sharing something personal at our morning meeting when the new office clerk got up and asked for coffee.]*

c. *Partner, please help role-play this situation. [Example: Play-act "sharing vulnerably" and while in the midst of talking, have your partner interrupt with "Oh, I just noticed that everyone got coffee! Is there a machine somewhere?"]*

d. *As soon as I hear or see the trigger, I can practice four simple steps.*

> i. *[Step 1: Breathe "EH?"]*
>
> *First I take a conscious breath, filling my lungs and then I slowly exhale while saying "EH?" to myself. "EH?" (pronounced like the letter "A" with a rising lilt) stands for "empathy" and "honesty." Together with the breath I took, "EH?" reminds me that my life is a constant flow of giving and receiving.*
>
> ii. *[Step 2: Focus on my own need.]*

I focus on needs: first my own. Silently I connect with whatever unmet need got roused for me in this exchange. In the example I used, my need might be for compassionate understanding (a caring response, emotional safety, genuine connection).

iii. [Step 3: Repeat breathing "EH?"]

Now I take another conscious breath. I receive the gift of breath into my lungs and then exhale while saying to myself "EH?"

iv. [Step 4: Focus on the other party's need.]

Now I am ready to focus silently on the other party's need. In the example I gave, I might guess that the new employee had a need to belong (to be in line with everyone else's experience) or that they valued effectiveness (in the form of wakefulness, especially on their first day at work).

Holding both our own and the other party's needs in our hearts is a powerful way to destroy enemies and to remember our common humanity. After breathing "EH?" through the four steps as I just demonstrated, we may choose whether or not to engage verbally. Should we decide to dialogue with the other party, we are more likely to be successful if our words come from an awareness of our shared humanity rather than from a place of enmity.

4. Summarize the instructions and make sure that everyone understands the activity:

   a. *Find a partner that you would like to work with.*

   b. *Take turns role-playing the situations you wrote down.*

   c. *The person who is practicing, remember the four steps:*

      i. *Consciously take a full breath in, and then as you breathe out, say "EH?"*

      ii. *Silently focus on your unmet need.*

      iii. *When ready, take another conscious breath, first receiving and then releasing saying "EH?"*

      iv. *Focus on the other party's unmet need.*

   d. *Take a moment of silence, and notice the experience of holding both needs in your heart. If you wish, share this experience very briefly with your partner before they take their turn to practice. You have 15 minutes altogether.*

DEBRIEF QUESTIONS:

1. Share an instance when you experienced diminished hostility after breathing "EH?" What do you think helped you to shift?

2. Share an instance when you continued to experience the same (or more) hostility after breathing "EH?" What do you think prevented the hostility from diminishing?

3. Share other ways you have successfully diminished hostility in a moment of anger or resentment.

4. What would help you to remember to breathe "EH?" the next time enemy images attack?

SUGGESTION FOR PRACTICE IN DAILY LIFE: Practice "EH?" in situations where you are angry with another party. ("Another party" may take the form of a public notice, a bicyclist on the road, a TV news commentator, etc.)

REFERENCES: Chapters 7, 8

ACTIVITY 18.3
Conflict Lineup

PURPOSE OF ACTIVITY:

1. To practice mediation through a fun and lively group activity

2. To free oneself from a stuck point of view, pattern, or behavior when experiencing conflict

BRIEF DESCRIPTION: Participants form two groups to represent opposing sides of an argument. They line up against each other, shout out arguments, and then "unpack" each statement by revealing the underlying needs. This is a very active exercise which some find useful after lunch if energy is low.

MATERIALS NEEDED:
☐ Board or flip chart

TIME REQUIRED: 60 minutes

GROUP SIZE: Ten to fifty

SPACE REQUIRED: An open space at the front of the room that measures at least 1 x 5 meters or yards

LITERACY LEVEL REQUIRED: None

PROCEDURE:

Part I—Choosing scenario and arguments

1. Ask the group:

    Do any of you feel frustrated about an ongoing situation in your life involving people whose behavior you just can't change? Are you able to describe the situation in one sentence? Let me give two examples by what I mean:

    a. *Every year at our annual family gathering, my husband Joe gets sloshed and ruins the party.*

    b. *I work full time; my partner works part time, but leaves all the housework to me.*

2. Solicit scenarios and decide as a group on one scenario to work with.

3. Invite the person (hence referred to as "protagonist") who volunteered the situation to come to the front of the room.

4. Have the protagonist invite someone in the group to represent the person (hence referred to as "antagonist") whose action has been triggering frustration for the protagonist.

5. Ask the antagonist to also come to the front of the room.

6. Ask participants to choose which side they would like to support. (The activity works best if there are even numbers of supporters on both sides.)

7. Divide the room so that the antagonist and those who support the antagonist huddle on one side while the protagonist and supporters huddle on the other side.

8. Give the groups the following task:

> *Find five or six statements or arguments that aim to prove the person on your side right and the other side wrong. Assign a different person to represent each of the five or six arguments. This person will be the voice for that particular argument.*

Part II—Forming the lineup

1. When the groups have completed the task, ask the protagonist, antagonist, and the ten or twelve people who have arguments to go to the front of the room. Ask the others to return to their seats.

2. Line up the people who are standing across the front of the room in the following formation:

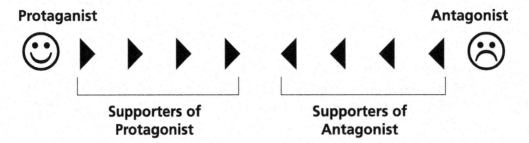

3. Ask everyone standing in the line to swivel their bodies so that they are facing in the direction of the opposing party. [At this point only the two persons standing furthest away from the protagonist and antagonist are able to look into each other's eyes. The protagonist and antagonist, who are each standing behind a row of supporters, are unable to see each other at all.]

    NOTE: Arrange for the two sides to be equal (or at least close) in numbers.

Part III—"Unpacking" the conflict

1. Give the following instructions to the people in the lineup:

    Now everyone, go ahead and tell the other side why you are right and they are wrong. You may raise your voice, gesticulate, and say anything you please, but please stay where you are in the formation. You have 1 minute to prove to the other side why you are right and they are wrong.

    Encourage the supporters of both sides to simultaneously vent and out-argue each other; meanwhile the protagonist and antagonist are neither able to see nor hear each other.

2. Signal the end of a minute and invite a moment of stillness for everyone to settle down. Then give the following instructions:

    With the help of the audience, we shall now "unpack" the arguments to reveal their underlying needs. We'll listen to the arguments, one by one, alternating sides, starting from those standing in the center and then moving outward. I'll ask each of you to state the argument you are representing. Those of you in the audience, please listen carefully and see if you can hear the need that is being expressed beneath the words.

3. Using a board or flip chart, write down the needs that the audience identifies. Put the number "1" on the left side of the board and list here the needs that underlie arguments made by the protagonist's party. Write "2" on the right side of the board where you will be listing the antagonist's needs.

4. When all the needs underlying a supporter's argument have been written on the board and the audience can offer no more guesses, say to the supporter who represented the argument, "Your job is complete; you may sit down now." Use this same phrase each time a supporter's argument has been "unpacked."

5. After all the supporters have had their arguments unpacked and have sat down, turn to the antagonist and protagonist and ask them to review the list of needs on their respective sides of the board. Ask if they have any needs in this situation that got left out. If so, add them to the list.

6. Ask the protagonist, and then the antagonist, which needs are most alive in this moment for them. Circle those words on the board.

7. Finally ask each of them whether they experienced a shift, and if so, to describe that shift.

8. Acknowledge all the needs that have revealed themselves over this process, and together with the whole group, take a moment to hold and honor the needs of each side.

DEBRIEF QUESTIONS:

1. [For those who participated in the lineup] As a representative holding on to an argument in support of your side, were you aware of any shift in feeling, outlook, or energy toward the end of the activity when all the arguments for both sides got "unpacked"?

2. [For those who served as audience] Over the course of this activity, did you notice anything about the people in the lineup or anything in yourself which you would like to share?

SUGGESTIONS FOR PRACTICE IN DAILY LIFE:

1. If you are in conflict with someone and find yourself stuck in a point of view or pattern of behavior, take out a piece of paper and fold it in half lengthwise. In the left column write down statements supporting your point of view; then connect to the needs underlying each statement and put them in the right column. Now turn the paper over, imagine yourself in the other person's shoes, and repeat the procedure: what statements or arguments might they make to support their view? What might be the needs underlying each statement? When you are complete, review the needs on both sides of the paper. Notice if you experience any shift in your point of view.

2. In the heat of the moment, stop, breathe, name your underlying need and imagine what the other person's underlying need might be.

REFERENCES: Chapters 5, 8, 10

ACTIVITY 18.4

Disarming Epithets

PURPOSE OF ACTIVITY:

1. To explore the needs underlying epithets, labels, and names we commonly use to judge others

2. To learn to hear the unmet needs of those who call us names

3. To transform "name-calling" into "naming needs"

BRIEF DESCRIPTION: Participants generate a list of "names" they often use to refer to others, explore the underlying needs, and practice NVC honesty to replace name-calling. They also generate a list of "names" by which they themselves have been called and practice connecting with possible unmet needs of the name-caller. This exercise may be demonstrated in one large group and practiced in triads or small groups.

MATERIALS NEEDED:

☐ Chalk/white/poster board

TIME REQUIRED: 30–60 minutes

GROUP SIZE: Flexible

SPACE REQUIRED: Adequate space for small groups to work without mutual interference, if small groups or triads are desired.

LITERACY LEVEL REQUIRED: None to minimal (Facilitator will be writing "names" on the board as participants generate them.)

PROCEDURE:

Part A—Recognizing needs behind the names we've been called

1. Even as children, most of us learned that "name-calling" is a sure-fire way to start or fan a conflict. How many of us remember being called a name? How many today experience anger or hurt related to a name we've been called in the past? What was that name?

2. List the "names" that participants offer. Allow time for participants to warm up in generating some of the more hurtful names—or you can name a few yourself (e.g., bullshitter, pervert, faggot, whore, chimo, thug, etc.)—and create a list on the board.

3. The title of this exercise is "Disarming Epithets." Practicing this powerful tool of NVC, we can deactivate even the nastiest names being hurled our way! Ready?

4. Point to one of the less-loaded epithets on the list: Let's disarm this one first. Take a moment to imagine being the person who is calling someone that name. *[Allow 10 seconds of silence.]*

5. What would you guess that person might be feeling and needing? Create a list of the need words and place them next to the epithet. (It is not necessary to write the feeling words on the board.)

6. Do one or more examples from this list, using increasingly more "loaded" epithets.

Part B—Recognizing needs behind the names we call others

7. Now I am wondering if any of us here have ever called anyone a name. Encourage a participant to volunteer an epithet they've used to either (a) address someone face to face, (b) refer to someone indirectly, or even (c) label someone in their own thoughts. Ask them to take some time to connect with the feelings and needs underneath the name-calling. Write the need words on the board next to the epithet they used. (Example: 'fascist,' I feel horrified by their views. My need is for compassion.)

8. Support participant in exploring their feelings and whether there may be more than one layer of needs when they call someone that name. (In the example given above: "When I call that person 'fascist,' in addition to my need for compassion, I also feel annoyed and recognize that I value being heard and understood. And when I stay with this further, I am aware of needs for inclusion and respect.")

9. Explore whether name-calling was successful in meeting the needs they listed. Discuss what needs, if any, get met through name-calling. (Example: "I called him 'fascist' out of my need to be heard and for my views to be understood. He might have heard the word I used but I still did not get the hearing or understanding I wanted.")

Part C (for more advanced groups)—Translating name-calling into NVC honesty

10. Encourage the same participant to translate their name-calling into "classical NVC honesty" using the four components: observation, feeling, need, and request. (Example: "When I hear you say, 'Round them up and execute them,' I feel horrified because I value compassion. Would you be willing to discuss alternatives that would address both our values?")

11. Invite the group to help render the classical NVC honesty (above) into colloquial expressions that can be used to replace the name-calling. (Example: "Oh, wow, ouch! I want to see more humane and creative approaches. Would you work with me on that?")

Part D—Small Group Practice

12. Continue working as above, either in the large group or in triads and small groups, giving each person an opportunity to practice each of the three parts:
    a. Recognizing needs behind the names we've been called
    b. Recognizing needs behind the names we call others
    c. Translating name-calling into NVC honesty (advanced level)

13. Five minutes before the end of the allotted time, ask each group to choose one of their epithets and to reflect on what they learned from working with it.

14. Bring everyone back together again and invite each group to contribute what they learned from the epithet they worked with.

DEBRIEF QUESTIONS:

1. Which epithets are easy for you to "disarm"? Which ones difficult? Why?

2. What did you learn from doing this exercise?

3. How would you apply what you learned here to "real life"?

4. What would happen to our society if our governments and institutions replaced labels with need language?

SUGGESTIONS FOR PRACTICE IN DAILY LIFE:

1. Create a personal list of epithets—names people might call you or judgments they might have of you—which would be most painful for you to hear. Next to each epithet or judgment, write down what the person might be needing and valuing if they were to address you or think about you in that way.

2. Make a list of the epithets and judgments you most commonly apply to other people. Translate each into unmet needs. Recognize that these may be prominent needs in your current life. Reflect on how much you cherish these needs and how you are meeting each one in your life right now.

3. As you move through your daily life, be aware of the epithets, name-calling, labels and judgments you hear. Take time to translate both the speaker's needs and the recipient's needs.

REFERENCES: Chapters 2, 5, 9, 10, 13

ACTIVITY 18.5

Stepping Into Another's Shoes

PURPOSE OF ACTIVITY:

1. To practice freeing ourselves of judgmental and demanding thoughts toward someone

2. To practice noticing our own and the other party's feelings and needs in situations of conflict or tension

BRIEF DESCRIPTION: Participants identify someone in their life who triggers judgmental thinking—thinking that is blaming, demanding, or critical of that person. They then reflect on how the other person might be experiencing the situation. The activity includes individual work and sharing in pairs.

MATERIALS NEEDED:

- ❑ Paper and pen
- ❑ Flip chart or board

TIME REQUIRED: 50 minutes

GROUP SIZE: Any size

SPACE REQUIRED: Minimal

LITERACY LEVEL REQUIRED: Able to write

PROCEDURE:

1. Make prior preparation for this activity by copying the four questions listed under #4 (below) onto a board or flip chart.

2. Introduce the exercise:

> *When we experience tension, disagreement, or conflict with someone, we may find ourselves blaming or diagnosing what's wrong with them. We may deny responsibility for our experience by attributing it to their behavior. We may have thoughts that demand them to behave differently or thoughts that say they deserve to be punished. All such images and thoughts prevent us from seeing the real person and from connecting to them from our heart.*
>
> *The kind of judgmental thinking I just described prevents us from hearing our own heart—hearing our own feelings and needs. It also prevents us from hearing the other person's heart—what they might be feeling and needing.*

3. Lead participants through the following procedure:

   a. *Bring to mind someone whom you judge or of whom you make demands. It may be that you do not express these judgments to others but just think them in your own head.*

   b. *Write down the name of the person.*

   c. *Imagine what this person might be thinking of you. In their mind, what labels might they apply to you? What might they think you "should" or "should not" say or do?*

   d. *Choose one label or "should-thought" they hold toward you (or you think they probably hold toward you).*

   e. *Can you imagine one observation they might have made that contributed to the label or "should- thought" you identified in (d) above? In other words, what might be one thing they heard or saw that could have led to their thinking about you in that way?*

   f. *What do you guess to be their feelings and needs behind that thinking?*

   g. *Now offer yourself empathy, connecting to your own feelings and needs after having "stepped into their shoes."*

4. Instruct participants to work in pairs, sharing personally to the extent that they feel comfortable. Read out loud the four questions you copied earlier on the flip chart:

   a. *What judgments or demands might that person have toward you?*

   b. *What might they have observed to have precipitated their judgment or demand?*

   c. *What might they be feeling and needing underneath their judgment and demand?*

   d. *What are you feeling and needing in this moment?*

5. Explain that the partner's task is to receive empathically with silent attention, using only an occasional word or phrase to let the speaker know that their words are being heard.

DEBRIEF QUESTIONS:

1. If you noticed a shift in energy during this activity, would you be willing to share that experience?

2. How might you apply this activity in your personal world?

SUGGESTIONS FOR PRACTICE IN DAILY LIFE—When you find yourself judging someone:

1. Imagine what they might be thinking of you, and

2. what they might have observed to have stimulated those thoughts.

3. Then—if you feel open to doing so—ask yourself what they might have been feeling and needing when they made their observation.

REFERENCES: Chapters 3, 8, 13

Cross-References—Toolkit Exercises and Marshall Rosenberg's Book

The following information is offered for those facilitators who organize practice sessions according to the chapters in Marshall Rosenberg's book *Nonviolent Communication: A Language of Life* (3rd edition):

1—Giving From the Heart: 1.1, 1.2, 1.3, 2.1, 2.2, 2.3, 8.5, 9.5, 10.2, 10.4, 11.1, 12.2, 12.3

2—Communication That Blocks Compassion: 3.1, 3.2, 3.3, 18.4

3—Observing Without Evaluating: 5.1, 5.2, 5.3, 5.4, 9.5, 10.2, 18.5

4—Identifying and Expressing Feelings: 6.1, 6.2, 6.3, 6.4, 6.5, 6.6, 6.7, 9.5, 10.2

5—Taking Responsibility for Our Feelings: 4.1, 4.2, 4.3, 7.1, 7.2, 7.3, 7.4, 9.2, 9.5, 10.1, 10.2, 13.1, 14.1, 18.3, 18.4

6—Requesting That Which Would Enrich Life: 8.1, 8.2, 8.3, 8.4, 8.5, 10.2, 10.4, 14.1

7—Receiving Empathically: 8.2, 8.4, 8.5, 11.1, 11.2, 11.3, 11.4, 11.5, 14.1, 18.2

8—The Power of Empathy: 11.1, 11.2, 11.3, 11.4, 11.5, 18.3, 18.5

9—Connecting Compassionately With Ourselves: 9.1, 9.2, 9.3, 9.4, 10.1, 12.1, 13.1, 13.3, 14.1, 17.1, 17.2, 17.3, 18.4

10—Expressing Anger Fully: 13.2, 14.2, 14.3, 16.1, 16.2, 16.3, 16.4, 16.5, 18.1, 18.3, 18.4

12—The Protective Use of Force: 13.3

13—Liberating Ourselves and Counseling Others: 1.1, 1.2, 1.3, 4.1, 4.2, 9.1, 10.1, 10.3, 12.1, 12.2, 12.3, 13.1, 14.1, 17.2, 18.4, 18.5

14—Expressing Appreciation in Nonviolent Communication: 15.1, 15.2, 15.3, 15.4, 15.5, 15.6

The Four-Part Nonviolent Communication Process

Clearly expressing how **I am** without blaming or criticizing	Empathically receiving how **you are** without hearing blame or criticism

OBSERVATIONS

1. What I observe *(see, hear, remember, imagine, free from my evaluations)* that does or does not contribute to my well-being: *"When I (see, hear) . . . "*	1. What you observe *(see, hear, remember, imagine, free from your evaluations)* that does or does not contribute to your well-being: *"When you see/hear . . . "* *(Sometimes unspoken when offering empathy)*

FEELINGS

2. How I feel *(emotion or sensation rather than thought)* in relation to what I observe: *"I feel . . . "*	2. How you feel *(emotion or sensation rather than thought)* in relation to what you observe: *"You feel . . ."*

NEEDS

3. What I need or value *(rather than a preference, or a specific action)* that causes my feelings: *" . . . because I need/value . . . "*	3. What you need or value *(rather than a preference, or a specific action)* that causes your feelings: *" . . . because you need/value . . . "*

Clearly requesting that which would enrich **my** life without demanding	Empathically receiving that which would enrich **your** life without hearing any demand

REQUESTS

4. The concrete actions I would like taken: *"Would you be willing to . . . ?"*	4. The concrete actions you would like taken: *"Would you like . . . ?"* *(Sometimes unspoken when offering empathy)*

Some Basic Feelings We All Have

Feelings when needs are fulfilled

- Amazed
- Comfortable
- Confident
- Eager
- Energetic
- Fulfilled
- Glad
- Hopeful
- Inspired
- Intrigued
- Joyous
- Moved
- Optimistic
- Proud
- Relieved
- Stimulated
- Surprised
- Thankful
- Touched
- Trustful

Feelings when needs are not fulfilled

- Angry
- Annoyed
- Concerned
- Confused
- Disappointed
- Discouraged
- Distressed
- Embarrassed
- Frustrated
- Helpless
- Hopeless
- Impatient
- Irritated
- Lonely
- Nervous
- Overwhelmed
- Puzzled
- Reluctant
- Sad
- Uncomfortable

 Some Basic Needs We All Have

Autonomy
- Choosing dreams/goals/values
- Choosing plans for fulfilling one's dreams, goals, values

Celebration
- Celebrating the creation of life and dreams fulfilled
- Celebrating losses: loved ones, dreams, etc. (mourning)

Integrity
- Authenticity • Creativity
- Meaning • Self-worth

Interdependence
- Acceptance • Appreciation
- Closeness • Community
- Consideration
- Contribution to the enrichment of life
- Emotional Safety • Empathy

Physical Nurturance
- Air • Food
- Movement, exercise
- Protection from life-threatening forms of life: viruses, bacteria, insects, predatory animals
- Rest • Sexual Expression
- Shelter • Touch • Water

Play
- Fun • Laughter

Spiritual Communion
- Beauty • Harmony
- Inspiration • Order • Peace

- Honesty (the empowering honesty that enables us to learn from our limitations)
- Love • Reassurance
- Respect • Support
- Trust • Understanding

Nonviolent Communication Research

You can find an up-to-date list of journal articles, dissertations, theses, project reports, and independent studies exploring various facets of Nonviolent Communication at: www.nonviolentcommunication.com/ learn-nonviolent-communication/research-on-nvc/

Some of these are qualitative, some quantitative, and some are mixed methods. Together they begin to offer an evidence base. If you have completed NVC research and would like to add your paper to the list, please contact us at: www.nonviolentcommunication.com/feedback-form/

 ## About Nonviolent Communication

Nonviolent Communication has flourished for more than four decades across sixty countries selling more than 5,000,000 books in over thirty-five languages for one simple reason: it works.

Nonviolent Communication is changing lives every day. NVC provides an easy-to-grasp, effective method to get to the root of violence and pain peacefully. By examining the unmet needs behind what we do and say, NVC helps reduce hostility, heal pain, and strengthen professional and personal relationships. NVC is being taught in corporations, classrooms, prisons, and mediation centers worldwide. And it is affecting cultural shifts as institutions, corporations, and governments integrate NVC consciousness into their organizational structures and their approach to leadership.

Most of us want the skills to improve the quality of our relationships, to deepen our sense of personal empowerment, or simply to help us communicate more effectively. Unfortunately, most of us are educated from birth to compete, judge, demand, and diagnose; to think and communicate in terms of what is "right" and "wrong" with people. At best, the habitual ways we think and speak hinder communication and create misunderstanding or frustration. And still worse, they can cause anger and pain, and may lead to violence. Without wanting to, even people with the best of intentions generate needless conflict.

NVC helps us reach beneath the surface and discover what is alive and vital within us, and how all of our actions are based on human needs that we are seeking to meet. We learn to develop a vocabulary of feelings and needs that helps us more clearly express what is going on in us at any given moment. When we understand and acknowledge our needs, we develop a shared foundation for much more satisfying relationships. Join the thousands of people worldwide who have improved their relationships and their lives with this simple yet revolutionary process.

About PuddleDancer Press

Visit the PDP website at www.NonviolentCommunication.com. We have a resource-rich and ever-growing website that currently addresses 35+ topics related to NVC through articles, online resources, handouts, Marshall Rosenberg quotes, and so much more. Please come visit us.

- **NVC Quick Connect e-Newsletter**—Sign up online to receive our monthly e-Newsletter, filled with expert articles on timely and relevant topics, links to NVC in the news, inspirational and fun quotes and songs, announcements of trainings and other NVC events, and exclusive specials on NVC learning materials.

- **Shop NVC**—Purchase our NVC titles safely, affordably, and conveniently online. Find everyday discounts on individual titles, multiple copies, and book packages. Learn more about our authors and read endorsements of NVC from world-renowned communication experts and peacemakers.

- **About NVC**—Learn more about the unique life-changing communication and conflict resolution skills of NVC (also known as Compassionate Communication, Collaborative Communication, Respectful Communication, Mindful Communication, Peaceful Communication, or Effective Communication). Find an overview of the NVC process, key facts about NVC, and more.

- **About Marshall Rosenberg**—Read about the world-renowned peacemaker, educator, best-selling author, and founder of the Center for Nonviolent Communication, including press materials, a biography, and more.

For more information, please contact PuddleDancer Press at:

2240 Encinitas Blvd., Ste. D-911 • Encinitas, CA 92024
Phone: 760-557-0326 • Email: email@puddledancer.com
www.NonviolentCommunication.com

About the Center for Nonviolent Communication

The Center for Nonviolent Communication (CNVC) is an international nonprofit peacemaking organization whose vision is a world where everyone's needs are met peacefully. CNVC is devoted to supporting the spread of Nonviolent Communication (NVC) around the world.

Founded in 1984 by Dr. Marshall B. Rosenberg, CNVC has been contributing to a vast social transformation in thinking, speaking and acting—showing people how to connect in ways that inspire compassionate results. NVC is now being taught around the globe in communities, schools, prisons, mediation centers, churches, businesses, professional conferences, and more. Hundreds of certified trainers and hundreds more supporters teach NVC to tens of thousands of people each year in more than sixty countries.

CNVC believes that NVC training is a crucial step to continue building a compassionate, peaceful society. Your tax-deductible donation will help CNVC continue to provide training in some of the most impoverished, violent corners of the world. It will also support the development and continuation of organized projects aimed at bringing NVC training to high-need geographic regions and populations.

To make a tax-deductible donation or to learn more about the valuable resources described below, visit the CNVC website at www. CNVC.org:

- **Training and Certification**—Find local, national, and international training opportunities, access trainer certification information, connect to local NVC communities, trainers, and more.

- **CNVC Bookstore**—Find mail or phone order information for a complete selection of NVC books, booklets, audio, and video materials at the CNVC website.

- **CNVC Projects**—Participate in one of the several regional and theme-based projects that provide focus and leadership for teaching NVC in a particular application or geographic region.

For more information, please contact CNVC at:
Ph: 505-244-4041 • US Only: 800-255-7696 • Fax: 505-247-0414
Email: cnvc@CNVC.org • Website: www.CNVC.org

Nonviolent Communication,

3rd Edition

A Language of Life

By Marshall B. Rosenberg, PhD

$19.95 — Trade Paper 6x9, 264pp
ISBN: 978-1-892005-28-1

What is Violent Communication?

If "violent" means acting in ways that result in hurt or harm, then much of how we communicate —judging others, bullying, having racial bias, blaming, finger pointing, discriminating, speaking without listening, criticizing others or ourselves, name-calling, reacting when angry, using political rhetoric, being defensive or judging who's "good/ bad" or what's "right/wrong" with people—**could indeed be called "violent communication."**

What is Nonviolent Communication?

Nonviolent Communication is the integration of four things:

- **Consciousness: a set of principles that support living a life of compassion, collaboration, courage, and authenticity**
- **Language: understanding how words contribute to connection or distance**
- **Communication: knowing how to ask for what we want, how to hear others even in disagreement, and how to move toward solutions that work for all**
- **Means of influence: sharing "power with others" rather than using "power over others"**

Nonviolent Communication serves our desire to do three things:

- **Increase our ability to live with choice, meaning, and connection**
- **Connect empathically with self and others to have more satisfying relationships**
- **Sharing of resources so everyone is able to benefit**

Available from PuddleDancer Press, the Center for Nonviolent Communication, all major bookstores, and Amazon.com. Distributed by Independent Publisher's Group: 800-888-4741. For Best Pricing Visit: NonviolentCommunication.com

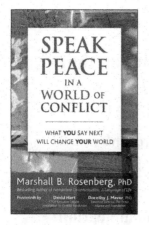

Speak Peace in a World of Conflict

What You Say Next Will Change Your World

By Marshall B. Rosenberg, PhD

$15.95 — Trade Paper 5-3/8x8-3/8, 208pp
ISBN: 978-1-892005-17-5

Create Peace in the Language You Use!

International peacemaker, mediator, and healer, Marshall Rosenberg shows you how the language you use is the key to enriching life. *Speak Peace* is filled with inspiring stories, lessons, and ideas drawn from more than forty years of mediating conflicts and healing relationships in some of the most war-torn, impoverished, and violent corners of the world. Find insight, practical skills, and powerful tools that will profoundly change your relationships and the course of your life for the better.

Nonviolent Communication has flourished for more than four decades across sixty countries selling more than 5,000,000 books for a simple reason: it works.

5,000,000 Copies Sold Worldwide • Translated in More Than 35 Languages

Comunicación No Violenta, 3era edición

Un lenguaje de vida

By Marshall B. Rosenberg, PhD

$19.95 — Trade Paper 6x9, 272pp
ISBN: 978-1-934336-19-9

What Is "Nonviolent" Communication?
It is the integration of 4 things:

Consciousness: a set of principles that support living a life of compassion, collaboration, courage, and authenticity

Language: understanding how words contribute to connection or distance

Communication: knowing how to ask for what we want, how to hear others even in disagreement, and how to move toward solutions that work for all

Means of influence: sharing "power with others" rather than using "power over others"

Available from PuddleDancer Press, the Center for Nonviolent Communication, all major bookstores, and Amazon.com. Distributed by Independent Publisher's Group: 800-888-4741. For Best Pricing Visit: NonviolentCommunication.com

Dementia Together
How to Communicate to Connect

By Pati Bielak-Smith

$17.95 — Trade Paper 6x9, 248pp
ISBN: 978-1-934336-18-2

Build a Healthy Dementia Relationship!

If you are looking to build and sustain a healthy relationship with someone who has dementia, this book is for you.

Dementia is an illness that causes no physical pain. Yet ask anyone who cares about someone with Alzheimer's or another dementia if their heart isn't aching. The pain in dementia comes not from the illness, but from feeling hopeless, alone, or disconnected from someone you care about. And a broken relationship can be healed.

"Practical and humane, this book is recommended for anyone caring for or about a person with dementia."

—**Tim Beanland PhD**, Head of Knowledge, Alzheimer's Society

The Healing Power of Empathy
True Stories About Transforming Relationships

Edited by Mary Goyer, MS

$17.95 — Trade Paper 6x9, 288pp
ISBN: 978-1-934336-17-5

Empathy Is a Learnable Skill!

Empathy is the cornerstone of good relationships—but it can be hard to access when it's most needed. Luckily, empathy is also a learnable skill, with the power to move conversations out of gridlock and pain.

- You'll see how anger and blame get translated and how productive dialogues are made possible.
- You'll hear the words used to repair arguments before they cause damage.
- You'll watch how self-empathy transforms relationships—without speaking any words at all.

Available from PuddleDancer Press, the Center for Nonviolent Communication, all major bookstores, and Amazon.com. Distributed by Independent Publisher's Group: 800-888-4741. For Best Pricing Visit: NonviolentCommunication.com

Being Me, Loving You: *A Practical Guide to Extraordinary Relationships* **by Marshall B. Rosenberg, PhD** • Watch your relationships strengthen as you learn to think of love as something you "do," something you give freely from the heart.
80pp, ISBN: 978-1-892005-16-8 • **$6.95**

Getting Past the Pain Between Us: *Healing and Reconciliation Without Compromise* **by Marshall B. Rosenberg, PhD** • Learn simple steps to create the heartfelt presence necessary for lasting healing to occur—great for mediators, counselors, families, and couples.
48pp, ISBN: 978-1-892005-07-6 • **$6.95**

Graduating From Guilt: *Six Steps to Overcome Guilt and Reclaim Your Life* **by Holly Michelle Eckert** • The burden of guilt leaves us stuck, stressed, and feeling like we can never measure up. Through a proven six-step process, this book helps liberate you from the toxic guilt, blame, and shame you carry.
96pp, ISBN: 978-1-892005-23-6 • **$7.95**

The Heart of Social Change: *How to Make a Difference in Your World* **by Marshall B. Rosenberg, PhD** • Learn how creating an internal consciousness of compassion can impact your social change efforts.
48pp, ISBN: 978-1-892005-10-6 • **$6.95**

Humanizing Health Care: *Creating Cultures of Compassion With Nonviolent Communication* **by Melanie Sears, RN, MBA, PhD** • Leveraging more than twenty-five years nursing experience, Melanie demonstrates the profound effectiveness of NVC to create lasting, positive improvements to patient care and the health care workplace.
112pp, ISBN: 978-1-892005-26-7 • **$7.95**

Parenting From Your Heart: *Sharing the Gifts of Compassion, Connection, and Choice* **by Inbal Kashtan** • Filled with insight and practical skills, this booklet will help you transform your parenting to address every day challenges.
48pp, ISBN: 978-1-892005-08-3 • **$6.95**

Practical Spirituality: *Reflections on the Spiritual Basis of Nonviolent Communication* **by Marshall B. Rosenberg, PhD** • Marshall's views on the spiritual origins and underpinnings of NVC, and how practicing the process helps him connect to the Divine.
48pp, ISBN: 978-1-892005-14-4 • **$6.95**

Raising Children Compassionately: *Parenting the Nonviolent Communication Way* **by Marshall B. Rosenberg, PhD** • Learn to create a mutually respectful, enriching family dynamic filled with heartfelt communication.
32pp, ISBN: 978-1-892005-09-0 • **$5.95**

The Surprising Purpose of Anger: *Beyond Anger Management: Finding the Gift* **by Marshall B. Rosenberg, PhD** • Marshall shows you how to use anger to discover what you need, and then how to meet your needs in more constructive, healthy ways.
48pp, ISBN: 978-1-892005-15-1 • **$6.95**

Teaching Children Compassionately: *How Students and Teachers Can Succeed With Mutual Understanding* **by Marshall B. Rosenberg, PhD** • In this national keynote address to Montessori educators, Marshall describes his progressive, radical approach to teaching that centers on compassionate connection.
48pp, ISBN: 978-1-892005-11-3 • **$6.95**

We Can Work It Out: *Resolving Conflicts Peacefully and Powerfully* **by Marshall B. Rosenberg, PhD** • Practical suggestions for fostering empathic connection, genuine co-operation, and satisfying resolutions in even the most difficult situations.
32pp, ISBN: 978-1-892005-12-0 • **$5.95**

What's Making You Angry? *10 Steps to Transforming Anger So Everyone Wins* **by Shari Klein and Neill Gibson** • A powerful, step-by-step approach to transform anger to find healthy, mutually satisfying outcomes.
32pp, ISBN: 978-1-892005-13-7 • **$5.95**

About the *Nonviolent Communication Toolkit* Creators

Raj Gill is the director of Prosperity Circles Coaching International in British Columbia, Canada. She is the cofounder of the Inclusive Leadership Adventures, a training program for youth leaders and a senior fellow at the Institute for Collaborative Learning (www. thei4cl.org). She began practicing Nonviolent Communication (NVC) in 2001 and currently serves as a CNVC certified trainer and life skills coach. Her work is informed and grounded in more than eighteen years of learning and working with Marshall Rosenburg, PhD. She is a strong believer in the power of compassion and human connection for resolving conflict and building universal success. Raj grew up in India, has lived on three continents and worked on five. She is the coauthor of the *Nonviolent Communication Toolkit for Facilitators* and has developed compassionate communication curricula and manuals for a variety of organizations, colleges, universities, and Correctional Service of Canada.

Lucy Leu first encountered NVC in 1995, after which she joined the CNVC Board, founded the Puget Sound Network for Compassionate Communication (PSNCC/NWCC), and cofounded the Freedom Project. She edited Marshall Rosenberg's book *Nonviolent Communication: A Language of Life* and wrote the *Nonviolent Communication Companion Workbook*. Lucy values seeing new generations of practitioners supported in their intention to effectively share NVC skills and consciousness. She has actively mentored Freedom Project trainers, helped create the CNVC certification program, and served as certification assessor in the U.S. Lucy grew up on Taiwan, has lived in various parts of the world, and currently appreciates the privilege of residing on the unceded ancestral lands of the Coast Salish peoples in Vancouver, BC, Canada.

Judi Morin, Sister of Saint Ann and CNVC certified trainer, was a prison chaplain for nearly thirty years. She is an educator by training and passion. Judi was first introduced to NVC in 1999 through Marshall Rosenberg's book *Nonviolent Communication: A Language of Life*. Judi decided that the best way for her to learn NVC would be to share it with others who are keen on exploring this new language. She thus invited several men in prison to join her in forming an NVC practice group and is delighted that this group continues to gather even to this day. Judi grew up in rural Vancouver Island and has lived most of her life on the west coast of Canada.

FIND MORE ONLINE!

Your purchase of this hardcopy *Exercise Manual* includes access to electronic downloads of Learning Aids, Handouts, and Instructional Video Clips for a complete Toolkit package. To access these materials, log on to: **nvctoolkit.org**, and enter in the customer username and password listed below, all in lowercase.

USERNAME: nvctoolkit

PASSWORD: rglljm